I Am Murdered

George Wythe, Thomas Jefferson,
and the Killing That
Shocked a New Nation

Bruce Chadwick

WILEY

John Wiley & Sons, Inc.

Published by John Wiley & Sons, Inc., Hoboken, New Jersey
Published simultaneously in Canada

Illustration credits: pages 4, 84, 150, 162, 172, 173 (top and bottom), and 220 courtesy of the Virginia Historical Society; pages 5, 41, 47, 49, 51, 65, 70, 71 (top and bottom), 74, 75 and 79 courtesy of the Colonial Williamsburg Foundation; pages 7, 8, 58 and 134 courtesy of Independence Hall National Historic Park; pages 190, 199 (top and bottom), and 200 courtesy of the Wellcome Library, London.

For general information about our other products and services, please contact our Customer Care Department within the United States at (800) 762-2974, outside the United States at (317) 572-3993 or fax (317) 572-4002.

Wiley also publishes its books in a variety of electronic formats. Some content that appears in print may not be available in electronic books. For more information about Wiley products, visit our web site at www.wiley.com.

Library of Congress Cataloging-in-Publication Data:

Chadwick, Bruce.
    "I am murdered" : George Wythe, Thomas Jefferson, and the killing that shocked a new nation / Bruce Chadwick.
        p.   cm.
    Includes bibliographical references and index.
    ISBN 978-0-470-18551-3 (cloth)
        1. Poisoning—Virginia—Richmond—History—19th century—Case studies.
    2. Murder—Virginia—Richmond—History—19th century—Case studies.   3. Criminal investigation—Virginia—Richmond—History—19th century—Case studies.   4. Wythe, George, 1726-1806—Death and burial.   5. Jefferson, Thomas, 1743-1826—Friends and associates.   6. Richmond (Va.)—History—19th century.   I. Title.
HV6555.U62R42 2009
364.152'3092—dc22
                                                                                2008015111

Printed in the United States of America

10 9 8 7 6 5 4 3 2 1

For Margie and Rory

He directed my studies in the law, led me into business, and continued, until death, my most affectionate friend.

—*Thomas Jefferson on George Wythe*

Contents

PART ONE: THE MURDER

1. "I Am Murdered"   3
2. The Funeral   17
3. Homicide: The Investigation, Part I   24
4. Williamsburg: George Wythe and Thomas Jefferson   40
5. Jefferson and Wythe Remake Virginia   63
6. Richmond: Boomtown and the Decadent Nightlife
   of George Wythe Sweeney   82
7. The Dying George Wythe Changes His Will   104
8. Moving Day: A Second Life in Richmond and the Return
   of George Wythe   108

PART TWO: THE INVESTIGATION

 9. The Arrest   123
10. The Investigation, Part II   126
11. For the Defense: William Wirt   132
12. For the Defense: Edmund Randolph   148
13. Mourning at the Executive Mansion   161

PART THREE: THE TRIAL

14. The Forensics Nightmare, Part I: Arsenic, the Poison
    of Choice   167

15. The Forensics Nightmare, Part II: The Autopsy   195

16. Lydia Broadnax: The Eyewitness   216

17. The Black and White Legal Codes   228

18. Washington, October 1806   235

    Epilogue   237

    Acknowledgments   241

    Notes   243

    Bibliography   263

    Index   273

PART ONE

The Murder

I

"I Am Murdered"

GEORGE WYTHE, the eighty-year-old high chancellor of the Virginia Chancery Court and one of the nation's founding fathers, sat up in bed on Sunday, May 25, 1806, and rubbed his eyes with his thin fingers. He yawned, tossed back his rumpled sheets, and rose just before 5 A.M., as he did each morning. He had just awakened in his elegant home on Shockoe Hill, the neighborhood where the wealthy resided in Richmond, Virginia's capital. It was a Sunday that seemed like any other. But on that quiet spring morning Wythe, the mentor and close friend of President Thomas Jefferson, and everyone in his household, would be poisoned, in one of the most shocking murders in the young nation's history.

Wythe had moved to Richmond in 1791. His bright yellow, well-appointed two-story home with a sturdy hip roof was located on the southeast corner of Fifth and Grace streets, near the very top of the hill. The house was one of the most elegant in the city and sat at the edge of a square surrounded by fine homes, including that of the mayor of Richmond, William DuVal. Also in this neighborhood were the dwellings of the city's and the state's most prominent lawyers, physicians, and politicians, as well as its richest merchants.[1] It was a subdued, pleasant part of town where men, women, and children greeted the dignified Wythe with friendly smiles when they saw him walking down the street.

3

The house on the steep hill, one of many hills within the city limits, had an unobstructed view of the slow-rolling James River below. From this height, one could also see the river's pretty, thickly forested small islands and the tiny village of Manchester on its southern bank.[2] Because the rapidly growing city, founded in 1737, had been built on the hills that overlooked the James, comparisons to ancient Rome were inevitable. "The aristocratic city of Richmond prided itself on being like Rome, built on seven hills," wrote the local sculptor Moses Ezekiel.[3]

"We believe [it is] one of the most beautiful [cities] in the Union," wrote a *Richmond Enquirer* reporter. "The situation of the city and the scenery surrounding it combines in a high degree the elements of grandeur and beauty. The river, winding among verdant hills, which rise with graceful swells and undulations, is interrupted by numerous islands and granite rocks, among which it tumbles and foams for a distance of several miles."[4]

The judge's house overlooked Richmond, which had become a raging American boomtown, an exploding urban mecca with something for everyone. There were dozens of raucous taverns where

In this painting, the Richmond of 1806, topped by Jefferson's capitol building, is viewed from Manchester, just south of the James River.

George Wythe lived in one of the finest homes in Williamsburg, or in all of the South, for most of his life. The two-story brick home overlooked one of the two village greens in town.

entertainment ranged from fiddlers to singers to exotic elephant acts. There were churches of every major sect; the city was home to the first Jewish synagogue in the South. The literati enjoyed two of the largest bookstores in Virginia. Three different respected theaters featured local groups plus traveling troupes from England with Britain's most honored actors. Well-stocked general stores offered everything from imported wines and rums to tickets for passage to Europe on the huge oceangoing ships that docked in the city's Rocketts section. The James River was lined with spacious wooden-and-brick tobacco warehouses and was jammed with dozens of tall, majestic tri-masted merchant ships. The vessels were either just in from, or bound for, exotic ports around the world, carrying shipments of Virginia's tobacco, the crop that made the state so rich.

Justice Wythe, for years a familiar figure as he walked about town, was one of the few remaining signers of the Declaration of Independence and architects of the U.S. Constitution. For decades, he had enjoyed his role as a guardian of the establishment, the wise old sage living among all the tough young lions of bustling Richmond. He was still regarded as one of the most prominent men in the United States, especially now in 1806, the thirtieth anniversary of the signing of the Declaration. He was beloved by all of the middle-aged men in town who had fought in the Revolution, some of them limping and still bearing the scars of war, yet he was just as admired by the well-dressed young lawyers and court employees. All of the students he taught liked the old judge, too. They saw him as a vibrant twenty-five-year-old man in an eighty-year-old body. His cheerful conversations, in which he repeatedly quoted Homer and Cicero, compared current events to the besieging of Rome by Carthage, or made references to the speeches of Pericles and his Greek antagonists, regaled all.[5] Searching for a title for the distinguished octo-genarian, who was still as feisty as ever, someone had nicknamed him the "American Aristides" after Aristides the Just, the greatly respected ancient Athenian soldier and statesman. An intelligent man who spoke five languages, the judge had earned the nickname with his well-rounded sophistication.

Wythe, a wisp of a man, had mastered Greek and Latin as a teen-ager, graduated college at nineteen, and was admitted to the bar as a lawyer at twenty. He was elected to the prestigious House of Burgesses, the Virginia state legislature, in his thirties, and was chosen by his peers there to be a delegate to the Continental Congress in 1774 and again in 1775.[6] He was an invaluable member of the delegation because of his legal skills. Whenever a delegate was perplexed by some legality at Congress, he would do what George Washington advised all of the assembled representatives: "Ask George Wythe." As a delegate, Wythe, a fierce patriot and a member of the Revolutionary movement for years, wrote the instructions for American diplomats in Europe to follow as they attempted to gain alliances with other nations through-out the war.[7] He worked with Thomas Jefferson and Edmund Pendleton from 1777 to 1779 to write an entirely new legal code for the state of Virginia. In 1778, he was named one of the three judges for Virginia's Chancery Court, the state's highest court for civil matters, and became chancellor, or chief justice, in 1789. He still held this extremely time-consuming position in 1806.[8] Due to age and infirmity, he had turned down an appointment to the State Supreme Court, as well as George Washington's offer to make him one of the first justices of the U.S. Supreme Court. His rulings from the bench shaped the political,

George Washington, Wythe's longtime friend, wanted to name him one of the first justices to the U.S. Supreme Court. Wythe, fearing extensive travel on the job, declined.

economic, and social life of perhaps the most important state in the Union. Virginia was the home to four of the nation's first five presidents as well as to Chief Justice John Marshall, numerous cabinet members, and important political figures such as Patrick Henry.

Everyone had enormous respect for George Wythe. Once, recommending the College of William and Mary, where Wythe taught, to the well-read son of a friend, Jefferson said that Wythe was "one of the greatest men of the age." To another, Jefferson wrote that Wythe was "the Cato of his country." After meeting Wythe, John Adams wrote that he was "a lawyer of high rank at the bar, a great scholar, a most indefatigable man and a staunch Virginian."[9]

Wythe, who always had a wry smile on his lips, was of "middle size," as one of his protégés, William Munford, later wrote in a description filled with color and detail. He was slightly stooped, "well formed and proportioned, and the features of his face manly, comely and engaging. In his walk, he carried his hands behind him, holding the one in the other, which added to his thoughtful appearance. In his latter days, he was very bald. The hair that remained was uncut and worn behind,

John Adams, who did not like most Southerners, struck up a friendship with Wythe as soon as the two met as delegates to the 1775 Continental Congress in Philadelphia. He considered Wythe one of the country's most intelligent men.

curled up in a continuous roll. His head was very round, with a high forehead, well arched eyebrows, prominent blue eyes, showing softness and intelligence combined, a large aquiline nose, rather small but well defined mouth; and thin whiskers, not lower than his ears.

"There were sharp indentations from the side of the nose down on his cheek, terminating about an inch from the corner of his mouth; and his chin was well rounded and distinct. His face was kept smoothly shaven; his cheeks considerably furrowed from the loss of teeth; and the crow's-feet very perceptible in the corner of the eyes. His countenance was exceedingly benevolent and cheerful. . . . He had a ruddy, healthy hue."[10]

Wythe was always immaculately dressed, although he would stoop over a bit on his cane as he took the three-block walk to his office in the gleaming new marble state capitol building. This American acropolis, with its commanding, columned Grecian portico, was designed by his lifelong friend Jefferson. In an era when most men died before they reached their fiftieth birthday, the sight of the frail, balding, happy justice, padding down the streets of Richmond with a well-worn law book or two under his arm, was reassuring. "He moved with a brisk and graceful step . . . a pleasing image of a fresh and healthy old man," remarked one observer.[11]

On this particular Sunday morning, however, one of the most distinguished jurists in America certainly did not look very distinguished. George Wythe was a man of habit, and every morning he followed the same routine. He slid out of bed, pulled a robe over his pale body, descended the narrow, creaking wooden staircase, and walked through the house to his large backyard. There, as the sun struggled to rise over the Virginia horizon, he passed his well-tended and now blooming garden, the kitchen outbuilding, the smokehouse, the dairy shed, the stables, and the carriage house. He lowered a large wooden bucket into his deep well with a thick rope and, after a moment, drew it back up, full of swirling ice-cold water from far below the ground. He carried the bucket to his back porch, where he had constructed an outdoor shower stall. Wythe stood on a chair and dumped the bucket of water into a reservoir connected to the porch ceiling. He slipped off his robe, stood in the narrow stall, pulled the reservoir cord down with his bony hands, and doused himself with the water.

The bucket shower was usually accompanied by an audible gasp as he shivered from the shock of the chilly water rushing over his body. The judge then soaped up, washed the suds off, and dried himself with a large towel. When he finished his morning shower, those who knew him well, such as Munford, said, "His face would be in a glow, and all his nerves were fully braced."[12] On most Sunday mornings, Wythe went back to his bedroom and dressed. He read the latest editions of the city's newspapers after ringing a bell to summon his maid, the freed black woman Lydia Broadnax, who brought up his morning breakfast. On those mornings, he could usually hear the inordinately intelligent sixteen-year-old former slave Michael, a mulatto, whom he had brought to live in his home as the latest in a long line of protégés, rummaging about the kitchen to the rear of the home—kitchens were disconnected from houses to prevent fires—either helping Lydia fix breakfast or making some for himself. The smell of eggs and toast wafting out of the kitchen windows filled the morning air.

Wythe sometimes heard his sister Anne's obstinate grandson, George Wythe Sweeney, running down the stairs to the kitchen, as his fast-moving feet created a thunderstorm of noise on the steps. Sweeney, now eighteen, had been named after the judge and frequently stayed with him. Few people in the city liked the brash boy, but the judge saw his sister's irresponsible grandson as a headstrong, impulsive, and misunderstood young man who merely needed a little guidance. Wythe had known his grandnephew since he was a small child. Anne often brought him to visit Wythe at his home in Williamsburg, where the boy had played happily with the toys Wythe and his wife kept in a closet for him. By the time he was sixteen, Sweeney had become the black sheep of the Wythe family, the reckless, always-in-trouble individual who turns up in just about everyone's family. George Wythe had seen the black sheep of hundreds of families in courtrooms over his sixty years in the legal profession. To him, his grandnephew was just one more of these misguided individuals. He, like his sister, simply hoped that maturity would cause the young man to calm down.[13]

That Sunday, as always, Wythe read the *Enquirer*:[14] three more slaves had run away from their Richmond masters in what had become an epidemic of black flight. In another item about blacks, William Cannon of nearby Buckingham County announced that he was selling seven of his slaves to raise money to pay his debts, a common practice. Horse races would be held the following Tuesday at the new Hanover Racetrack, which had joined Fairfield as one of the newer and better racetracks in the South. Large crowds of brightly dressed, enthusiastic wagerers always jammed the tracks on race days. Homes and land were for sale. A brand-new school, the Rumford Academy, was holding a lottery to raise money for its planned library. For the first time, stagecoaches would run back and forth to the summer resort town of Staunton, Virginia, which in only a few short years had become a gambling mecca. And in international news, Napoleon celebrated his first anniversary as the emperor of France.[15]

The stories reflected the meteoric growth of Richmond. It had been a city in turmoil ever since the state capital was transferred there from Williamsburg at the height of the Revolution in the spring of 1779.[16] Two years later, in 1781, the traitor Benedict Arnold, who had sold out his country in order to become a British general, attacked Richmond with his English forces. He burned part of the town and nearly captured Governor Thomas Jefferson, who managed to flee on horseback at the last moment. In 1788, the city had played host to the state's Constitutional Convention, which had ratified the new national Constitution after weeks of verbal war between the Federalists and the Anti-Federalists. The Federalists were led by James Madison and George Wythe.[17] In 1798 and 1799, Richmond was riven by political craziness again when debates raged over Congress's controversial Alien and Sedition Acts, which restricted free press and limited immigration.

The town had been severely shaken in 1800 when a disgruntled slave on a local plantation, Gabriel Prosser, nearly carried out a widespread rebellion that would have included murdering a dozen prominent citizens and seizing numerous public buildings. The leaders hoped that success would encourage a broader uprising of the several hundred thousand slaves throughout Virginia, where half of the population was enslaved, and in the Southern states.[18] The conspirators were caught and hanged before a crowd of more than a thousand anxious local residents. Ever since, Richmonders had feared more trouble from the thousands of slaves and freed blacks who lived in Richmond. The tension between blacks and whites kept the city on edge and would continue to do so for years to come.

Richmond had grown dramatically in size after being named the capital. The population had jumped from just 1,500 in the 1790s to 5,300 in 1800 and nearly 10,000 in 1810. The number would double again by 1820.[19] The population rolls were swollen not only with whites, freed blacks, and slaves, but with large numbers of Europeans, including Portuguese who had immigrated to Richmond from Brazil, a major trading partner with Virginia. They were joined by Frenchmen who had fought in the Revolution on the American side and come back to live in a state that had captured their imagination. There were also large numbers of Frenchmen who had fled Haiti in 1802 during its savage slave revolution.

Richmond's city fathers had never been able to manage the town properly. The city had poor public transportation, inefficient garbage collection, a badly organized fire department, and only a few police constables. City streets often flooded when the James River crested during heavy rains, and residents sometimes had to use boats to move from block to block. The population explosion forced many people to live in overcrowded boardinghouses or warehouses refurbished into numerous small rooms. The newcomers to the city, who were mostly young men, consisted of tavern owners, hucksters, con men, and panhandlers; there were also hundreds of prostitutes, who boldly plied their trade in taverns and brazenly sashayed through the streets in search of customers.

Gambling had reared its head early. Gambling in taverns and heavy betting at the local Richmond racetrack was always combined with drinking, and unruliness often followed.[20] As early as 1752, a Virginia governor, Alexander Spotswood, had become alarmed at runaway gambling and begged his constituents to stop because they lost money, drank too much, and wound up in brawls.[21] By 1806, gambling had become a disease in Richmond, especially for the thousands of young men who immigrated there in search of work or who lived in town, such as Wythe's grandnephew George Sweeney.

The rowdy taverns, the unchecked prostitution, and the cramped living quarters bred crime. Pickpockets and armed gunmen descended on Richmond to profit from its newfound affluence. Horse thieves thrived. Counterfeit rings flourished. Arsonists prospered. As early as 1782, public officials led by Edmund Randolph, who would soon become the first attorney general of the United States, were petitioning the governor for assistance in curbing crime. The officials cited "the nocturnal depredations and robberies which have been lately so much practiced among us."[22] Just two weeks prior to Wythe's murder, Abel Clements, a local farmer, had used two axes to bludgeon his wife and eight children to death in a crime that stunned Virginia.[23] In fact, the number of criminals in the city had increased so dramatically during the 1790s that a city jail plus a state penitentiary, one of the largest in the nation, had to be built to hold them, and the local militia was called in to run the new prison.[24]

In the spring of 1806, however, George Wythe was more interested in winding down the court calendar and preparing for summer than he was in furthering discussions about what had gone wrong with Richmond. He also wanted to spend the summer months helping his impetuous grandnephew Sweeney settle down by finding him a full-time job that would keep him away from the racetrack and the gambling dens where he spent nearly every evening and lost all of his money.

SWEENEY HAD COMPLETE FREEDOM in Wythe's house. Judge Wythe had concluded that letting the headstrong, relentlessly demanding teenager do what he wanted was easier on everybody than trying to make him follow the guidelines that governed the lives of everyone else in the household. His grandnephew was free to come in and leave at any hour of the night or morning that he chose. He was never questioned about his nocturnal whereabouts or unkempt friends and was encouraged to help himself to food and drink in the kitchen.

Lydia Broadnax and Wythe's protégé Michael were told to give "Mars George," as Broadnax called Sweeney, anything that he wanted. The teenager enjoyed the same status in the house as if he had been Wythe's son. He had lived there on and off for so long that he referred to Broadnax, age sixty-six, as "Aunt Liddy."

On the morning of May 25, 1806, as George Wythe dried himself with a towel in the back-porch shower stall, Broadnax began to cook her typical Sunday morning breakfast for the household: eggs, usually poached, toast, sweet breads, and coffee. Everyone in Richmond loved to drink coffee in the morning. The city was the main southern port for the import of different blends of exotic coffee from South America, especially Brazil. And coffee was a sturdy American drink, unlike British tea. Its aroma drifted through the open windows of the house as Broadnax moved about the kitchen. George Sweeney walked into the outbuilding at the rear of the main house that contained the kitchen and waved to Broadnax. The pair had known each other for years. Broadnax had been a servant for Wythe since 1783, when he lived in Williamsburg, and she had remained with him after he granted her her freedom in 1787. Broadnax, like many freed slaves, found it comfortable to continue to live with and work for her former owner as a paid employee. Besides, she had always liked the judge and enjoyed taking care of him in his sunset years.

"Aunt Liddy, I want you to give me a cup of coffee and some bread, because I haven't time to stay for breakfast," the young Sweeney said, apparently in a great hurry.

Broadnax frowned. "Mars George, breakfast is nearly ready," she said. "I have only got to poach a few eggs and make some toast for the old master, so you had better stay and eat with him." She wanted the teenager to be well nourished and not sickly, which would give the old man even more headaches.

"No," he insisted. "I'll just take a cup of hot coffee now, so you can toast me a slice of bread."

She protested again, but he waved her off as if she were a pest. Sweeney watched her toast a large piece of bread for him. He approached the iron griddle where a pot of coffee sat over the fire, with the flames underneath keeping it very hot. He took a cup from the countertop with one hand, and with another he raised the pot and filled the cup, making certain that Broadnax saw him do so.

Sweeney put the iron kettle back on the griddle and quickly moved his hands over its top. Broadnax then saw him toss something into the fire: a small piece of white paper he'd been clutching in his fingers. She watched it dissolve in seconds in the flame. The maid thought nothing of this at the time.

Sweeney turned, walked several steps, and then sat down at the large wooden kitchen table. He leaned back in the chair and gulped some coffee from his cup. He sank a wide knife into a tub of butter that sat on the table and smeared the butter over the thickly sliced toast that Broadnax had set in front of him. With quick bites, he finished the toast. He stared at Broadnax while he drank the rest of his coffee, making certain that she saw him finish the cup. He once again reminded her that he had to leave and then pushed back his chair. He stood up and yelled "Good-bye!" to Michael, who was seated at the table across from him, and left the kitchen. He walked across the back lawn on a slate pathway toward Grace Street.

Moments later, Broadnax heard the bell that Wythe used to summon her from his upstairs chambers. The "old master," as she always called him, was dressed and ready for his breakfast. Broadnax put a plate of eggs and toast on a tray, along with a small pot of coffee that she'd filled from the large main pot. She carefully carried the tray up the staircase to Wythe's second-floor bedroom. She found the judge reading in a comfortable chair in the corner of his room.

"Thank you," he said, as Broadnax put the tray on a small table next to him. He asked her whether she had the keys to his desk. The room had grown brighter as the sun rose high in the morning sky. Broadnax reminded him that he had given the keys to George Sweeney the night before because his grandnephew wanted to read some papers that Wythe had put there.

The chancellor was puzzled. "I fear I am getting old, Liddy, for I am becoming more and more forgetful every day. Give Michael his breakfast, and get your own," he said. Wythe then started to drink his coffee in slow, even sips as his eyes scanned the pages of the newspaper.

The maid went back to the kitchen and poured herself some coffee from the pot. Michael Brown drank several cups of hot coffee with his eggs. Broadnax then rose to wash the dishes with a well-worn towel. After she finished, she began to clean the coffee pot. She dumped out the grounds, washed the kettle with warm water, and dried it with a kitchen rag.

She placed the kettle on the counter next to the sink and suddenly felt an awful, crippling pain in her stomach. It was so sharp, she felt as if she were being cut in two by a woodsman's saw. She clutched her stomach as a wave of cramps swept over her. The maid clenched her teeth and her eyes widened. She had never felt so much pain in her life.

Broadnax slowly turned to ask Michael for help, but he could not respond. The boy was bent over in his chair. He, too, held his stomach, with his face contorted in an awful grimace. Between spasms of searing pain, he cried out that he felt terribly sick. The teenager was so stricken, he could not move from his chair.

Upstairs in the main house, Chancellor Wythe continued to read the newspaper while he finished eating breakfast and drinking his coffee. As the coffee raced down his throat into his stomach, he suddenly felt stabbing pains throughout his abdomen and chest. A seizure shook him, and he doubled over. He grabbed his sides with his thin, bony hands. Intense pain ravaged his body, a pain more terrible than any he had ever experienced before. He managed to rise from the chair ever so slowly before he vomited all over the room's wooden floor. His mouth felt extremely dry, despite the eruptions, and his now-empty stomach hurt.

He started for the bedroom door, holding onto furniture and leaning against the wall as he tried to keep himself steady. The old man moved slowly; his legs were weak and could barely hold up his small body. He felt frightened by the tingling throughout his nervous system and the severe pains in his joints. His skin felt quite hot. His arms and legs ached as they never had before, even during severe cases of the flu. He knew that he needed help but was too incapacitated to open his mouth to shout. His eyes hurt and he felt very disoriented, uncertain how to move forward. Yet the chancellor was determined to climb down the stairs to find Broadnax, Michael, or George Sweeney and get assistance.

The aging jurist carefully held onto the mahogany banister and made it down the staircase to the first floor, one step at a time. As he stumbled out the back door to the kitchen, he found his maid and his protégé as violently ill as he was. Broadnax's face revealed extreme discomfort, and she held her stomach with both hands while leaning heavily against the counter. Michael Brown was still in the chair, his trembling upper body prone on the table. An empty cup of coffee and a plate of half-eaten food sat in front of him. He would be dead within a week.

Staring incredulously at the other two members of his household, a wide-eyed and frightened Wythe gasped to Broadnax, "Send for the doctor."[25]

Later, when his physician arrived, along with a friend who was a lawyer, Wythe struggled to prop himself up on his elbows. Weak, bedridden, and barely able to move, he whispered to them, "*I am murdered.*"[26]

2

The Funeral

JUDGE WYTHE lingered until Sunday, June 8, 1806, two weeks after he fell ill, and then died. Michael lived for a week. Lydia Broadnax survived, although she had been quite sick. The poison would permanently damage her eyesight (Thomas Jefferson helped pay her medical bills in later years).[1] Everyone in Richmond was shocked and saddened when the judge succumbed, but no one suffered his loss more than his protégé and longtime close friend President Jefferson, who was preparing for another oppressively hot summer in Washington, D.C.

Mayor DuVal informed Jefferson of the judge's death, providing as many details as he could. He promised swift prosecution. The president was depressed. He told DuVal, "No purer character [than Wythe] ever lived. His advanced years left us little hope of retaining him much longer, and had his end been brought on by the ordinary decays of time and nature, although always a subject of regret, it would not have been aggravated by the horror of his falling by the hand of a parricide—such an instance of depravity has been hitherto known to us only in the fables of the poets. He was my antient master, my earliest and best friend, and to him I am indebted for first impressions which have had the most salutary influence on the course of my life. I had reserved with fondness, for the day of my retirement, the hope of inducing him to pass much of his time with me. It would have been a great pleasure to recollect with him first opinions on the new state of things which arose soon after my acquaintance with him; to pass in review the long period which has elapsed since that time."[2]

Jefferson had loved the judge so much that he had given Wythe his personal copies of the Declaration of Independence (the first draft), the Religious Bill of Rights for Virginia, and the Constitution of Virginia, all of which Jefferson had authored.

The mourning for Wythe extended throughout the entire city of Richmond, not only on top of Shockoe Hill and in the shadows of the glistening white marble capitol building. In an unprecedented step, the editors of the *Virginia Argus*, one of Richmond's two newspapers, devoted the entire front page to articles about his mysterious death and the funeral. So did the rival *Richmond Enquirer*. The front pages of both the *Argus* and the *Enquirer* carried thick black borders of ink to denote both papers' sorrow over the judge's passing. The citizens of the city had expected him to die any day, and when he finally expired that Sunday, all were grief-stricken. Clergymen of every denomination ordered their church bells to toll loudly as soon as they heard the sad news. The bells rang solemnly all afternoon, and everyone in the greater Richmond area heard them and knew that the beloved old judge had breathed his last.

The Common Hall, the city council of Richmond, gathered in its chamber and planned the funeral of the judge for Wednesday, June 11, following the official autopsy. Its heavy-hearted members, who for days had feared the worst, had discussed the funeral, its size and scope, and its length. The old man was so popular, and the expected mourners so numerous, that no mere church funeral would do. The city fathers felt obligated to stage a grand ceremony that would rival the funeral of a president of the United States or the monarch of a powerful European nation so that people throughout America would know how much Virginians had loved the old man.

The Common Hall declared thirty official days of mourning and ordered the wearing of black armbands during that period, the only time this had been done since the death of President Washington in 1799. On June 10, Wythe's body, in a closed casket, lay in state all day in Richmond's elegant Hall of Delegates on top of Shockoe Hill so that friends, neighbors, and members of the general public could pay their last respects. Long lines of bereaved people extended out of the capitol building, along the street, and down the steep hill from sunup until sundown. Bankers and paupers, blacks and whites queued behind one another to see the judge for the last time. Hundreds had arrived on horseback and in carriages from many miles away. The funeral itself began at 4 P.M. the next day in the Hall of Delegates, where the governor of Virginia, the state's U.S. senators, congressmen, judges, city councilmen, and members of the state legislature were joined by hundreds of clergy, merchants, mayors, newspaper editors, and city and state residents, all wearing black armbands. They gathered to hear Wythe's protégé and longtime friend William Munford deliver a stirring oration.

In his lengthy eulogy in the packed chamber, a somber Munford, perhaps Wythe's most devoted protégé, with the exception of Thomas Jefferson, told the crowd that Wythe was a "patriot and sage." He said that Wythe was a man among men in an age when so many distinguished individuals took the political stage during the Revolution, the Constitutional Convention, and the founding years of the nation under the administrations of Washington, John Adams, and Jefferson. "Others may have excelled him in genius," said Munford, probably referring to Jefferson, "but he certainly never was surpassed in patriotism, learning, and judgment."

As Munford looked out at the mourners in the elegant legislative chamber, he chronicled the chancellor's life in personal terms. He expressed his own love for the old man and traced Wythe's devotion to Virginia and the nation from the mid-1770s onward. He reminded everyone that the judge had tried to enlist in the military at the age of fifty, musket in hand, only to be gently rebuffed. Munford outlined Wythe's services at the Continental Congress and as a signer of the Declaration of Independence. He said, "He was one of those who signed that ever memorable declaration by which they pledged their lives, their fortunes, and their sacred honor to maintain and defend the violated rights of their country. He was an active, useful, and respected member of that body, the most enlightened, patriotic, and heroic that perhaps ever existed in the world."

Munford went on to recount Wythe's service throughout his life and at the Virginia Convention to ratify the Constitution and thanked

Wythe for taking him under his wing as a young man. He told the crowd assembled in the capitol that they would never see another individual like Wythe. In conclusion, Munford reminded everyone that throughout his life, Wythe had served as a professor and a jurist and had declined private law service, which might have made him a wealthy man. He was, Munford told the crowd, "a venerable patriot." Munford, choked with emotion and barely able to speak at times, said that "a kinder heart never throbbed in the bosom of a human being."[3]

But then, toward the end of his eulogy, to everyone's surprise, Munford angrily denounced Wythe's grandnephew Sweeney, without directly naming him. Sweeney was now the chief suspect in what had become a murder investigation. Munford told the crowd that Wythe's charity "extended to every human being, no matter how low and humble his station, because he was always striving to do good." Then Munford glared out at the huge throng and told them that the judge's benevolence went too far.

"It may be said indeed that in one deplorable instance (which it strikes me with horror even to mention), his benevolence was placed on an unworthy object and repaid with *black ingratitude*."

Following Munford's moving words, a long line of well-dressed clergymen joined him in leading the lengthy funeral procession down Shockoe Hill to Main Street. This was the city's longest thoroughfare, which ran parallel to the James River and anchored the central business district of town. The large assemblage of mourners then followed the casket on its horse-drawn carriage for the nearly three-mile walk across the Shockoe Bottom district, near the congested shipping wharves at Rockett's Landing. They trudged uphill to St. John's Church for a service and a burial, with the roaring of the James River's waterfalls easily heard on the quiet afternoon. It was at St. John's long ago that Wythe and others had been thrilled by Patrick Henry's call for a revolution, which ended in his renowned plea, "Give me liberty or give me death!"

Munford and the clergy walked in front of George Wythe's funeral carriage as part of the assigned order of marchers devised by the city council. The carriage was followed by a large group of eminent doctors, including those who had participated in the autopsy: James McClurg, James McCaw, and William Foushee. The trio of doctors wore glum faces. Each had been an intimate friend of Wythe's. Foushee was so close to Wythe that the judge not only used him as a private doctor, but let him handle much of his financial work, such as reselling his Chesterville plantation in 1795.[4] The physicians were followed by Wythe's relatives, who had traveled to Richmond from all over the state for the funeral. Next came all of the state, county, and local judges in Virginia, who had arrived to mourn their colleague on the bench. They were followed by hundreds of lawyers, all of the people who worked for the Chancery Court in any capacity, then every court employee in the capital, the governor and members of the city's Common Hall, all of the officers of the state and city governments, the mayor, and the aldermen. Falling into formation behind the mayor and the aldermen were hundreds of citizens of Richmond and Virginia, with their heads down and black armbands on their sleeves. They walked slowly and wore sad looks, anxious to pay their last respects to the spry old man they had loved for so long. Each person seemed to have a story about the judge, along with many memories.

As the procession gradually moved toward St. John's, thousands of residents lined the streets to pay their last respects to the high chancellor. The wealthy filed down from their splendid homes on Shockoe Hill, and the poor trekked over from the tightly packed neighborhoods of warehouses and wooden boardinghouses near the river. They were joined by the dockworkers and the sailors at Rockett's Landing and its shipyards. All of the stores in town were closed, and their merchants either joined the procession or gathered along the street. There were people who ran the bakeries and the candy stores that Wythe frequented with great delight and booksellers whom he spent so much time with as he carefully selected volumes in Greek and Latin that had newly arrived from Europe. There were members of reading groups he had joined, poetry circles he had frequented, and schools he had visited. Even colleagues from the Society for the Advancement of Useful Knowledge showed up. They had listened to Wythe discuss experiments he had conducted over the years, many of them with his friend Jefferson.

It was the biggest funeral in the history of Virginia up to that time. (George Washington's funeral in 1799 had been a private service at Mount Vernon.) Sizing up the thousands of people in the procession that filled much of Main Street, a newspaper editor wrote, "There is not perhaps another man in Virginia" whose death would attract such a crowd of mourners.

Thomas Ritchie, the editor of the *Richmond Enquirer* and a close friend of President Jefferson and Wythe, may have put it best: "Let the solemn and lengthened procession which attended him to his grave declare the loss which we have sustained. Kings may require mausoleums to consecrate their memory; saints may claim the privileges of canonization, but the venerable George Wythe needs no other monument than the services rendered to his country and the universal sorrow which that country sheds over his grave."[5]

Ritchie and other editors mourned the loss of their "patriot and sage," but they grieved even more the loss of a historic figure who had exerted considerable influence over the history of Virginia and the United States. He had been a delegate to the Continental Congress and the Constitutional Convention, a signer of the Declaration of Independence, an author of Virginia's laws, the nation's first law professor, and a man who had spent years on the state's highest court.

Newspaper eulogists remembered, too, that throughout his life, whether at age twenty-eight or seventy-eight, he had maintained a high moral ground in whatever occupied his attention. He had never been involved in political or personal scandal. "Few have more strongly evinced the height of moral and intellectual excellence to which man is capable of ascending," wrote one.[6]

In their obituaries and articles about his passing, the editors reminded their readers, however, that perhaps Wythe's greatest impact was as the teacher of some of the most distinguished public officials in the country. Ritchie wrote, "For some years, the private tuition of youth was his favorite employment and amusement. The illustrious president of the United States, with gratitude and affection, boasts himself as a pupil of this modern Socrates. Hundreds in America are gratified in acknowledging themselves his disciples."[7]

One of the most important disciples he trained was young U.S. senator Henry Clay from Kentucky, who would go on to become one of the most distinguished political leaders in American history. He was unable to attend the funeral. Later, he wrote of his feelings upon hearing the news of the judge's death: "It is painful and melancholy to reflect that a man so pure, so upright, so virtuous, so learned, so distinguished and beloved, should have met with an unnatural death."[8]

Everyone who gathered in Richmond for the funeral that summer day, regardless of his or her social standing, knew that the judge had been physically frail over the last few years and had been a victim of the forgetfulness and perhaps untidy habits that others of that advanced age sometimes evinced. They forgave him everything, though. One Richmond resident, William Brown, who complained to a friend that the judge sometimes seemed a bit disoriented in his last months, added, "Yet when we look at him so venerable in his appearance and with such unsullied dignity he behaves, he involuntarily claims our respect and commands the low bow of respect, such is the man who notwithstanding his imperfections, yet seems to have gained the esteem of all his Citizens."[9]

Munford's chilling denunciation of Sweeney in his oration was remembered by all as they walked toward St. John's for the burial. His words especially affected the bright, aggressive young prosecutor in the case, Phillip Norborne Nicholas, who was marching in the procession. Nicholas had been assured by Mayor DuVal, Lydia Broadnax, and Munford that the judge had been poisoned. If the horror of the citizens of Virginia did not impress upon Nicholas the need to bring Wythe's murderer to justice, Munford's stinging public accusation and the enormous crowd that had gathered for the judge's funeral certainly did.

3

Homicide:
The Investigation, Part I

GEORGE WYTHE SWEENEY was the immediate target of the early homicide investigation. After news of the judge's sudden illness traveled around Richmond, among the first men to arrive at Wythe's home were Dr. William Foushee, the doctor who had treated Wythe most frequently during the judge's last years; the attorney Edmund Randolph, who handled his personal legal work; and Mayor DuVal, a friend and a neighbor. They were told by Lydia Broadnax that Sweeney had put some substance into the coffee. He had then destroyed the evidence by dropping the paper containing the substance into the fire that burned in the stove beneath the coffee pot. Everyone who drank the coffee, including Broadnax herself, became ill within minutes.

"I gave Michael as much coffee as he wanted and then I drank a cup myself," Lydia Broadnax eagerly told every visitor to the Wythe home that day.

Following her trip upstairs to bring Judge Wythe his breakfast, Broadnax returned to the kitchen to clean up, as the fastidious maid did after every meal. "With the hot water in the kettle, I washed the plates, emptied the coffee grounds out, and scrubbed the coffee pot bright, and by that time I became so sick I could hardly see, and had a violent cramp. Michael was sick, too," she said "and the old master was as sick as he could be."

Dr. Foushee said that the maid pointed the finger of guilt directly at Sweeney. She recounted to him the same story she had told others, adding, "All these things made me think Mars George must have put something in the coffee pot. I didn't (exactly) see him, but it looks monstrous strange."[1]

Again and again, she told each man who called on the dying Wythe that the three had become desperately ill within minutes after drinking the coffee that Sweeney had laced with some substance. He drank his own cup of coffee before he tampered with the pot, she swore, and that explained why he had not fallen ill. It would be solid evidence: if he had poisoned the coffee, why did he not become sick? It must have been poison of some kind, she speculated, or why would everyone who drank the coffee from the same kettle become sick immediately? And with identical symptoms?

The two men who listened to Lydia Broadnax's account most often and questioned her repeatedly were two ministers whom Wythe had befriended, the Reverend John Buchanan, an Episcopalian, and the Reverend John Blair, a Presbyterian. Blair was considered one of the most distinguished men in Richmond. Buchanan, a Scotsman, was a jovial minister admired by all. Buchanan was usually dressed in a large coat with a long vest underneath it and wore bright silver shoe buckles. He was, a chronicler wrote, "lively and genial in manner."[2] The two clergymen visited the judge as soon as they heard he had been stricken ill. They came back nearly every day and remained at his bedside for hours. They spent much time talking to Lydia Broadnax. They relayed everything she said to the physicians, who soon arrived. The ministers must have told the doctors, too, although the doctors already knew, that Broadnax had worked with Wythe for more than twenty years, was well-known to his friends, and was considered by all to be an honest and reliable person.[3]

Wythe insisted that he had been poisoned. Fortunately for him, he thought, the three friends who examined him were among the best physicians in the country and had been honored by medical journals, city councils, and state legislatures for their brilliant medical work over the years. The heralded doctors were Dr. James McClurg, a longtime friend and neighbor who had treated Wythe for years and was the author of medical textbooks printed in several languages; Dr. Foushee, Wythe's personal physician; and Dr. Samuel McCaw, another noted Richmond doctor, whose son, a doctor, and other descendants would continue a veritable medical dynasty in Virginia for the next seventy years.

Surprisingly, these men, the best and the brightest medical specialists of the era, dismissed Wythe's claims that he had been poisoned. They suggested that the symptoms did not indicate arsenic or any other toxin but cholera morbus. It turned out to be a mistaken diagnosis and the first in a long line of mistakes that transformed the Wythe murder case into a colossal medical and forensics nightmare and made the trial one of the most closely watched and intriguing in the nation.

The victim of cholera morbus suffers severe, sudden stomach cramps, frequent diarrhea, and extensive vomiting. He has acute pains in his stomach, bowels, and joints and can barely move. His skin takes on a silver-bluish color and wrinkles, his eyes sink into their orbs, and the areas around them darken. The body becomes very cold and is covered with excessive sweat; the nail beds at the ends of the fingers turn blue. The veins of the liver and the bowels fill with blood, the intestines are distended with air, the gall bladder fills with dark bile, the muscles go soft, and the victim's lungs collapse in only a few hours. The pulse weakens, the victim breathes rapidly, and the voice goes hoarse. In a twenty-four-hour period, the victim vomits or is attacked by virulent diarrhea twenty or more times. The body dehydrates quickly, and the victim rushes toward death. One doctor, when trying to explain the rapid deterioration of the bodies of cholera patients, wrote graphically that the disease "cadaverizes them," and they always die within forty-eight hours.[4]

Cholera always struck in warm-weather regions of the world, such as India, southern Asia, or Africa, or in northern countries during the summertime when people consumed large amounts of water. The British press reported that in India, ships carried cholera from one port to another during the summer and that in cholera epidemics, between 10 and 50 percent of those stricken died. The judge became ill during the last week of May, as warm weather set in throughout Virginia.

Medical authorities of the early nineteenth century had no resources to stop the deadly disease. Quarantining victims and administering the primitive medicines of the day, such as calomel, opium, castor oil, carbonate of magnesia, and numerous laxatives, did nothing to halt cholera. In fact, doctors of the era knew so little about the cure of any medical malady that they simply drained quarts of blood from the victims of any sickness. They were certain that removing tainted blood would make patients better. As late as 1799, just seven years before Wythe was stricken ill, the doctors attending George Washington drained several quarts of blood from him when he fell ill. The removal of the blood did not help; it merely made the ex-president weaker, and he died the following day.[5]

Most American doctors had a simplistic view of medicine and were convinced that good living alone could prevent all diseases. The best physicians in the nation, led by Dr. Benjamin Rush of Philadelphia, the chief surgeon of the Continental Army and a congressman, preached that breathing clean air and drinking good water were all that people needed to avoid any sickness. Their view, accepted throughout the United States, made it impossible for the medical profession to combat the epidemics that struck the United States and Europe during that era by attempting to find medicines that could help people.[6]

Even though they knew little about most ailments, medical experts continually reassured the public that they knew how to stop any epidemic, regardless of its size or ferocity. In 1820, following a cholera outbreak in India that sent the British into a panic, the editors of the University of Edinburgh's *Edinburgh Medical and Surgical Journal* told its readers that medicine had a cure for cholera if it reared its ugly head on the streets of London. And this came from no less an authority than the leading medical publication in the world, which was published by the alma mater of both McCaw and McClurg. An editor writing on a cholera outbreak in Bombay told *Journal* subscribers that his article "would make our readers thoroughly acquainted with the history of the epidemic and what rarely occurs in our professional pursuits, of the means by which it may be almost stripped of its terror." Later, another editor at the same medical journal wrote in a review, "The treatment of epidemic cholera forms one of the greatest and most undoubted triumphs of modern physic."[7] British medicine's defense against cholera, which amounted to little more than purging, failed miserably four years later when a horrific cholera epidemic swept through Great Britain and claimed the lives of more than 23,000 people.

There were also social beliefs concerning cholera that prevented any substantive cure until the middle of the nineteenth century, when doctors isolated its source in contaminated water.[8] Many prominent Europeans and Americans believed that diseases infected the poor and not the rich because the poverty-stricken somehow deserved it. These people were destitute, the theory went, because they refused to educate themselves, work, or remain clean. They dressed in shabby clothes, drank beer and rum, had bad diets, lived in run-down tenement dwellings, and, when outdoors, gathered in crowds where illness was rampant. Diseases were not merely nature's punishment but were God's retribution for their failure to climb out of poverty. The tens of thousands of immigrants arriving in America became an important part of this rather convoluted thinking. Americans did not like the immigrants. The hordes of newcomers caused enormous overpopulation problems, particularly in cities and especially those that were seaports and river ports. The immigrants lived in the poor areas when they arrived, and so, Americans felt, diseases such as smallpox and cholera were God's punishment not only for being poor, but for being foreign.[9] Later, in 1832, when a brutal cholera epidemic struck the United States and hit mostly the lower classes, John Pinard, a prominent merchant and the founder of the New York Historical Society, breathed a sigh of relief that he was rich and safe. He wrote that cholera was "almost exclusively confined to the lower classes of intemperate[,] dissolute and filthy people huddled together like swine in their polluted habitations."[10]

Cholera is a toxic bacillus, *vibrio cholerae*. The bacillus causes nerve cells in the stomach to misfire. The stomach and the intestines then fill with water that drains out salt and brings on vomiting, diarrhea, convulsions, dehydration, and death.

Cholera usually exists in contaminated water. It can appear in the flood basins of rivers that overflow and pour water into city streets or yards to form stagnant pools. It can be found in any body of water that people have defecated or urinated in. Cholera tends to occur in poorer areas that are unsanitary and strewn with garbage and where people drink water from pumps or directly from rivers or creeks. During the nineteenth century, hundreds of thousands of residents of India drank water directly from dirty rivers. Cholera struck city populations where unsanitary conditions were the worst and where little attention was paid to the source of water or to drinks mixed with water or foods washed by water.[11] This bacillus festered in unsanitary water in warm-weather areas; the first great pandemics were in India, at the delta of the Ganges River, a large watery area with unsanitary water contaminated by garbage and human refuse that were carried downriver from the city of Calcutta. At the time, physicians associated most diseases with water and automatically assumed that if there was bad water nearby, diseases had to be in it.[12]

Cholera was first mentioned as a lethal gastrointestinal disease in the writings of Hippocrates in ancient Greece. Indian historians claimed that the first great epidemic struck India in 1325, with additional outbreaks there in 1438 and 1503. Cholera outbreaks were reported in Java in 1629 and 1689, and in Ceylon in 1782, 1790, and 1804. Macpherson's *Annals of Cholera* reported sixty-four incidents of cholera worldwide between 1503 and 1817, ten of epidemic proportions.[13] There were more epidemics in India in the late eighteenth century. The first, in 1768, killed more than 60,000 people. A second epidemic struck British army troops in India in 1781, killing several hundred of them. That epidemic moved across the country, in just eight days killing 20,000 religious pilgrims who arrived on the banks of the Ganges at the holy city of Hurdwar. Three more cholera outbreaks seized India in 1787, 1790, and 1794. Since England had a large military presence in India and lost many troops to the disease, reports of the dreaded cholera surfaced routinely in the British press. British physicians who studied diseases had written extensively about cholera in medical journals in India since 1774.[14]

One oddity of cholera is that it did not cause sickness in everyone. Five men who drank from a polluted stream might come down with cholera, but a sixth man would not. There were reports that doctors and nurses who accidentally drank from cholera-infected water felt no ill effects at all.[15]

The possibility of a savage cholera outbreak beginning in the home of George Wythe must have frightened McClurg, McCaw, and Foushee.[16]

The doctors thought they had several valid reasons to believe that the desperately ill people in the Wythe household were victims of cholera. Although the disease is usually found in water supplies, cholera sometimes infects people who have eaten fruits and vegetables that have been washed with unsanitary water or are under- or overripe. The night before Wythe was stricken, he had consumed a bowl of strawberries that someone noted had a whitish hue to them. The doctors assumed that the strawberries were rotten, had developed a white mold, and gave him cholera; others in the house who had fallen ill had also eaten strawberries from the same source.

Cholera's terrible symptoms do not strike immediately but occur within a period of twenty-four hours after infection, so the consumption of the strawberries some sixteen hours before the physical symptoms made perfect sense to the doctors. Arsenic has an immediate effect, however, and would have acted quickly on each of its victims if it had been in anything they ate or drank that morning, such as the coffee. The doctors discounted this because the delayed time frame seemed to fit cholera.

Why didn't young Sweeney come down with cholera, too? The doctors were aware that not every member of a household always contracts cholera; the disease may have simply passed Sweeney by. They also knew that medical experts believed that cholera, like the bubonic plague of the fourteenth century, was carried from place to place by infected people traveling on ships and that it struck in warm-weather climates. The wharves of Richmond's bustling seaport were filled with ships that had arrived from ports in South America and the Caribbean. Several slave traders had sailed there from Africa.

Cholera, along with yellow fever, often develops when dirty rivers or streams flood or when rainstorms leave large areas of land underwater for days, causing the water to stagnate. Richmond and the surrounding area were often flooded by the James River after spring and summer downpours. Not only did the river flood, but a creek that ran right through the city always overflowed when it rained. A natural bowl of land near Shockoe Hill filled up quickly with rainwater and turned into a pond that did not drain for months, due to the peculiar soil and rock base beneath it. Children swam in it during the summer and ice-skated on it in the winter. The stagnant dirty water could have served as a breeding ground for cholera.[17]

And why was their friend the judge so alert, despite his condition? Alertness is an unusual side effect of cholera and occurs in no other disease. To the nationally renowned doctors, there was no doubt that cholera explained the ailments of the trio of stricken people in the Wythe home.

The physicians were so ready to embrace cholera as the reason for the debilitating condition of Wythe and the others that they did not consider other obvious, predisposed conditions for cholera that would immediately rule it out.

Cholera almost always emanates from a contaminated water supply and never from private, underground, fresh-water wells. Wythe drank his water from a private backyard well. All the water in his home, including the water that was used to wash the food and make the coffee, came from the untainted well. Even the judge's showers required buckets of fresh spring water from the well.

In those days, cholera was rife in poor and overcrowded city neighborhoods. Wythe was wealthy and lived in a well-to-do neighborhood, high up on a hill and far from Richmond's overpopulated areas. He spent little time in the congested districts of town near the warehouses and the wharves.

Cholera may have contaminated fruits, vegetables, and other provisions in the hurly-burly markets of poor neighborhoods, but the judge purchased his food from the best stores in town. Cholera, the medical journals said, was somehow carried by people wearing tattered clothing who maintained unkempt homes, had unhealthy diets, and lived in unsanitary conditions. No home in Richmond was better maintained than Wythe's, which was cared for by a maid who also carefully prepared all of the meals for the members of the household. Everyone in the home dressed well and adhered to a well-balanced diet (the judge was a vegetarian, so cholera in bad meat had to be ruled out).

And the doctors ignored the most important reason of all: there had never been a single case of cholera in the United States up to that time. The disease had infected people throughout India and in certain other tropical Asian and African nations but had not traveled to North America. With absolutely no history in the Americas during the nearly two hundred years since settlers had arrived in Jamestown, Virginia, why would cholera suddenly turn up in the kitchen of George Wythe?

Why, given these facts, did the doctors cling to their initial diagnosis when Wythe was so insistent that he had been poisoned? When everyone around Wythe and his closest friends insisted he was poisoned? When Lydia Broadnax had provided a vivid eyewitness account of the poisoning?

THEY DID so because the Americas and the tropical Caribbean islands had been hit with numerous other epidemics over the previous fifty years, mainly yellow fever and smallpox. The first ones were smallpox outbreaks in Boston in 1721 and New York City in 1731, which took the lives of 15 percent of both communities' populations.

Smallpox had decimated America. The pox terrorized people because they had read of its infamous death tolls around the world. Smallpox, brought to Mexico by Spanish invaders in the sixteenth century, reportedly killed several million Aztec Indians during the military campaigns of Hernando Cortez.[18] More than a dozen severe epidemics hit London between 1718 and 1774 and claimed the lives of tens of thousands of city residents, nearly 12 percent of the metropolis's population. Epidemics that struck other European cities had killed an average of 5 percent of the population. European leaders such as Prince William II of the Netherlands, King Luis I of Spain, Czar Peter II of Russia, and King Louis XV of France had died from smallpox.[19] Several thousand died in epidemics that swept through Geneva, Switzerland, and Berlin, Germany, during those same years. More than forty thousand residents of Belem, Brazil, died in a smallpox epidemic in 1750.

Canada's Indian tribes had been crippled by the pox in the 1750s; several thousand Indians contracted the disease and more than 500 died. An epidemic that struck Charleston, South Carolina, in 1760 took the lives of 10 percent of the city's population. A 1768 smallpox epidemic in Reading, Pennsylvania, claimed the lives of several hundred residents, a high percentage of them children. Another smallpox disaster hit Canada in 1775, when the American army invaded during the first year of the American Revolution. During the failed attack, more than 2,000 soldiers fell to smallpox and more than 500 died, in addition to several hundred Canadians. Hundreds of Indians died in another smallpox outbreak in Canada between 1780 and 1782, as did several hundred residents of Connecticut during the early 1790s and in Virginia in 1794 and 1802.[20]

The dreaded yellow fever was carried by female mosquitoes (*aedes aegypti*) that ingested the yellow fever flavivirus from contaminated water in ships' barrels during ocean voyages or from stagnant water, polluted streams, puddles, or privies, usually in hot climates. Yellow fever first struck the Americas during the mid-seventeenth century in Cuba, Brazil, and Mexico. Yellow fever causes headaches, chills, and fever, followed by nausea, muscular pain, vomiting of black bile, and a yellow jaundiced skin, and it often kills its victim. The mosquitoes thrive in unsanitary conditions where stagnant, contaminated water or garbage can be found. Yellow fever was prevalent in all colonial cities in the seventeenth and eighteenth centuries.[21]

Yellow fever struck the American colonies for the first time in 1693 at the port of Boston and killed several hundred city residents.[22] Small outbreaks occurred throughout the century, particularly in New York. The worst was in Philadelphia during the summer of 1793, when the fever claimed the lives of 10 percent of all the residents; similar outbreaks killed several thousand people in New York, New Haven, Charleston, and Baltimore during that decade.

Virginia, however, was the most frequent hot zone for yellow fever. Thousands of people were employed in its shipping industry, and they spread the disease quickly in that warm climate once they had it. Individuals were easily infected in the congested port towns.[23] The worst epidemic raced through the eastern counties of Virginia during the summer of 1798, killing hundreds. There were other yellow fever outbreaks throughout the state between 1798 and 1806, and in each one, not only did hundreds die, but their cities were paralyzed for months as the residents fled in terror and many businesses closed down. The fever hit the town of Alexandria, on the southern bank of the Potomac River, in 1800, 1801, 1802, 1803, and 1804. During each epidemic, half of the city's residents fled to avoid infection. Fredericksburg was a victim of yellow fever in 1800, 1802, and 1803. It struck Petersburg in 1801. In 1806, around the time that Wythe died, there was a small outbreak of yellow fever in the state penitentiary at Richmond. Severe yellow fever epidemics killed hundreds in the seaport of Norfolk in 1793, 1800, and 1801. Two-thirds of Norfolk's population fled the city during the 1800 epidemic, which was reportedly started by infected seamen who arrived on a ship from the Caribbean.

Doctors at the time did not realize that mosquitoes carried yellow fever and thrived on the unsanitary conditions in the nation's cities, particularly in seaports and river ports. This ignorance delayed the discovery of preventive measures for nearly one hundred years.[24]

Thousands of soldiers from European countries who were sent to South American and Caribbean countries during that era died from smallpox and yellow fever, especially from the latter. The British sea captain Francis Wheeler lost 1,800 of the 2,100 sailors in his Caribbean task force to yellow fever in 1694. The British naval force that attacked Cartagena, Colombia, in 1741 lost 8,400 of its 12,000 men to the fever. Twenty thousand French troops who invaded Haiti in 1804 to put down a slave rebellion died of yellow fever.[25]

Altogether, smallpox and yellow fever had claimed the lives of some 50,000 people in North America and the Caribbean during the previous fifty years. As they left George Wythe's bedroom on the first day they examined him, the three Richmond doctors who treated him, all veterans of disease epidemics, were terrified that they had another epidemic, perhaps the worst ever, on their hands.

No one was more conscious of epidemics than McClurg, McCaw, and Foushee. Epidemics had made them famous. Each doctor not only had been involved in treating victims of widespread epidemics of yellow fever, malaria, and smallpox over the last decade in Virginia, but had supervised dozens of other doctors' epidemic cases in Richmond and other regions of the state.

Much of Dr. James McClurg's fame came in 1800 when, as mayor of Richmond, he insisted that all of the men and the women who had traveled to the city from Norfolk be placed in an isolation ward so that, if infected, they could not spread the fever throughout the city. His efforts were credited with preventing a medical catastrophe in the capital.[26]

Dr. McCaw had inoculated hundreds of Richmonders during the smallpox epidemics of 1794 and 1802, which had threatened to take the lives of a high percentage of the city's population. He had been instrumental in restoring calm after panic swept the region.

The fear of smallpox was so great that at one point in the 1794 smallpox epidemic, the residents of Manchester blockaded the bridge that spanned the James River and connected them to Richmond, to bar any Richmonders from entering their city. A mob of Richmonders gathered on their side of the bridge and threatened violence unless it was opened. The governor had to send the state militia to open the bridge and permit Richmonders to cross, but only on business and for short periods of time. The panic was not uncommon. During other epidemics, residents of Boston burned down a hospital where smallpox patients were recuperating, and in Norfolk, nervous neighbors torched an entire block of recently evacuated ramshackle wooden tenement buildings that had been home to hundreds of people stricken with smallpox, fearing that the buildings still harbored the disease.[27]

Dr. Foushee and his brother had inoculated hundreds more Richmond residents at their city office during the smallpox epidemic of 1802. McClurg had worked with others in stemming that same epidemic. McClurg's familiarity with epidemic treatments extended all the way back to his childhood. His father, Walter, was a doctor and a British smallpox expert. He had been sent to America in the 1720s specifically to combat an outbreak of smallpox in Hampton, Virginia, and set up one of North America's first smallpox hospitals there.[28]

The doctors' work in each epidemic was seen as heroic by all. They went into infected areas and tended to dying patients as everyone else was fleeing those same neighborhoods in panic, fearful for their lives. The doctors' exploits were recounted in melodramatic tones everywhere. One admiring newspaper editor in a city stricken with yellow fever wrote, "The city was wrapped in gloom. All of the stores and the dwellings of the absentees were closed; few were seen passing in the streets on foot, and these on some errand of mercy or necessity. . . . Most of the inhabitants present were either confined at home by sickness, or in attendance of the sick . . . and though there was the perpetual din of carriages, continually passing, from early dawn till a late hour of the night—the physicians carriages, and hacks conveying nurses . . . and the hearses, and the ever moving 'sick wagon,' rattling and rumbling to and fro in every direction—there was no sign of wholesome animation."[29]

Everyone in Richmond respected the work of Doctors McClurg, McCaw, and Foushee during the epidemics. The city council even passed official citations thanking them for their emergency service to the city.[30]

So, naturally, when the doctors found Wythe, Broadnax, and Brown all ill from the same symptoms, they suspected an epidemic-like disease. Cholera fit perfectly.

WYTHE ANGRILY REJECTED their diagnosis. The judge was certain that Sweeney had poisoned him and, though barely able to sit up in bed, wanted to prove his point. He asked DuVal and Randolph to search the young man's room for any evidence of arsenic powder or other poisons. If Sweeney had poisoned Wythe that morning, perhaps he had more of that toxic substance hidden in his room. They refused. The esteemed doctors were convinced that the old man suffered from cholera, not arsenic poisoning, and saw no need to search through his grandnephew's possessions. Although their friend the judge knew everything about the law, they felt, he did not know anything about diseases. The doctors did. Two days passed. Feeling much worse and vomiting constantly, an angry Wythe once again insisted that his friends go to Sweeney's room and badgered them to search it.

By then, the doctors had haltingly begun to question their diagnosis of cholera, because the disease always killed its victims within forty-eight hours. Nearly three days had passed, and Wythe and Brown were still alive. Their illness must have been due to something else. The physicians also learned that the authorities had zeroed in on young Sweeney as the suspect, which lent strength to the judge's claim that he had been poisoned by his nephew for some nefarious reason.

Finally, the doctors reluctantly gave in to his demands for a search of Sweeney's room. They were shocked by what they found: a glass vial of what seemed to be a mixture of arsenic and sulfur, giving the appearance of yellow arsenic, and a bowl of six strawberries with a whitish hue that might have been a fungus or a powder. Mayor DuVal no longer needed to be convinced about the cause of death. He dismissed the physicians' diagnosis of cholera and insisted it was arsenic poisoning. The mayor was certain that Sweeney had tried to murder everyone in the household. He wrote to President Jefferson, "Many other strong circumstances concurred to induce a belief that he had poisoned the whole family."[31]

William Claiborne, a longtime Virginia political figure, the father of the governor of the New Orleans territory, and Wythe's next-door neighbor on the square, knew the judge, his maid, Michael Brown, and Sweeney well. He knew that the judge had suffered from a variety of ailments as he had aged, including increasingly painful bowel problems for which his doctors had treated him for several years. Claiborne had rushed to the house when he heard that the judge had been stricken ill. Lydia Broadnax told him that Sweeney had poisoned the old man, but Claiborne wondered whether that was true. How could the nephew, for whom the judge had done so much all of his life, try to murder Wythe?

Then Claiborne had an idea. He made a hurried visit to Mayor DuVal. Claiborne told DuVal that in Wythe's will, he left half of his money to Sweeney but designated the other half for his black protégé Michael Brown. There was a codicil to the will, however, that gave all of the money to Sweeney if Michael Brown should die before him. Now Michael Brown was very sick and might die, and Sweeney would stand to inherit all of the money if the judge, lingering on in pain for days, did not survive. It was a compelling motive, and Claiborne assured Wythe's friends that Sweeney knew the contents of the will. Wythe's money and assets from the sale of his plantation and his home were considerable, enough to tempt an impulsive and greedy teenager to commit murder.[32]

DuVal agreed. "[Claiborne] expressed his opinion that the family were poisoned and suspected [Sweeney]," he said. Claiborne also told DuVal and others that during the years he had known Sweeney, the young man had repeatedly told him that Judge Wythe would provide for him generously in his will, a reassurance that seemed to please Sweeney. He certainly seemed to have no motive to murder the judge, Michael, and Lydia Broadnax. That's why Claiborne was at first so surprised when Broadnax told him that she was sure Sweeney had poisoned them all. Now, however, remembering the will, the originally reluctant Claiborne became certain that Sweeney had poisoned the judge.

Lydia Broadnax told Mayor DuVal and anyone else who would listen that Claiborne was right; young Sweeney was very familiar with the will. In fact, she had found him reading it by candlelight in the judge's office the night before he poisoned everyone. Sweeney expressed no surprise when Broadnax caught him. He nonchalantly said that he had been given the key to the desk where the will was kept by his uncle and was just going through it for no great purpose. The next morning, the judge asked Lydia whether she had the key to the desk because he did not. She told him that he had given it to Sweeney, and he nodded his head in puzzlement. He said that he had become quite forgetful lately and that if Sweeney had the key, he must have given it to his grandnephew. Lydia Broadnax was convinced that the nephew stole the key in order to read the will.

Wythe's friends knew that Sweeney was a headstrong and irresponsible young man who gave little thought to the consequences of his actions. They were aware that he owed a lot of money to gamblers. How had he become so overpowered by Richmond's out-of-control gambling, brawling, prostitution, and drinking? What was it about the chaotic, congested, rapidly growing boomtown of Richmond that caused a young man from one of the finest families in Virginia to commit the most heinous murder in the nation's young history?

To some people, the judge's murder by his own nephew was a reminder that there were black sheep in many families. To others, the slaying was the logical next step in the harrowing downward spiral of Richmond. In a little more than twenty years, since it was named the state capital, the city had become raucous, dirty, and polluted. It was a magnet for newly arrived residents from dozens of different countries who constantly bickered with one another. Richmond was a racial time bomb, a town with one of the largest black populations in the country, both slaves and freedmen, who repeatedly clashed with the white residents. The town was still recovering from an abortive slave insurrection in which the murders of hundreds of whites had been planned. The state capital was a mecca of sin, a town overrun with racetracks, gamblers, prostitutes, con men, embezzlers, horse thieves, and counterfeiters. So much beer was consumed nightly at the wild taverns that Richmond even had its own city brewery to produce an endless supply of it.

In two decades Richmond had become one of the most violent cities in the country, with an army of nighttime burglars, dozens of murders, soaring assault convictions, and, it seemed, thieves lurking around every corner. And there were so many hangings, attended by thousands of residents, that city fathers had to erect a permanent gallows at the corner of Broad and Fifteenth streets. Had the awful aspects of the city turned Sweeney into a killer?

George Wythe was buried in Richmond as one of the nation's most revered judges, but it was in Williamsburg where the judge had built his enviable reputation as a lawyer, a jurist, and a legislator. In Williamsburg, he had tutored so many of the nation's leaders. It was there where he had been sent to the Continental Congress to sign the Declaration of Independence and, later, to the Constitutional Convention. There, he had enjoyed well-deserved happiness with his loving wife and the college students who had been his surrogate children.

It was also in that town, so long ago, where George Wythe had first met the tall, thin, red-headed, brilliant boy with the fiddle, Thomas Jefferson.

4

Williamsburg: George Wythe and Thomas Jefferson

G EORGE WYTHE first met Thomas Jefferson when the young man enrolled at the College of William and Mary in Williamsburg. It was the autumn of 1759, in the middle of the French and Indian War. Jefferson appeared emotionally rudderless when he arrived in the lovely capital city of Virginia. His father, Peter Jefferson, had died when the boy was just fourteen. For two years Tom had served as the nominal male head of his household, trying to help his mother care for six sisters and a younger brother. A teenager, he needed the guidance of older and wiser men. In 1787, looking back on his youth, he wrote to Alexander Donald of his fears of being "thrown on a wide world, among entire strangers, without a friend or guardian to advise so young a man, too, and with so little experience of mankind." He wrote that as a teenager, with no male influence in his life, he had spent much time foxhunting, gambling, going to the racetrack, and associating with "various sorts of bad company." He was surprised that he had not ruined his life and "become worthless to society."

Then he came to Williamsburg, where he took the first of many classes with Wythe at the College of William and Mary, following two years of education at a boarding school where he had learned Latin and Greek.

"I had the good fortune to become acquainted very early with some characters of very high standing, and to feel the incessant wish that I could even become what they were . . . Mr. Wythe [was one of these men]," Jefferson wrote, adding that Wythe had helped him decide to make a future for himself as "the honest advocate of my country's rights."[1]

Jefferson described Wythe, who was thirty-five years old when they first met, as "my faithful and beloved mentor in youth, and my most affectionate friend through life."[2]

Few men in American history were so much alike, despite being from different generations. Jefferson, like Wythe, saw higher education and the study of law not as a path to a career, but as training for a political life. Both men hated slavery. Both had a deep love of books, and they competed with each other in amassing the largest collection of books in Virginia (Jefferson's library would eventually include 6,500 books and become the foundation for the Library of Congress). The two claimed to have read every book they purchased.[3] Wythe had so imbued Jefferson with the love of books that when a sudden fire

Wythe's most famous pupil was Thomas Jefferson, who became the third president of the United States. The young Jefferson worked side by side with Wythe as his student for four years and then as his law clerk for five more years. The two remained extremely close friends all of their lives.

destroyed his family home at Shadwell in 1770, it was the loss of his books and papers, not the loss of the building, that sent young Jefferson into a depression. He wrote, "I am utterly destitute."[4]

The two were devoted to sciences and any sort of machinery. Jefferson's home at Monticello included the nation's first automatic doors and dumbwaiters and was filled with machines he used to conduct scientific experiments. Wythe's house in Williamsburg was similarly stocked with his "philosophical machines," which he used to conduct intellectual experiments with his students—devices such as telescopes and microscopes—as well as jars filled with dead animals that he loved to dissect.

The pair enjoyed a love of gardening, instilled in Jefferson by Wythe when he tended the gardens around his home in Williamsburg. They regularly exchanged grapevines and grafts for fruits such as nectarines and apricots to be replanted in each other's gardens. Elizabeth Wythe sent Jefferson newly grown peas, and he mailed her plants he had obtained from the East Indies. Wythe forwarded Jefferson garden catalogues he had purchased. Wythe and Jefferson developed new types of mulch and strains of seed that they shared with each other.[5]

Both men loved the Greek language and the culture of ancient Greece. The love of Greek that Wythe gave Jefferson filled the future president's days with joy. Jefferson read not only Homer, Pericles, Socrates, and Plato, but also the famous Greek playwrights, such as Sophocles.[6]

The pair loved to discuss the issues of the day with anyone and everyone they met, and Williamsburg, the capital, was always full of interesting people from whom the professor and his pupil could learn much. As an example, Jefferson and Royal Governor Frances Fauquier became close friends when the governor discovered that Jefferson, like himself, kept daily meteorological diaries that recorded the depth of snow, incidents of rainfall, and wind velocity. Fauquier, Wythe, and Jefferson often dined together. Jefferson wrote of his discussions with Wythe and Fauquier, "I have heard more good sense, more rational and philosophical conversation than in all my life besides."[7]

Life under the intellectual wing of George Wythe broadened quickly for Jefferson as his mentor introduced him to all of the important men in the colony's government, along with men and women who were the pillars of high society in Virginia, such as George Washington, Patrick Henry, and George Mason.

Jefferson and Wythe were both early risers who felt that getting out of bed at 5 A.M. was an opportunity not merely to add more hours of activity to the day, but to read more books. In a letter to Benjamin Moore, a friend who had asked for a reading list, Jefferson chronicled what he read in college each day. He suggested that Moore, like him, should try to get up at dawn and plunge into his books well before breakfast. "Before 8 A.M. . . . employ yourself in physical studies, ethics, religion and natural law." Jefferson advised reading law books from 8 A.M. until noon and politics from noon until 1 P.M. Moore should spend the entire afternoon reading history, Jefferson said, and admonished him to save the evening hours to read novels, criticism, rhetoric, and oratory. In telling Moore about his studies, Jefferson explained, in modest lines, his own enormous intellectual training under Wythe at the college. He told Moore that for the study of law, "a sufficient ground work must be laid. For this purpose an acquaintance with the Latin and French languages is absolutely necessary. Mathematics and natural history are so useful in the most familiar occurrences of life and are so peculiarly engaging and delightful as would induce every person to wish an acquaintance with them. . . . Mathematical reasoning and deductions are therefore a fine preparation for investigating the abstruse speculations of the law."

Jefferson wrote down the names of numerous books and concluded that all of this reading and these books were a mere foundation for the knowledge that he had gained and that he advised all prospective attorneys to have. "They will give him a respectable and useful and satisfactory degree of knowledge in these branches, and will themselves form a valuable and sufficient library for a lawyer."

Jefferson saw in Wythe the perfect teacher, a man who was obviously one of the world's leading intellectuals and yet could make the understanding of complicated legal, historical, and political theories easy for any student. He was "a man of unaffected modesty," according to Jefferson, "whose suavity of manners endeared him to everyone. . . . He was of easy elocution, his language chaste, methodical in the arrangement of his matter learned and logical in the use of it . . . profound in penetration and sound in conclusion."[8]

Just about everyone who met Wythe felt the same way. The Marquis de Chastellux, a French diplomat with the French army and a visitor to the College of William and Mary during the Revolution, wrote, "George Wythe . . . may be looked upon as [a] living book, in which both precepts and examples are to be found." He added that it was well-known that many of the most important men in Virginia had been Wythe's students.[9]

Jefferson's diligence as a student became legendary. There were dozens of attractive temptations for students at the college, whose campus covered the western end of Williamsburg. The city offered a racetrack, gambling, taverns, prostitutes, seemingly endless rounds of parties, and a ceaseless parade of visitors with sordid backgrounds from all over the country. Yet Jefferson never seemed to let any of those diversions get in the way of his education. He enjoyed stringent self-discipline, which perhaps was inborn or may have been engendered by his relationship to Wythe. John Page, later the governor of Virginia and a fellow student of Jefferson's at the college, was, like Wythe and Jefferson, a man who loved astronomy and inventions. Yet he was jealous of Jefferson's educational discipline. Page himself could not study that hard, he wrote, "for I was too sociable and fond of the conversations of my friends, to study as Mr. Jefferson did, who could tear himself away from his dearest friends to fly to his studies."[10]

Throughout his life, Jefferson maintained that workaholic discipline. He attributed it to intellectual inquiry and good health. He favored very weak wines; ate as little meat as possible; possessed, he said, a strong digestive tract; tried to get six to eight hours of sleep each night; and always read for an hour prior to going to bed. He never had more than tea or coffee for breakfast, consumed a light afternoon dinner, and did everything in moderation. At Williamsburg, perhaps inspired by Wythe's practice of dousing himself with a bucket of freezing well water each morning, Jefferson began his own morning ritual of soaking his feet in a tub of ice-cold water. He ascribed much of his good health to that odd practice.[11]

Writing of Jefferson's education by Wythe, U.S. Supreme Court Justice Lewis Powell wrote in 1990, "In sum, the tutoring of Wythe was the equivalent for Jefferson of the most demanding university education. Indeed, far more demanding than what is called a university education today." (Justice Powell reportedly always asked his prospective law clerks whether they had heard of George Wythe; if they had not, he refused to hire them.)[12]

Thomas Jefferson saw George Wythe as a master teacher, but he may have also considered Wythe a second father, one whom the growing teenage boy very much needed. Wythe, in turn, who had no children with his two wives, perhaps saw in Jefferson the son he never had. They seemed, said all who knew them, a perfect pair.

GEORGE WYTHE was born in Chesterville, Virginia (now Hampton), in Elizabeth City County in 1726, to a family that had sailed to America from England in the 1670s. His father, Thomas, who died young, was a successful farmer. Thomas Wythe developed the Chesterville Plantation into a 1,050-acre farm, which he ran with two overseers and a slave force that ranged, over the years, from twenty-six to thirty-two members. On the farm, the Wythes grew hay, corn, wheat, and barley; raised several hundred head of cattle, sheep, and hogs; and maintained vast orchards that included numerous apple trees. In addition to the main brick manor house, there were slave quarters, an office building, a stable, storehouses, and a granary that held sixty tons of farm produce. The Wythes also built a school for area children to attend, which they leased to the county.[13]

George Wythe was descended from a long line of Quakers, who had been involved in the antislavery movement. His great-grandfather was George Keith, the noted traveling preacher who formed "the Keithians" as a Quaker sect. He published An Exhortation and Caution to Friends Concerning Buying or Keeping of Negroes in 1693. His mother, Margaret, was one of the best-read and -educated women in the colony and one of its few Quakers, a strident one. She educated George herself, except for a brief period of time when he boarded at the grammar school run by the College of William and Mary. He became proficient in Latin and Greek and was urged by his mother to study new subjects throughout his life.[14]

When he was twenty, Wythe passed the bar exam and became a lawyer. He practiced in Fredericksburg, where his sister Anne had just married and begun to have children, instead of the Chesterville area.

Anne's grandson George Sweeney, who was later accused of murdering Wythe, would be born there.

He worked as a junior partner with a prominent attorney named Zachary Lewis, traveling a court circuit through the four northernmost counties in Virginia. In 1747, Wythe married Lewis's daughter, Anne. She died one year later. Despondent, Wythe left Lewis's law firm and moved to Williamsburg permanently, to start a new life. He became a member of the thriving Benjamin Waller law firm. The politically connected Waller introduced Wythe to legislators in the House of Burgesses, who in turn got him interested in the political life.

House members appointed Wythe as their committee clerk, to benefit from his talents and make him feel like a part of the legislature. As the clerk, he sat at the table in the middle of the people's chamber, the lower house of the two houses (the king's chamber was the other). He was surrounded by the several dozens of legislators in two rows of wooden benches and the speaker, who sat on an ornate ten-foot-high wooden chair. Light streamed into the chamber through three circular and three rectangular windows.

In 1752, Wythe's life took an unexpected turn when Royal Governor Robert Dinwiddie named him to replace Peyton Randolph as speaker of the house for a year while Randolph traveled to England on legislative business. It gave Wythe, just twenty-six, his first taste of governmental responsibility and immediate prominence. A year later, the voters of Elizabeth City County elected him to the House of Burgesses, as they had elected members of his family for years. In 1755, his brother, who had inherited the plantation, died. He left everything to George Wythe, making him a comfortable man.

Later that year, Wythe met and married Elizabeth Taliaferro, the attractive daughter of the very wealthy Richard Taliaferro, a sophisticated planter who also served as a county judge and had long admired Wythe, the lawyer. Taliaferro gave the pair the use of his handsome, 3,900-square-foot, two-story Georgian-style brick mansion in Williamsburg, on an acre of land, as a wedding present, and later bequeathed its ownership to them in his will.[15] Behind the home were small wooden buildings, including a stable, a laundry, a smokehouse, and a kitchen. The house, with a spacious garden in the rear full of various sweet-smelling flowers, sat on the same street as the Governor's Palace.

The handsomely designed House of Burgesses was home to the Virginia State Legislature until it moved to Richmond in 1778. The building's chambers were the scene of some of the greatest speeches in American history. Wythe worked there for years as the body's clerk and then later as a longtime elected member.

It overlooked a rectangular village green that extended from the palace to the shops and taverns of busy Duke of Gloucester Street, which was often filled with strolling couples or running children. Elizabeth, like other daughters of wealthy Virginians, was well read, educated, and as familiar with literature as she was with dancing and music. She was "amiable in her disposition, engaging in her manners, and possessed of every virtue which could render her beloved," said a friend.

To many in Williamsburg, they seemed an unlikely pair because Wythe, at nearly thirty, was fourteen years older than his teenage bride. People who knew them well saw a compatible couple; they both loved reading, education, parties, and fine clothes. No one ever completely approved of Wythe's staid Quakerish dress, with his traditional gray coat, breeches, and long-out-of-style silver-buckle shoes, but they admired his willingness to shower his wife with the latest gowns, dresses, bonnets, and handkerchiefs. The couple even ordered stylish monogrammed riding saddles for their horses. The pair purchased dozens of shoes and other garments from London, along with expensive china sets, teacup settings, comfortable bed quilts (and similarly warm quilts for their servants), and breeches and stockings. When Wythe ordered goods from classy London stores, there was always something for his students, such as mathematical measuring instruments. He ordered telescopes for himself. And, always, there were books. One order included the works of Theophilus in Greek and Latin, in two volumes, plus books by Granville, Bracton, Britton, and Fleta; Greek common prayer books; and a volume of Erasmus's adages.[16]

The couple did not have children, and so the Wythes, who would be married for thirty-two years, luxuriated in making George's college students their surrogate children. Over the years, they took in many students as boarders and welcomed hundreds of students and their girl-friends or wives to their home as guests while the men were enrolled at the college and later in their lives.[17]

The home they entertained in was one of the most elegant in Virginia. The first floor contained a parlor, a dining room, and a down-stairs bedroom that the Wythes slept in for coolness in the oppressively hot summer months. The rooms were separated by a twelve-foot-wide hallway that bisected the house. The hallway was often used for dancing at their parties, and the Wythes dined there, with the front and rear doors flung open for ventilation, on excessively hot evenings.

At the rear of the first floor of the Wythe house was the scholar's fifteen-by-twelve-foot study, where he did his work and tutored Jefferson and his other students. It was jammed with books, instruments, news-papers, magazines, globes of the world, and large, colorful maps. The study was anchored by a circular wooden table, which was surrounded by large, comfortable chairs. Wythe and the students working at the table were bathed in light from windows on the southern and western sides of the room and in the winter were warmed by a fireplace on the eastern side. Nearby was an optical viewer that everyone had fun with as they viewed a succession of drawings through its magnifying glass. Wythe's jars of dead animals were on top of a bookcase. All of the rooms seemed even larger because of their ten-foot-high ceilings.

The Wythes' main bedroom was upstairs, facing the village green. Next to it was a guest bedroom, where Jefferson slept when he was in town. To the rear was a large children's room, filled with toys ordered

This aerial view shows the entire Wythe estate in Williamsburg. A large, well-kept lawn at the rear of the home is surrounded by a series of outbuildings—a kitchen, a laundry, and stables—and the main house is to the left. Wythe lived there for more than thirty years.

from London, where the family's nieces and nephews, including George Wythe Sweeney, stayed on their numerous visits.

The judge probably had more of an attachment to young Sweeney than to any of his other nieces and nephews because Sweeney's father, also named George Wythe Sweeney, worked as the manager of the judge's plantation at Chesterville from 1786 until Wythe sold it in 1792. Whenever Judge Wythe visited, he saw the manager and his family, along with his young son. Wythe knew young Sweeney well and showered him with pocket money and gifts throughout his life.[18]

The Wythes owned a dozen slaves, who lived in the various out-buildings. Lydia Broadnax, the cook, stayed in a room in the large kitchen outbuilding. Ben, the coachman, lived in the carriage house, and Fanny, the laundress, lived in the laundry with her two sons.

In 1750, the residents of Williamsburg elected Wythe an alderman, and in 1758, the aldermen chose him as mayor. Wythe would serve a total of eighteen years in city government. In addition to his role as mayor, he was a vestryman at Bruton Parish Church, the most prominent in the state. He was also on the boards of various organizations, including those of the local hospital and the nation's first insane asylum. In 1761, he was named a justice of the Elizabeth City County courts, his very first judicial role.[19]

George Wythe, thirty-six, had become one of Virginia's most distinguished teachers, lawyers, and judges and an influential state legislator. He was a happily married man who flung open the doors of his home to students and friends for parties and numerous organizational meetings. He loved riding through the countryside and spent hours nestled in a comfortable chair in his study, reading as many books as he could, in as many languages as possible. Young Thomas Jefferson could not have had better fortune in choosing the man who would become his mentor, adviser, and close friend for life.

Jefferson's work at the College of William and Mary developed into an enthusiastic interest in law and politics. Wythe was happy that his protégé had decided to follow him in the legal profession and agreed to take Jefferson on as his clerk. Jefferson had spent four years as Wythe's pupil and would spend every day of the next five years at the elbow of his teacher, studying law, writing and reviewing briefs, and discussing how law impacts society. No one saw more promise in Tom Jefferson than George Wythe did, and Wythe designed a complex apprenticeship for the fledgling lawyer from Henrico County. In addition to going over cases with his mentor, writing briefs on his own to assist Wythe, and going to court with Wythe for his cases, Jefferson was urged to attend court as an interested observer.[20]

Wythe also urged young Jefferson to spend as much time as he could at the state legislature, where he could listen and learn from all of the politicians attending the sessions each October and April. Wythe explained carefully to all of his students that it was not enough to simply become good lawyers; his protégés had to be leaders, too.

At the House of Burgesses, Jefferson became an eyewitness to the turbulent history of the colonial era. Because there was no visitors' gallery at that time, Jefferson had to lean against a wall near a wooden doorway to listen to the loud debates. He cut quite an impressive figure even then. One man wrote, "He was tall, slender, and remarkably erect, with a small head and thin hair, mild sparkling blue eyes."[21]

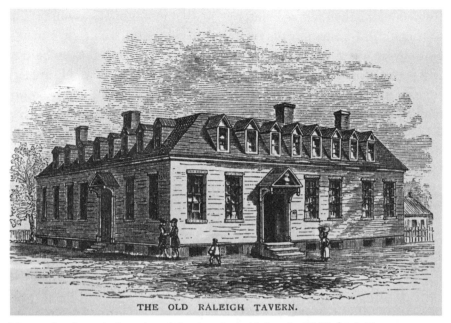

THE OLD RALEIGH TAVERN.

Virginia legislators had meals and drank and gambled at the Old Raleigh Tavern in Williamsburg. They met there whenever the angry royal governor dismissed the House of Burgesses.

It was in the House of Burgesses, in 1765, that Jefferson heard a boisterous Patrick Henry deliver a soaring denunciation of the Crown during a series of debates on the Stamp Act. This was one of many controversial tax bills passed by Parliament to obtain money from the colonists to pay for the Crown's costs in the recent French and Indian War.

Jefferson was impressed by Henry's fiery oratorical skills. He observed "the splendid display of Mr. Henry's talents as a popular orator. They were great indeed." Henry's speeches were "such as I have never heard from any other man. He appeared to me to speak as Homer wrote."

Henry filled the legislative chamber with "torrents of sublime eloquence," Jefferson wrote. "He was in his element and captivated all with his bold and splendid eloquence."[22]

Wythe said that people had to live with a strong moral code, a basic sense of right and wrong unencumbered by political agendas.

Remembering that, Jefferson later wrote that morality was as important to a man or a woman as his or her physical senses, and that a man's conscience was as critical as his limbs. "It is given to all human beings in a stronger or weaker degree," he said after the Revolution. He argued that people's morality did not depend on their wealth or education and that it was the foundation of whatever success Americans were going to have as a people. "State a moral case to a ploughman and a professor. The former will decide it as well, and often better than the latter, because he has not been led astray by artificial rules."[23]

Wythe had become one of the most industrious men in Virginia. The legislator rose at dawn and plunged into the day's work, whether it was planning lectures for his classes, researching legal cases for his law practice, or attending committee meetings at the state legislature. At the same time, he traveled back and forth to Elizabeth City County to serve as a judge and tend to his plantation there, becoming the quintessential country squire.[24]

Wythe himself was a poor politician. He hated campaigning for public office, detested listening to the many long-winded speeches in the legislature, and had no lust for power. His own speeches were sophisticated, elegant, and informational but bored his audiences. They were lengthy, rambling orations filled with passages from Greek and Latin scholars and were sometimes even read in those languages. Wythe's speeches were organized around brilliant ideas and original concepts, but Wythe had none of the oratorical flourishes of most politicians in Williamsburg.[25]

One of his many protégés, Nathaniel Beverley Tucker, wrote, "In his ordinary motives and modes of action he differed altogether from other men. . . . Without ambition, without avarice, he was by nature addicted to solitude and his active mind found its only enjoyment in profound research."

Wythe the lawyer was much like Wythe the politician, a man who was so consumed with presenting a strong case, based on exhaustive research and merit, that he had no time for the courtroom theatrics that rival attorneys, despite their lesser legal and intellectual credentials, often used to win cases.

One lawyer wrote of Wythe's losing cases to flamboyant barristers: "He [Wythe] was too open and direct in his conduct and possessed too little management either with regard to his own temper or those of other men, to cope with [a] cool and skillful adversary." Another lawyer wrote that in court, Wythe's demeanor was full of "dignity and of grace," but that he had no regard for his effect on the judge or the jury. "While the stern integrity and unyielding firmness of Mr. Wythe's character carried him always straight to his object, as soon as he was convinced it was proper, and he in the pursuit of what he [believed] right, he was heedless of and utterly indifferent to after effects." Yet another added that Wythe could make a good case but was weak under the crossfire of rebuttal, that "he failed to rally until the day was lost." And, many complained, Wythe could not resist enthusiastically dropping in lines of Horace, Cicero, and other ancient scholars that seemed to put everyone to sleep.[26]

Wythe never defended a client whom he believed was guilty, and he left the necessary legal defenses of murderers, robbers, and embezzlers to other attorneys.

His mother had instilled in him a moral code derived from her own altruistic Quaker heritage. She urged him to do what he could to help the mentally ill, Native Americans, slaves, and freed black men and women; to urge coeducational public schooling, assistance for the physically disabled, alms houses for the poor, the teaching of applied sciences in schools and colleges, and the separation of church and state. He championed these causes throughout his life.[27]

His personal attributes were not those of the traditional politician in Virginia or the other colonies, either. He did not drink more than a glass of wine with friends and he shunned the taverns, where the other state legislators and successful merchants ate and drank until the early hours of the morning. He dressed well but not ostentatiously and abhorred the powdered wigs and the frilly jackets of the rich. He did not gamble or spend hours at the racetrack, like so many of the legislators, especially his friend George Washington, who often dined at his home and for whom he did legal work.[28] Wythe did not curse or tell bawdy stories, and he respected women. He never attended cockfights or joined an audience to watch public wrestling matches. He disdained gossip, and although he did read the novels and the short stories of the day, he was always quick to retreat to his library and the Greek and Latin classics.

All of the characteristics that made him a weak and uninspiring politician, however, combined to make him a distinguished and venerated figure in Williamsburg. He was a rarity in politics: a gentleman and a scholar.

Andrew Burnaby, an Englishman who traveled through the South, said that Wythe was a throwback to the ancient times of Rome and Greece. "I cannot resist the inclination to mention George Wythe, who to a perfect knowledge of the Greek language . . . and of ancient, particularly platonic, philosophy had joined such a profound reverence for the Supreme Being, such respect for the divine laws, such inflexible rectitude and integrity of principle as would have dignified a Roman senator, even in the most virtuous times of the Republic."[29]

He had become, to all, the "American Aristides."

GEORGE WYTHE'S ROAD to the American Revolution, like that of many others, began with his opposition to the Stamp Act in 1765. Parliament imposed the tax on newspapers and all legal documents. The Stamp Act began a series of taxes on tea, glass, paint, lead, paper, and even doorknobs, along with trade restrictions against the colonies. These culminated in the Crown's decision to try Americans in London as political prisoners and to send a small army to America in 1768 to put down any civil disorders that might arise.

In 1765, in 1769, and again in 1774, the royal governor of Virginia dissolved the state legislature for its increasingly critical activities. Virginia's legislators eventually authorized a militia to prepare for war if it came. Wythe, shaking his head, told them that a simple militia was not enough and that an army of more than ten thousand troops would be needed. Prophetically, he warned them that England would send a huge military force to put down any American rebellion.[30]

In the spring of 1775, Virginia sent George Wythe to Philadelphia as one of its representatives to the Continental Congress. There, delegates were surprised at the radicalization of Wythe. They all knew of Patrick Henry's bombast but had heard that Wythe was a mild-mannered scholar and not one of the rebels. They also looked upon Wythe, age fifty, as an elder statesman and not one of the young turks. Yet the professor was as radical as anyone else in screaming for independence.

In one of his first public stands, Wythe rose to his feet in the
assembly hall, straightened out his gray coat, and not only condemned
several actions by Governor Dunmore of Virginia, but demanded his
arrest. He rebuked those who did not believe that America could build
a navy or outfit merchant ships into naval vessels. He reminded them
that the Romans had had no navy and that they had built one for their
war against Carthage. He encouraged universal trade with all European
countries during the war and castigated those who thought otherwise.
And, foremost, he reminded everyone that America would not lose
this war. "We shall sometime or other rise superior to all the difficulties
they may throw in our way," he said.[31]

The delegates, impressed with Wythe, appointed him to committees
to oversee the construction of the first U.S. navy; to dispense British
merchant ship cargo captured at sea; to investigate the reluctance of
the colonists to spend the Continental Congress's new paper currency;
to settle land disputes between colonies; to produce published journals
of the work on Congress; to work with New York to help it unravel its
political difficulties; to communicate with the generals in charge of the
failed invasion of Canada; to persuade states, such as New Jersey, that
were reluctant to break with England to do so; and to work for peaceful
coexistence with Indians. He impressed everyone. John Adams wrote,
"[He] is a learned and very laborious man." Georgia delegate William
Pierce wrote, "He is one of the most learned legal characters of the
present age. . . . He is remarked for his exemplary life and universally
esteemed for his good principles."[32]

Adams and Wythe became great friends in Philadelphia. Many
in Congress did not like the abrasive Adams. The New Englander
had a dim view of Southerners; he considered them primitive and
uncultured and no match for proper New Englanders like himself. The
intellectual and gracious Wythe did not fit his stereotype. They had
several things in common that created a bond. He and Wythe were
both lawyers; had solid marriages to strong, independent, intellectual
women; and had the vision to see the need for a federal government,
and not a collection of states, put into place once the Revolution was
over. Adams wrote to Wythe, "You and I, my dear friend, have been
sent into life at a time when the greatest lawgivers of antiquity would
have wished to live. How few of the human race have ever enjoyed an

opportunity of making an election of government for themselves or their children!"[33]

In the steaming hot summer of 1776, Congress appointed a committee to write a Declaration of Independence. The committee, composed of Thomas Jefferson, Benjamin Franklin, Robert Livingston, John Adams, and Roger Sherman, turned to Jefferson to write the final document. For advice, Jefferson turned to Wythe and asked him to write a statement on independence that Jefferson could use for reference. In it, Wythe wrote, "Whilst you are asserting the rights of mankind, and delivering your country from bondage, those who fall cannot die in a better cause, nor can those who survive with victory earn a nobler triumph. . . . What do men who know the value of liberty think too great a price to purchase it with! And what is property worth, or rather can we have property, if we enjoy not liberty."[34]

It was not the soaring oratory that Jefferson would write in the Declaration, but it was emotional and moving. Jefferson treasured his friend's statement and kept it all of his life.

Throughout June and into early July, the delegates engaged in heated debates over independence. "We must declare ourselves a free people!" Wythe insisted.[35]

Jefferson was surprised that in Philadelphia, Wythe used very direct and persuasive language—no Greek or Latin phrases—to convince the delegates to declare independence. Jefferson told everyone that his friend did not haggle on "halfway principles as others did."[36]

Benjamin Rush of Pennsylvania saw Wythe as most people did, a brilliant man who was possessed of unusual common sense. "He seldom spoke in Congress, but when he did his speeches were correct, sensible and pertinent. I have never known a man [to] possess more modesty or a more dove like simplicity and gentleness of manner."[37]

Wythe was not in Philadelphia when independence was approved and the Declaration signed. He had been called back to Virginia with some others to preside over the colony's own constitutional convention. He came back in the fall. In Philadelphia, out of respect, the Virginians who did sign the Declaration left a vacant spot at the top of their column of names for him to sign when he returned. He did so with a great flourish of his pen.

On the day the Virginia convention began, George Wythe seemed younger than anybody in the room. A man there wrote that he was "erect and active, that overarching forehead with its wide, magnificent sweep, and those dark grey eyes that beamed beneath it, that Roman nose, those finely chiseled lips on which the flame of conscious inspiration seems yet to burn, that broad and well defined chin, all making up a profile which would be singled out of a thousand."[38]

Upon his return to Philadelphia, Wythe plunged into work on yet more committees, including those to procure gunpowder for the army and to develop American money to replace the British pound. He mingled with the most influential men in America on these committees, serving on four with John Adams, on three with Benjamin Franklin, and on the military committee that worked with George Washington and his generals; there he lobbied hard for the creation of an American navy.[39] His most important committee was to oversee the work of diplomats who were sent to France to convince that nation to come into the Revolution on the American side. The intervention of the French, with their troops, money, and huge navy was the only way America could win the war, Wythe warned Congress. He also advocated outfitting merchant ships with cannons and letting them operate as privateers.[40] He wrote an address to the thousands of Hessian soldiers serving in the British army, in an attempt to get them to leave America and go back home.[41]

It was his final assignment. He was called home to Virginia with Jefferson and was asked to serve on a committee with Edmund Pendleton to revise all of the laws and the government of their new state.

As a legislator prior to the war, Washington had continually sought the opinion of George Wythe on any political matters connected to legal issues. He was pleased that Virginia elected Wythe to the Continental Congress in 1775 and 1776 and was frustrated that Wythe left to return to Virginia after his second term. Washington had relied on several Virginians in Congress for help in the early days of the Revolution, and he missed them when they retired. In December 1777, a bitter Washington grew frustrated with Congress's inability to help his army during the terrible winter at Valley Forge and charged that the best men in the country were not there. He wrote to a friend, "Where is Mason—Wythe—Jefferson?"[42]

Wythe was just as eager to fight as the young men in Virginia were. He had been a part-time militia volunteer years earlier. He attempted to join a militia company in Williamsburg, arriving with his musket

Edmund Pendleton was Wythe's judicial rival in Virginia for many years but teamed up with him to help get the U.S. Constitution passed at the state's ratification convention in 1788.

on his shoulder, but was gently rejected because of his age. Although never proven, a story circulated for years that in the fall of 1781, Wythe and three friends went hunting and spotted a group of British soldiers disembarking from a ship. Wythe and his friends fired at the Redcoats, who then ran back to the ship. Wythe, it was said, was thrilled that he wound up in the war after all, even if for one shot.[43]

GEORGE WYTHE LOVED Williamsburg. It had been built as the capital of the colony, two miles from the James and York rivers. It was not a large community, having only fifteen hundred year-round residents. The main avenue was the wide, tree-lined Duke of Gloucester Street, where the largest taverns and inns were located, along with small shops and residential homes. The mile-long street was anchored at one end by the red-brick, H-shaped House of Burgesses, the colony's legislative assembly, set amid a grove of trees, and at the other by the stately College of William and Mary. Numerous narrow lanes intersected the

Duke of Gloucester Street. They contained tiny, two-room, white clapboard homes, outbuildings, and stables.

The town was home to the Bruton Parish Church, the Governor's Palace, a one-story brick courthouse, a jail, a formidable gunpowder warehouse, and several stables where the town's merchants kept their horses. Much of the architecture emulated buildings in England that were designed by Sir Christopher Wren. The thriving community impressed everyone who visited it. A Hessian soldier stationed there during the Revolution wrote, "It [is] among the beautiful cities of America. . . . It has some beautiful churches and steeples with clocks to see, and also some buildings otherwise worth seeing. The broad and straight main street of the city is nearly one mile long. There is also a beautiful large statehouse, where the general court assembles."[44]

Visitors to the town found the people gracious. Lord Adam Gordon, a British noble traveling through the town in 1765, wrote that "the people are well bred, polite and extremely civil to strangers." Gordon, who noted the lovely countryside around Williamsburg, added that he had met many people in his travels and the Virginians of Williamsburg impressed him the most. "They far exceed in good sense, affability, and ease any set of men I have yet fallen in with, either in the West Indies or on the Continent," he wrote and said that if he had to live in America, he would live in Williamsburg.[45]

Many people found the William and Mary teachers just as enchanting as the town. The Marquis de Chastellux, a French diplomat, wrote that the College of William and Mary was "a noble establishment which does honour to Virginia" and that it was "distinguished merit of several professors [Wythe]."[46]

The population of Williamsburg tripled during October and April, the two months of the year when both the legislature and the courts were in session. Anyone who had business with the government or the judicial system came to Williamsburg then; many stayed for a week or more.

The sleepy capital came alive during those months. The town's racetrack, one of the first in the country, held seasonal meets with races and betting; planters offered large purses for the winners of races. Athletic teams gathered in meadows to play an early form of baseball called "trap ball," in which batters swung at balls hurled through the air by a crude mechanical pitching machine. There were foot races of all kinds. Balls, parties, and receptions were held from one end of the town to the other, and men and women dressed in their finest clothes for them.

The event of the year was the annual ball at the Governor's Palace on the king's birthday. It was attended by the wealthiest residents of the colony, and their families and servants arrived in Williamsburg with them.[47] One young lady who attended wrote that the ball "consisted of more beauty and elegance than I had ever witnessed before."[48]

The more successful merchants in Williamsburg owned luxurious carriages, but these paled in comparison to the handsome carriages that the rich legislators, businessmen, and planters rode up in during the legislative seasons. Residents and boarders hosted dinners in their homes or at taverns and rented out buildings for parties (some rented the courthouse itself). Planters who lived nearby invited guests to their farms for fox hunting and outdoor fairs in good weather. The royal governor always hosted music concerts at the palace and sometimes invited local student musicians to play (Thomas Jefferson appeared there frequently with his violin).

Entertainers established street carnivals and earned money in generous tips from residents and visitors. A year-round theater was established, one of the first in the colonies, which offered Shakespearean drama and contemporary British plays such as *She Stoops to Conquer* and *The Beggar's Opera*. The theaters also produced vaudeville-style shows, complete with musical numbers staged within elaborate sets, some of which were illuminated by fire. The theater was routinely attended by Wythe and other residents of town, plus visitors such as Thomas Jefferson, Patrick Henry, and George Washington.[49]

Parties were numerous and celebrated every conceivable event, from birthdays to anniversaries, engagements, graduations, recoveries from illness, and christenings ("The drinks flew about in vast abundance," noted one student).[50]

NOT ONLY DID Williamsburg's College of William and Mary quickly grow into the finest institution of higher education in Virginia, but over the years an extraordinarily high number of its graduates became leaders of the state's political, economic, and cultural communities. As an example, an 1861 study showed that more than half of all the Supreme Court appeals judges in Virginia's previous one hundred years had been graduates of the College of William and Mary.[51]

The college had always had a rigorous curriculum. To obtain a bachelor's degree, students had to study theoretical and practical mathematics; read eight books of Euclid; learn plain trigonometry, heights and distances, surveying, algebra, and natural philosophy in relation to the general properties of matter, as well as mechanics, electricity, pneumatics, hydrostatics, and optics; and master the first principles of astronomy. Students were required to take classes in logic, letters, rhetoric, natural law, the law of nations, civil history, law enforcement, and the general principles of politics. Each student also had to have a competent knowledge of geography and ancient and modern languages.

Student Littleton Tazewell, later a governor of Virginia and a U.S. senator, called Wythe "a great and good man." He remembered arriving at Wythe's brick home just after sunrise and studying Greek and Latin with him, particularly the works of Herodotus, Aeschylus, and Cicero. Whatever Tazewell did not know, he said, Wythe taught him with great enthusiasm. They usually worked for several hours and then took a break. Tazewell returned at noon and studied Latin with Wythe for two hours. Following a two-hour break, he returned at 4 P.M. to study mathematics and French. In the evening, the teacher and the student read and discussed English novels.[52] Students complained that they had far too much homework (Jefferson reportedly spent fifteen hours a day in class and studies, with three hours for his violin practice and six hours for sleep) and spent too many hours in tutorials with professors. Later, though, all agreed that they had received a remarkable education. Munford wrote of students that "After being buried for five or six years, we see them emerge from their hiding places and shine forth with a splendor that dazzles the continent."[53]

Wythe's desire to educate young people knew no boundaries. He also taught slaves in Williamsburg to read and write and took some in as sideline students. In an experiment, he tutored one white boy from a prestigious Virginia family and a slave boy at the same time. Under his guidance, both performed well in their studies. They were proof, he said, that blacks were not inferior to whites and that given the same opportunities in life would perform just as well.[54]

George Wythe had, by the late 1770s, established himself as a unique man in a unique town.

5

Jefferson and Wythe
Remake Virginia

W HEN JEFFERSON became the second governor of Virginia in
1779, the College of William and Mary named him to its
Board of Visitors, the governing board of the institution. As
a new member and a powerful alumnus, Governor Jefferson persuaded
the board to restructure the college. He saw no need for the grammar
school and abolished it, along with professorships in divinity and language. He insisted on one professorship each in anatomy, medicine, and
chemistry; one in modern languages; and the nation's first professorship
in law. The governor named his old mentor and friend George Wythe,
now fifty-three, to the law post. Jefferson was determined to remake the
already prestigious college into an institution of higher learning that
did not merely produce educated young men, but graduated men who
would be trained and equipped to become useful members of Virginia's
political life.

Wythe, of course, was eminently qualified for the first professorship
of law as envisioned by Jefferson; he was held in high esteem by all.
"No man ever left behind him a character more venerated than George
Wythe," Jefferson wrote later. "His virtue was of the purest tint; his
integrity flexible and his justice exact, of warm patriotism and devoted

as he was to liberty and the natural and equal rights of man. He might truly be called the Cato of his country . . . for a more distinguished person never lived."

Jefferson told everyone that Wythe, the new law professor, was a man of high moral character who believed in religious freedom for all and a system of laws that benefited the rich and the poor equally. Jefferson added that Wythe led a "life of exemplary virtue."[1]

The relationship between the two had become even closer as Jefferson moved into politics. The pair worked together on committees when Jefferson returned to Williamsburg as a member of the state legislature, and they corresponded regularly. They were so close that when Jefferson came to Williamsburg on his own or with his wife, Martha, he usually stayed with Wythe. (Jefferson was a generous tipper, giving tips to Wythe's house slaves for driving him in the judge's carriage, purchasing goods at local stores, and cleaning his clothes. Jefferson and his wife took an early liking to the cook, Lydia Broadnax; she received larger and more frequent tips from the Jeffersons than any other servants did.)[2] It was to Wythe's comfortable brick home, in September 1776, that Jefferson returned following his authorship of the Declaration of Independence in Philadelphia. His pregnant wife met him at Wythe's house, and there, in Wythe's spare bedroom, their first child, an unnamed baby boy, was brought into the world with the help of Wythe and his servants (the baby died two weeks later).[3]

No one was happier than Jefferson when Wythe was elected Speaker of the House in Virginia in the spring of 1777; his mentor and friend had now become his most important political ally. Jefferson wrote of the new speaker that "his pure integrity, judgment and reasoning powers gave him great weight."[4]

Perhaps the most important reason Jefferson had such great confidence in George Wythe was because of their previous three years together as members of the Board of Revisors. The committee consisted of Jefferson, Wythe, and Edmund Pendleton, another judge. Pendleton fell and dislocated his hip early into the work, however, leaving the bulk of it to Wythe and Jefferson. The trio was charged with revising the entire legal code of Virginia. The leaders of the House of Burgesses wanted not only to revise antiquated statutes, but to pass new legislation to improve the judicial system in the state and make it

This portrait of George Wythe captured the man in his forties. He died at eighty, one of the oldest men in the South.

a shining example of jurisprudence when the Revolution was won and independence secured.

The trio set up a whole new court system. Under it, there was a Chancery Court, to hear civil cases; a General Court for criminal cases; and an Admiralty Court for cases that concerned the shipping industry. Judges from each court met together to form a Court of Appeals and a State Supreme Court. Wythe was adamant that all of the judges in Virginia had to be scrupulously honest. They had to swear "to do equal right to all manner of people, great and small, high and low, rich and poor, of what country or nation so ever they be without respect of persons. You shall not take, by yourself, or by any other, any gift, fee or reward of gold, silver or any other thing, directly or indirectly, of any person or persons great or small, for any matter done by virtue of your office. . . . You shall faithfully, justly, and truly, according to the best of your skill and judgment, do equal and impartial justice, without fraud, favor, affection or partiality."[5]

The most important legislation they wrote concerned crime, education, and religion. All three areas were controversial in Virginia, which in both size and population was the largest of the new states, with the number of residents increasing each year.

Crime was a particularly thorny issue because the state's system of punishment, like that of other states, was undergoing a dramatic transition. The American criminal codes were far more streamlined than those of the British. Punishments were less severe, and there were fewer crimes that brought about harsh penalties. England had a criminal code, dubbed "the bloody code," in which a felon could be hanged for any one of more than two hundred offenses, including stealing a neighbor's fence post. Americans wanted fewer capital crimes. The trio who revised the criminal codes also wanted more lenient punishments than the draconian sentences that England had handed down for generations in hopes that severe punishment would deter criminals. None of the three Virginians believed in the centuries-old British tradition of extreme punishment for a minor crime. As an example, they wrote a law that a man who punched another in a dispute would be imprisoned for a period of time. In England, the penalty for that same act in 1779 was chopping off the hand of the man who threw the punch; in earlier years in England, it was death.

Jefferson and Wythe insisted that the death sentence had to be eliminated for all crimes except murder and treason and that hard labor should replace prison time for many other offenses. Rape and sodomy were punishable by death in many states; Jefferson, Wythe, and Pendleton downgraded the punishment to castration for men and ordered one-half inch of cartilage removed from the noses of women guilty of sexual assault. They insisted on mere reprimands for certain people who took the lives of others in self-defense. To achieve leniency, they asked for two murder grades, simple murder for a premeditated killing and manslaughter for all other slayings. "An eye for an eye, and a hand for a hand, will exhibit spectacles in execution whose moral effect would be questionable," wrote Jefferson.[6]

But Jefferson also prescribed quirky punishments. The elitist legislator asked for a four-year prison sentence for burglars who robbed the homes of wealthy men like himself but only a three-year term for the robbery of anyone else's home. Although Jefferson was opposed to "eye for an eye" punishment, he strangely demanded the severing of a convicted brawler's ear if in the fight a man bit off another's ear.

In a suggestion that he would consider ironic years later, he also wanted a man convicted of murdering someone with poison to suffer death by poison himself.[7]

Their criminal code was far more lenient than those of other states. The Virginians asked for a six-year prison term for counterfeiters; most states hanged them. The trio asked for gradations of punishment for robbery, depending on the circumstances, but restricted all punishments to prison terms. Most states hanged robbers; in Pennsylvania, one man was hanged for stealing nine dollars. In the majority of states, a man who committed murder while trying to rob another of his goods was hanged. Jefferson and Wythe turned that into manslaughter with a prison term. Massachusetts decreed death for anyone practicing witchcraft. Jefferson, Wythe, and Pendleton thought that dunking the local witch fifteen times in the community pond was sufficient punishment.

The trio proposed a sweeping new educational system. They called for a restructuring of the curriculum at the College of William and Mary, the construction of a large public library in Richmond, and a series of free public schools throughout the state that were accessible to the poor.[8]

"We examined critically our several parts, sentence by sentence, scrutinizing and amending until we had agreed on the whole . . . [revising] all of the British statutes from Magna Carta to the present day."[9]

In their general bill on slavery, both Jefferson and Wythe wrote an optional amendment calling for the emancipation of all slaves. They knew that it had no chance of passing, so in the body of the bill itself they simply reworded the current legislation on slavery, calling for no change. Jefferson complained bitterly about the continuation of slavery. He told Jean Nicholas Demeunier that "we must await with patience the workings of an overruling providence and hope that that is preparing the deliverance of these suffering brethren. When the measure of their tears shall be full, when their groans shall have involved heaven itself in darkness, doubtless a God of justice will awaken to their distress."[10] He added, "Nothing is more certainly written in the book of fate than that these people are to be free. Nor is it less certain that the two races, equally free, cannot live in the same government. Nature, habit, opinion has drawn indelible lines of distinction between them. . . . If, on the contrary, [slavery] is left to force itself on, human nature must shudder at the prospect held up."[11]

The trio also dismissed any changes regarding criminal activity by slaves and court procedures and mandated punishments for it. "The public mind would not yet bear the proposition[s]," Jefferson wrote of the ideas.[12]

None toiled harder for the new legal codes than James Madison, whom Jefferson lovingly referred to as "the unwearied Mr. Madison." He managed to have a Richmond printer publish the entire code as a pamphlet for wide public distribution, convinced that this, along with the public debates across the state that the publication would inspire, would help the code's passage. Madison called the legal code of his friends "a mine of legislative wealth."[13]

It took seven long years for the state legislature to completely revamp the criminal code and reorganize the state government. Of the 126 bills the three legislators proposed, more than 50 were approved, but the state library was defeated along with universal education and the formal reorganization of the College of William and Mary by the state.[14] The legislators' plea for public labor instead of jail time was also rejected. Their bill to divide murder charges into first and second degree to lighten most homicide convictions—"second degree" referred to slayings that resulted from domestic disputes or arguments, with gradations of punishment for each individual offense—was initially rejected but was approved ten years later.

"[Despite] endless quibbles, chicaneries, perversions, vexations and delays of lawyers and demi-lawyers, most of the bills were passed by the legislature with little alteration," Jefferson happily reported. The new laws represented some of his finest work, he wrote near the end of his life. He considered the laws "forming a system by which every fiber would be eradicated of ancient or future aristocracy and a foundation laid for a government truly republican." Virginia's new code soon became a legislative model for other states, particularly those in the South.[15]

The three legislators were proudest of the freedom of religion bill. The state of Virginia had previously funded the Anglican Church, despite loud protests from other churches, especially during the previous twenty years. Under the bill, that support ended and there could be no ties between any church and the state government. The bill served as a model for similar bills in other states and for the separation clause in the Constitution.

The three men had spent a considerable time writing all of their bills and defending them. Was the new set of laws as thorough as it might have been? Did they miss anything? If they did, they were so pleased with their work at the time that they did not dwell upon any omissions.

IT WAS WYTHE'S INTEGRITY that Jefferson bragged about when discussing the professorial appointment in 1779. Speaking of the students at the school, Jefferson said, "They are under the direction of Mr. Wythe, one of the most virtuous of characters."[16]

Wythe's view of teaching law was entirely different from that of the traditional British system. In England and in America prior to Wythe, students read and memorized law but did not spend much time analyzing it or discussing its use in society. They spent some time in the classroom, but most coursework consisted of an apprenticeship to a lawyer who drilled the student on case precedent. Most youths found the study of law boring. John Adams called it "a dreary ramble."[17]

Wythe was different. He employed three methods of instruction: lectures, discussions of readings, and his own marvelous educational invention—moot courts and legislatures.

Wythe's classes were regimented. Each morning, students read William Blackstone, the eminent British legal scholar, plus copies of British and American legal decisions, and discussed them with one another and their professor. In Wythe's discussions with students about law, he urged them to analyze everything they read in order to achieve their own personal perspective on the law and to reread documents in order to gain a complete understanding of them. Munford, one of Wythe's protégés who lived in his Williamsburg brick mansion with him for three years, always remembered that. Munford wrote, "He instructed me in the course (of law) pursued by himself in studying law, saying don't skim it; read it deeply, and ponder what you read."[18]

At noon every Tuesday and Thursday, Wythe lectured his forty or so students. Following his lectures, students again discussed law texts with Wythe and were given time to study the works of David Hume and Baron Charles Louis de Montesquieu, two favorites of Wythe. Hume's theory, developed in his *Treatise of Human Nature*, was that the

These drawings portray the buildings that made up the College of William and Mary in the 1760s. Wythe taught there as America's first professor of law.

foundation of a stable nation was a system of property ownership, defined by detailed legal sales and personal rights. Wythe also saw this as crucial in the ever-expanding territories of the American colonies and, later, the United States. Montesquieu argued that the most successful government had three branches—executive, legislative, and judicial—and that one should not dominate the others.[19] Montesquieu's theory was in perfect unison with that of Wythe, who always told pupils that the study of politics was "a training ground for Republican citizenship."[20]

One of his pupils, John Tyler, who served as governor of Virginia and whose son John became the tenth president of the United States, wrote of the value of Wythe's classes: "There being so much of his own sound reasoning upon great principles, not a mere servile copy of Blackstone, and other British commentators, a good many of his own thoughts on our constitutions and the necessary changes they have begotten, with that spirit of freedom which always marked his opinion."[21]

Wythe started the Phi Beta Kappa Society in the United States at the College of William and Mary. He was also the first to order students

In this comfortable study of George Wythe's home in Williamsburg, Thomas Jefferson, James Monroe, John Marshall, and his other students discussed the world's great books, as well as history, law, and politics, with their mentor.

John Marshall, one of Wythe's most brilliant pupils, went on to become the chief justice of the United States Supreme Court and modeled some of his most important legal opinions on those handed down by Wythe.

to keep what he called the "law notebook," a thick book into which they copied key legal decisions in dozens of areas of the law. One of the most famous notebooks was that of John Marshall, whose compilations extended to 238 pages and included notes on Wythe's lectures, case law, and book chapters (the esteemed future chief justice's intellectual notes were often interrupted, in his handwriting, with the name of his girlfriend, Polly Ambler).[22]

Wythe's most creative forms of teaching were the moot court and legislature. In his moot court, law students were assigned cases to prosecute and defend, and other students were given roles as defendants, litigants, and witnesses. Wythe and other lawyers in Williamsburg served as the judges at the court, which usually met once a month. They guided students through simulated trials of crimes and cases that Wythe provided, some of which were fictional and others based on actual cases. To furnish an authentic atmosphere for the legal proceedings, Wythe held his moot court in the actual one-story brick courthouse in town.

The moot legislature was run the same way and was held at the House of Burgesses. There, Judge Wythe served as the speaker of the House and presided over a student legislature. Students introduced bills to rectify what they thought were weaknesses in Virginia state law, and then all forty members of the moot legislature debated or amended the law, or both. The goal was not merely to train his law students in legal and parliamentary proceedings, but to encourage them to think for themselves and to consider the problems of the state and possible solutions. In the moot legislative sessions of 1779 and 1780, Wythe had his students argue the merits of the new Virginia laws that he had written with Jefferson and Pendleton. They discussed and voted on them in a single semester; the Virginia legislature would take six years to do the same. His purpose, Wythe told John Adams, was "to form such characters as may be fit to succeed those which have been ornamental and useful in the national councils of America."[23]

The moot court and legislature not only gave students a real taste for the legal and political life, but also made learning engaging. These teaching situations enabled students from Virginia's cities to team up with those from rural areas to back legislation, for students with both liberal and conservative views of government to share these, and for everyone to gain an understanding of the democratic process and how it worked, especially after the Revolution and the emergence of the new American government.

The moot chambers often affected the lives of students. Thomas Shippen, one of Wythe's students, believed that the moot court and legislature helped him gain personal confidence. He wrote, "[I] surmounted the difficulties which were opposed to me by my diffidence, my youth and the solemnity of the occasion, much better than I myself or any of my friends expected. And the applause I met with, tho' I did not think I deserved it, repaid me for the pain and anxiety I felt on the occasion."[24]

John Brown, a student at the College of William and Mary in 1780, wrote that Wythe's entertaining legislative days turned his life around. "I take an active part in both these institutions and hope thereby to rub off that natural bashfulness which at present is extremely prejudicial to me. These exercises serve not only as the best amusement after severe studies, but are very useful and attended with many important advantages."

The then confident Brown graduated several years later and went on to a distinguished career as a U.S. senator from Kentucky.[25]

Wythe's moot court idea, considered a radical educational tool at the time, was quickly adopted by other law schools across the country and in Europe, following its great success at the College of William and Mary. Within a few decades, the moot court took its place as the cornerstone of every major law school in America, and it remains so today.

Wythe's students admired him. John Marshall, especially, was grateful to Wythe. He had joined the army when the Revolution began and arrived as a war veteran to study at the College of William and Mary. Marshall, who impressed Wythe immediately, studied at the college for only a single semester, then moved to Richmond to get married. Wythe was so enamored of Marshall and his voluminous notes and speaking prowess that he talked Marshall into joining the debating team and insisted that Marshall be voted into Phi Beta Kappa. Marshall went on to serve six terms in the state legislature, was a delegate to the Constitution ratification convention with Wythe in 1788, and, when he moved to Richmond in 1791, purchased a large home just a few blocks from where Wythe resided. Marshall often sat in Wythe's courtroom to listen to him hand down decisions.[26]

When Wythe moved to Richmond in 1791, he continued his practice of personally tutoring young men. His first pupil there was Henry Clay, pictured here, who went on to become a longtime congressman from Kentucky and one of the most important figures in the history of the United States.

No one was more forceful in his assessment of Wythe than Henry Clay, Wythe's protégé during his last years. Clay, who went to work for Wythe as a clerk at sixteen and dazzled the old man with his intellectual brilliance, wrote, "To no man was I more indebted, by his instructions, his advice and his example for the little intellectual improvement which I made, up to the period when, in my first year, I finally left the city of Richmond."[27] Many of Wythe's former students, most prominently Jefferson, referred to him as a "second father."[28]

Munford was always grateful (Wythe paid his college tuition and let Munford live in his home). "For what I know of Greek, Spanish and Italian I am indebted to him. He devoted himself without reward to my instruction, giving me the best and most excellent advice, and imparting knowledge which I never could have acquired otherwise. He was . . . one of the most remarkable men I ever knew."[29]

No one could add up all of the students who arrived at Wythe's doorstep because they had been strongly recommended to attend the College of William and Mary merely so that they could learn from

James Monroe, the nation's fifth president, came to the College of William and Mary as a Revolutionary War hero. He left very reluctantly after only a year of working with George Wythe, when his friend Thomas Jefferson asked Monroe to move to Richmond to serve as his aide.

Wythe. Jefferson sent dozens of students to him, and so did prominent men in Virginia and other states.[30]

Those who left Wythe's classes did so with great reluctance. James Monroe, a wounded army veteran, returned to Williamsburg in January 1780 and enrolled in Wythe's law class. That winter, he became close friends with the newly elected governor, Thomas Jefferson.[31]

The governor asked Monroe to move with him to Richmond, the new capital, and become one of his aides. Jefferson promised to tutor Monroe there so that he could finish up his collegiate studies. Monroe reluctantly told an understanding Wythe that he had to go to Richmond. He left with the professor's blessing.[32]

Over the years, Wythe educated some of the most important public figures in Virginia and the United States in his classroom, moot court, and legislature and in the comfort of his home. Among them, in addition to Jefferson, were John Marshall, the chief justice of the U.S. Supreme Court; John Wickham, the president of the Virginia Bar Association; Spencer Roane, a Virginia Supreme Court of Appeals judge; John Breckinridge and John Brown, both U.S. senators from Kentucky;

George Nicholas, an attorney general of Kentucky; Littleton Tazewell, a U.S. senator and a governor of Virginia; William Giles, a U.S. senator and a governor of Virginia; and George Izard, a territorial governor of Arkansas. In addition, dozens of Virginia state legislators and prominent attorneys and judges studied under Wythe at Williamsburg.[33]

Jefferson always advised students to study with his old friend. His letter to Ralph Izard about his son's college education was typical. Jefferson wrote, "I cannot but approve your idea of sending your eldest son, destined for the law, to Williamsburg. . . . The pride of the institution William and Mary is Mr. Wythe, one of the Chancellors of the State, and professor of law in the college. He is one of the greatest men of the age, having held, without competition, the first place at the bar of our general court for thirty five years, and always distinguished by the most spotless virtue. . . . I know of no place in the world, while present professors remain, where I would so soon place a son."[34]

The students were glad to be there. Jefferson's nephew Peter Carr was one of them. Carr wrote to Jefferson, "Mr. Wythe has given me a very friendly invitation to his lectures on law. I have likewise the good fortune to be a private pupil and am now reading with him: Herodotus, Sophocles, Cicero. . . . Besides the advantages of his literary instructions, he adds advice and lessons of morality which are not only pleasing and instructive now, but will be (I hope) of real utility in the future. . . . Mr. Wythe has just put Lucretius into my hands, whose sects and opinions men generally think dangerous but under so good a guide I fear not his opinions whatever they may be."[35]

Throughout his life, Jefferson thanked Wythe for all of his help. "I know that to you, a consciousness of doing good is a luxury ineffable," Jefferson once wrote. "You have enjoyed it already beyond all human measure and that you may long live to enjoy it and to bless your country and friends is the sincere prayer of him who is with every possible sentiment of esteem."[36]

It wasn't only the college students who admired Wythe. The small children in town loved him, too. The children had a much different view of him, though. They knew him as the man who always stopped to talk to them as he walked about town, who bought them candy at local shops, who petted their cats and dogs, or who, with wide-eyed wonder, showed them the bees' nests attached to the windows of his home, which he studied intently in one of his innumerable experiments with nature. He gleefully showed them the half-dozen dead animals he kept in jars in his study for dissection, or his telescope, his microscope, or any of the inventions he was usually working on. Wythe himself had the unbridled excitement of a child.

One of his students' children said of Wythe's relationships to the young people in Williamsburg, "He was one of those that a child could approach without hesitating or shrinking—would talk to, in its innocent prattle, without constraint of fear—would lean upon, and, looking in his face, return a sympathetic smile. He was one of those before whom a surly dog would unbend, and wag his tail with manifest pleasure, though never seen before."[37]

BY THE LATE 1780s, the state government and courts and the business that they had once generated had moved to Richmond, and this loss caused a dramatic decline in the overall life of Williamsburg. The deterioration was felt financially, as well as in the erosion of Williamsburg's community and cultural life. Since there were no legislative sessions, the town never again played host to the thousands of visitors who arrived for the political seasons and stayed for weeks. The town's prosperity dwindled, some of its famous taverns closed, and the fancy women's shops that sold clothing to the planters' and merchants' wives were shuttered. Attendance slumped at the once famous racetrack, social life sputtered, and the population of the college never fully rebounded after the war. The Reverend Jedidiah Morse, who visited the community during those years, was saddened by what he saw. He wrote, "Everything in Williamsburg seems dull, forsaken and melancholy, no trade, no amusements but the infamous one of gaming, no industry and but very little appearance of religion."

One man wrote during that time that Williamsburg was "daily crumbling into ruins."[38]

The decline of the city was felt at the College of William and Mary, too, where disputes among administrators, professors, and students became more frequent during the 1770s and affected enrollment and interpersonal relations. Several professors quit at the end of the Revolution and enrollment dropped.

The students' reputation for rowdiness did not help. George Washington refused to send his stepson Jack there when he was ready for college in 1773. By the 1790s the students' hooliganism had become worse. Drinking among students had risen to such a dangerous level that in 1791, the college finally banned the consumption of alcohol.

Even defenders of the college had to admit that the school's image had suffered severely. "An idea lately has gone abroad, and seems to be lately gaining ground, that there is not a school in this country [William and Mary] at which a parent can trust his child," one man wrote in a letter to the *Virginia Gazette* in 1786. One lawyer there wrote that "The college . . . permits their youth to run riot in all the wildness of dissipation."[39]

One man, fed up, called Williamsburg "Devilsburg."

The conditions in Williamsburg were not unlike those in other small cities in Virginia during that era, all of which were drained by the exodus of residents and businesses to the new capital. Petersburg was equally run down. "The coach braces before we arrive, the roads in ruts, the fields uncultivated, the houses tumbling down, groups of free negroes, mulattos and whites lounging around . . . the town half depopulated," wrote one visitor to the town.[40]

George Wythe had lived in Williamsburg for much of his adult life, but he felt depressed over the town's general collapse, combined with the removal of the government and most of his prominent political friends, especially Thomas Jefferson. He had lost interest in the College of William and Mary, too, after unhappy relationships with the administration and other professors at the school. He quit.

"Mr. Wythe has abandoned the College of William and Mary, disgusted with some conduct of the professors, and particularly of the ex professor [John] Bracken, and perhaps too with himself for having suffered himself to be too much irritated with that," his friend Jefferson, then secretary of state, wrote in a curt note. "It is over with the College."[41]

Then, in 1787, George Wythe's wife, Elizabeth, forty-eight, his mate for thirty-one years, fell desperately ill at the same time that he had been sent to Philadelphia by the state of Virginia to help write the new Constitution of the United States. In early June, Wythe received word that Elizabeth had taken a turn for the worse and was bedridden.

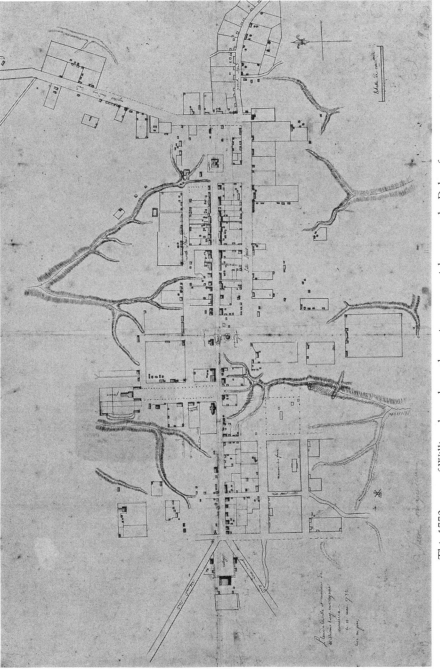

This 1770s map of Williamsburg shows the main commercial avenue, the Duke of Gloucester Street, the House of Burgesses, taverns, and the Bruton Parish church. Wythe's house was located in the area shown in the upper-left corner of the map, near the palace of the royal governor.

He left Philadelphia immediately and raced home to Williamsburg. There, he found his wife in very poor condition.

He wrote to members of the Constitutional Convention that he would probably not return. "Mrs. W's state of health is so low, and she is so emaciated, that my apprehensions are not a little afflicting, and, if the worst should not befall, she must linger, I fear, a long time, in no other circumstances would I withdraw. . . . I shall not return to Philadelphia."[42]

Elizabeth Wythe, whom he had married when she was seventeen, grew weak throughout the summer and finally died on August 23, 1787. She passed on, a writer for the *Virginia Gazette* told his readers, "after a very long and lingering sickness which she bore with the patience of a true Christian."[43]

Wythe was lost without his wife. He took in students as boarders. He retained his faithful cook, Lydia Broadnax, to whom he had given her freedom, and she helped him get through the most difficult time in his life. Still, his wife's death plunged him into grief. He could not accomplish household chores or pay his bills, and he seemed disoriented. Her death caused him "much more trouble than he could sustain. The necessary domestic duties occupied so much his time. . . . He was irritated and vexed by a thousand little occurrences he had never foreseen," wrote the student Littleton Tazewell at the time.[44]

Dozens of residents of Williamsburg mourned with him and invited him to their homes to help him get through the difficult time. Friends from around the world wrote him letters of condolence, and those who knew Elizabeth Wythe well, such as Jefferson, were shaken by her passing.

Public figures in the state knew that Wythe needed an important activity to get his mind off his wife. They sent him to Richmond to serve as the chairman of the special convention that had been called to determine whether the new U.S. Constitution should be ratified by Virginia. There was substantial opposition to the Constitution throughout the nation because it did not have a bill of rights to protect the people's individual freedoms and it seemed to favor an overly strong federal government. In Richmond, Wythe ran the convention just as successfully as he had run the state legislature in Williamsburg as its speaker.

As Wythe grew older—he was sixty-three in 1789, when the Constitution was ratified—he found it increasingly laborious to make the necessary lengthy trips to Richmond to attend to his job as the chancellor of the Virginia Chancery Courts. His overall demeanor had soured, too, since the passing of his wife. He withdrew from many of his friends, was rarely seen at parties, and acknowledged acquaintances he encountered on the streets of Williamsburg with little more than a nod of his head. The judge spoke so little that children devised shrewd games to get him to say something when they saw him shopping on the Duke of Gloucester Street.[45]

The disputes between the College of William and Mary's faculty and administrators and the declining student population, the rowdiness and the drunkenness, the wearying travel, and the death of his wife all contributed to George Wythe's stunning decision to leave Williamsburg and permanently move to Richmond, where he could tend to his judicial work.

The judge knew that Richmond was a rapidly growing city beset with problems, huge waves of every type of immigrant, and a rising crime rate. Even so, Wythe certainly did not think that he would be murdered there.

6

Richmond: Boomtown and the Decadent Nightlife of George Wythe Sweeney

T HE POPULATION OF RICHMOND had skyrocketed since the city became the state capital in 1780. The rapid growth of the river capital matched that of other river ports, such as Philadelphia, and seaports such as New York and Boston. Between 1800 and 1850, the percentage of people living in U.S. cities would leap from 9 percent of the total American population to more than 20 percent, and during that same time, the population of the country would grow by nearly 700 percent.[1]

Richmond's population surged to nearly ten thousand residents by the spring of 1806. They included people from dozens of countries around the world, slaves, and one of the largest Jewish populations in America.[2] The overabundance of people resulted in overcrowding. There was little regulation in housing, transportation, sanitation, or health care, and city fathers found it difficult to cope with the exploding growth of their communities. Men were moving from farms to cities. Urban areas on rivers or oceans, especially, experienced an invasion of immigrants, all coming to America for better opportunities.

The congestion and the rowdiness of Richmond had grown considerably since George Wythe had moved there in 1791. The increase in bars and gambling casinos and the arguments and the fights that ensued on their premises had turned the quiet community into a turbulent city. "An astonishing amount of blood shed at taverns, around gambling tables, and at the race track," wrote one Richmond resident at the turn of the century.[3] This surprised even hardened Virginians who had grown up in what was considered a violent state. Nothing had changed much in the honky-tonk culture of Virginia over fifty years; there was just more of it now. In 1752, an exasperated governor, Alexander Spotswood, had pleaded with assemblymen on their way to their home counties "to discourage gaming, swearing and immoderate drinking," to ban gambling, and to shutter any taverns that permitted it. That year, gaming was such a danger that a minister who was asked to address the state legislature called it "a dangerous contagion." No one paid any attention, and the social problems of the state had only grown.

In fact, crime, drunkenness, and rowdiness had grown so much over the years that in the winter just before Wythe died, several grand juries, appalled at the mayhem in the city, took it upon themselves to issue special rebukes to community and state authorities and to plead for the enforcement of existing laws, the passage of new ones, and a police force to keep the peace. They charged that blacks and whites were drinking not only at the city's numerous taverns, but at illegal bars, too. The jurors denounced the local constables as inept and the city council for permitting the town to become an open market for pickpockets, robbers, burglars, and street brawlers.

The grand jurors and thousands of citizens were terrified that Richmond had turned into a colonial Sodom and Gomorrah.[4]

THE TAVERNS were the source of much of the gaming trouble that beset Richmond. They were crowded with the rich and the poor, black and white, travelers and residents, and thousands of newly arrived immigrants and sailors. They were centers for gambling, drinking, and womanizing. Early Virginian historians targeted drinking as a common problem throughout the Commonwealth. As early as 1687, residents complained of drunken townspeople and continually linked the consumption of alcohol in taverns to gambling and its woes. A planter noted at the end of the seventeenth century that Virginia was awash in rum imported from the West Indies and that it "breaks the Constitution, vitiates the morals, and ruins the industry of most of the poor people of this country." A British soldier in America in the colonial era sneered that Virginia planters have a drink at 8 A.M. before they begin breakfast. A French visitor to Virginia wrote in 1765 of a tavern he visited, "At night [there was] carousing and drinking in one chamber and box and dice in another, which continues till morning commonly."[5]

"Frolicking" was a favorite pastime in Richmond. The heavy concentration of men in Richmond, approximately twice as many men as women in 1800, with most of them young and unattached, and all of them with physical needs, made the town a mecca for prostitutes.

By 1806, the ladies of the evening, and any other time of the day, had been part of the landscape in America for nearly one hundred years. The spread of prostitution to the America's seaports seemed natural. Prostitutes thrived where the business was: in the rapidly growing seaports and river towns such as Boston, New York, Philadelphia, Norfolk, and Richmond.

Most prostitutes solicited men in Richmond's taverns, but many did so on the streets and in the local theaters. Some Richmond women worked on their own and others in brothels.[6]

Prostitution flourished in all of the big cities of the United States in 1806, not only in Richmond, because the furious urban population explosion usually resulted in far more male residents than women. The success of cities as mercantile centers also meant that thousands of men visited them each year to conduct business. In addition, the seaport and river-port cities, such as Richmond, attracted thousands of workers in the shipping business and sailors who had been at sea without female companionship for a year or more. The prostitution business boomed. By the late 1820s, New York City alone was home to more than two hundred brothels and two thousand prostitutes. Houses of ill repute also flung open their doors with regularity in Virginia cities, especially the ports of Richmond and Norfolk. There are no

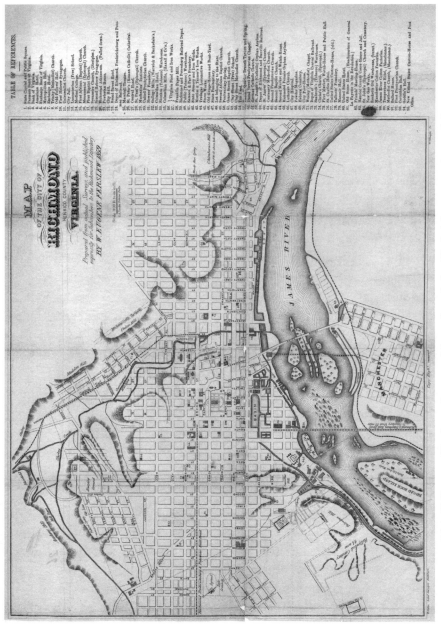

TABLE OF REFERENCES

1. State Capitol and Public Square.
2. Governor's House.
3. Bank of Virginia.
4. Exchange Bank.
5. Farmers Bank of Virginia.
6. Metropolitan Hall.
7. Exchange Hotel.
8. Trinity (Methodist) Church.
9. Odd Fellows' Hall.
10. Universalist Church.
11. Fred Hebrew Synagogue.
12. City Hall.
13. Lancasterian (Free) School.
14. Medical College.
15. First African (Baptist) Church.
16. Monumental (Episcopal) Church.
17. First Baptist Church.
18. Sycamore Church, (Disciples)
19. Second Hebrew Synagogue.
20. Richmond Athenaeum. (Pulled down.)
21. Powhatan House.
22. City Hall.
23. Broad Street Hotel.
24. Depot of Richmond, Fredericksburg and Potomac Railroad.
25. St. Peter's (Roman Catholic) Cathedral.
26. Central Hotel.
27. St. Paul's (Episcopal) Church.
28. Mechanics' Institute.
29. United Presbyterian Church.
30. Brewery
31. Gallego Mills, (Warwick & Barksdale's.)
32. Columbian Hotel.
33. Tredegar (Tobacco) Warehouse
34. Spotswood Hotel.
35. Columbian Mills, (Haxall & Co's.)
36. Stove Works.
37. Franklin Paper Mill.
38. Richmond and Petersburg Railroad Depot.
39. Public (Tobacco) Warehouse.
40. State Armory and Iron Works.
41. Belle Isle Manufactory.
42. Martin's Tanner's Tan Works.
43. Tredegar Locomotive Works.
44. Iron Works.
45. State Penitentiary.
46. Lunatic Asylum for the State.
47. Second African Baptist Church.
48. Grace Street Baptist Church.
49. Clay Street Methodist Church.
50. Leigh Street Baptist Church.
51. Fair Ground.
52. Spring Garden, Drench Tavern and Spring.
53. Grand Street Presbyterian Chapel.
54. St. Joseph's (Catholic) Orphan Asylum.
55. Depot of Virginia and Danville Railroad.
56. St. James' (Episcopal) Church.
57. Centenary Methodist Church.
58. Second Presbyterian Church.
59. Second Baptist Church.
60. Leigh Street and Wells House.
61. Richmond Female Orphan Asylum.
62. Laburnum Church.
63. City Hospital.
64. Powder Magazine.
65. Almshouse (old.)
66. City Poor-House.
67. Wesley (Methodist) Chapel.
68. Depot of Virginia Central Railroad.
69. Crenshaw's (Tobacco) Warehouse.
70. Clarke's Church, (Episcopal.)
71. First Armory, Watch-House and Public Hall.
72. Christian Church.
73. United States Custom-House, (old.)
74. Theatre.
75. Masonic Hall.
76. Globe Sugar Hotel.
77. Old State House, (Headquarters of General La Fayette in the Revolution.)
78. Crystal Meeting House.
79. Henrico County Court-House and Jail.
80. John's (Episcopal) Church and Cemetery.
81. New Gas Works.
82. Sycamore Cotton Factories.
83. James River Cotton Factories.
84. Manchester Cotton Factories.
85. Methodist Church, (Manchester.)
86. Baptist Church.
87. First Presbyterian Church.
88. Episcopal Church, (Manchester.)
89. Corinthian Hall.
90. Goddin's Hall.
91. New United States Custom-House and Post Office.

This 1859 map of Richmond is one of the earliest. Judge Wythe's home is at the top left, near the capitol building designed by his friend Thomas Jefferson. Wythe's funeral cortege traveled eastward on Main Street, just north of the James River, to St. Paul's Church, lower right, where he was buried.

statistics available on the exact number of prostitutes in Richmond, but court records show that in 1806, when Wythe died, the city was home to dozens of whorehouses. Most were owned by white men and women and featured white prostitutes, but eighteen were owned by blacks and had black prostitutes. By the 1850s, the mayor of Norfolk wrote in a police report that his city had two hundred brothels; by then, Richmond probably had even more.[7]

Many prostitutes worked at packed dance halls, where they earned money from the emporium's manager to dance with patrons and then made more by sleeping with their dance partners. A study showed that dance halls constituted 28 percent of the places where prostitutes solicited men. Any man in Richmond who won a considerable amount of money gambling soon found himself with an attractive prostitute on his arm, who was eager to unburden him of his winnings. Or he found himself walking to the nearest brothel, usually within a block or two of Main Street, with his winnings weighing down his pockets. During that era, prostitution became such a prosperous industry that a Richmond side street where many bordellos flourished soon acquired the nickname "Pink Alley." The alley was a raucous place, reported the Richmond Daily Dispatch, "so notorious in the police annals of Richmond as are the Five Points in those of New York."[8]

By 1806, the madams of Richmond and their ladies had become an industry. The women were young, generally in their early twenties, although some 4 percent were under eighteen; single; childless; and mostly white. They sold their bodies, they said in surveys conducted at the time, because they could not find work in a male-dominated workforce, and the work they did find as domestics, tailoresses, or waitresses paid only about 20 percent of what they could earn in a brothel, which was usually $3 to $4 per week. Women in Virginia were some of the lowest paid in the country, too. Free white women working in Virginia's cotton industry, as an example, earned only half the pay of men working in the same trade in Virginia and half the pay of women in the same trade in New England.[9]

Richmond civic officials denounced it, ministers flailed their arms in condemning it, refined women sneered at it, and newspaper editors deplored it, but by 1806 prostitution was a thriving industry in

Richmond and would remain so for many years to come. Its women were sexual magnets for young men like George Wythe Sweeney.

YET IT WAS GAMBLING that brought on Sweeney's woes. Gambling appeared during the first months of the Jamestown settlement in 1607, when men competed for money in street bowling. It was embedded in the Virginia culture by the 1680s, when men drank and played cards for money in taverns or at one another's homes until the early hours of the morning. Virginia became an American oasis of gambling. Throughout the colonial era, men and women could purchase lottery tickets, bet on their favorite steeds at the horse races, and even wager on political campaigns. The love of gambling was so great that when the dreaded yellow fever struck Philadelphia in 1793, killing 10 percent of the city's population, men in taverns placed bets on the final death toll.[10]

Lotteries began in Virginia during the early years of the eighteenth century, when governments and civic organizations, such as churches, that were in need of money to operate resorted to holding lotteries. They were instantly popular, and soon anyone who needed revenue ran his own lottery. Tickets were sold to raise funds to construct barns, repair the roofs of houses, build new homes, and purchase land. Many Virginians, rich and poor, ran lotteries to pay off their debts. Lotteries were heavily advertised in local newspapers. The payoffs were substantial, as they are today, but the bulk of the money went to the organization or the individual who ran it. Who could resist the chance to win thousands of dollars—and assist the town or a neighbor—with the purchase of a single ticket for just a few cents? During the Revolution, lotteries were even held to raise money to fund the Continental Army.

Everyone, rich or poor, refined plantation owner or city blacksmith, played the lottery in Virginia. One of its biggest benefactors was George Washington. The gentleman gambler was a fanatic about lotteries of all kinds. While playing cards one night in a tavern in Williamsburg, he saw a man selling lottery tickets across the room. Washington could not resist. He borrowed money from a friend and on a whim bought several thousand dollars' worth of tickets. Washington once purchased $3,600 in lottery tickets from a man who rode all the way down from New Jersey to sell them to him.[11] In 1793, the federal government ran a lottery to raise money for the construction of its new capital, Washington, D.C. First prize was an actual hotel, Blodgett's. The first ticket was purchased by President Washington.[12]

Women were enthusiastic lottery players, too. A popular form of lottery for the ladies in Richmond and elsewhere was the store merchandise raffle. Shop owners raffled off numerous items of clothing, shoes, and jewels to the hundreds of women who had purchased tickets.[13] Some people were so hooked on lotteries that they had their portraits painted as they proudly held out winning lottery tickets, and they hung the paintings in their homes for all to see.[14]

So many Americans lost money on cards and dice that when George Washington became commander in chief of the Continental Army, he banned gambling among the troops. He wrote, "There are few vices with more pernicious consequences than gambling" (he stopped playing cards himself, which must have taken enormous self-restraint for the notorious gambler).[15]

Some women in Virginia were just as addicted to gambling as the men were. They played card games in their homes with other women or their husbands and wagered money at racetracks. Even young girls were hooked on betting. An eleven-year-old girl in Fairfax County wrote in her diary in 1771 that she regularly played "checks," a game involving peach stones, against men and women for money and took great delight in 1771 when she "won ten shillings of Mr. William [playing] at Chex."[16]

Winning at gambling, against anyone, by any means, was considered great sport. Most of the men who owned plantations or businesses gambled. They saw it as competition and as a way to mingle with other men, drinks in hand, as well as a chance to get away from their wives and families. Gambling marked them as competitors, not only in cards or at the track, but in life itself. It was part of a gentleman's persona.[17]

George Washington owned horses that he entered in races and bet heavily on. He and his family also attended races in Annapolis and other cities. He played cards for money at taverns in any town he visited; with Lord Dunmore, Britain's last royal governor of Virginia; and at parties at the Governor's Palace. He hosted card games at receptions and balls at Mount Vernon. Washington bet heavily, wagering about $35,000 a year in today's money on his various gambling activities. Another gambler was Wythe's close friend Thomas Jefferson, who spent the evenings of the summer when he wrote the Declaration of Independence in Philadelphia playing cards, buying lottery tickets, and going to the racetrack. Yet another was young Henry Clay, one of Wythe's law clerks, who fell in love with gambling during his years working for Wythe in Richmond. Later, as an adult, Clay wagered as much as $60,000 a night at cards, and once he told a friend that he preferred gambling to politics.[18]

Gambling was opposed by civic leaders and ministers, because it had become an addiction for thousands. Men spent their wages on cards and lottery tickets and wound up penniless. Gambling addiction caused rifts in marriages and friction among families and brought about the loss of jobs for many who stole money from their stores to gamble. Clergymen complained about it from their pulpits for years; several even lectured the state legislature on the evils of gambling in much publicized speeches.[19] It was a major social problem in the eighteenth century, and by the time the new century arrived, gambling had become much worse in major cities, such as Richmond, where residents had easy access to racetracks, gambling houses, and lottery parlors. (By the 1820s, New York City would have nearly a thousand lottery parlors, which were similar to the Off-Track Betting parlors of the twentieth century, where residents could walk in and buy tickets for that day's lottery.)

Yet it was traditional casino-style gaming—cards, roulette, dice, and other games of chance—that was the heart of gambling in Richmond. This was the kind of gaming that helped make the city so decadent and ruined men such as young George Wythe Sweeney, who was devoured by the city's gambling dens every night.

Court records from the era indicate that more than a hundred gambling houses of some kind flourished in Richmond, each one more crowded than the next.[20] There seemed to be a betting emporium on every street corner in that congested city, from the dingiest tavern with its card tables in dimly illuminated back rooms to the finest hotel in town. The recently opened Eagle Hotel, at Twelfth and Main streets, midway along Brick Row, whose construction cost a then-astronomical $125,000, served as the elegant social hub of the state capital. People who traveled claimed that the hardwood floor of the

Eagle's ballroom was the best for dancing in all of the Southern states. The Eagle featured one of the finest restaurants and the best bars in the city, elegantly appointed hallways, an impressive lobby, and beautifully furnished rooms. Rich planters and wealthy merchants spent much time there dining and dancing. Travelers loved to stay in its comfortable rooms with unobstructed views of the James River to the south.

The centerpiece of the Eagle was not its dance floor or bar, but its large, colorful wheel of fortune, which was said to be the biggest in the country. Thousands of gamblers took out their money and bet on the numbers that the wheel would stop at (it was then, and still is now, the worst percentage bet in all of gaming). The wheel was like a magnet to Richmonders, attracting people from all over town and providing enormous profits for the hotel owner. There were other wheels of fortune in hotels and gaming emporiums in other cities and they, too, caused addiction. Uncontrollable betting on the spins of the wheel became such a problem for people in Washington, D.C., that the nation's capital outlawed the wheels several years later.[21]

Nearby, on Brick Row and the adjoining streets, were more than a dozen crowded gambling casinos, run by colorful and well-dressed owners. The casinos were patronized by the rich and the poor of Richmond, who mingled with sailors newly arrived from the Caribbean and tobacco sellers. It was noted with a wink of an eye that ministers gambled, too, but in private homes to avoid detection. One plantation tutor chortled about a clergyman at a party. "There was Parson Gibbern, ill of his last week's bout; he was up three nights successively, drinking and playing cards so that the liquor and want of sleep put him quite out of his senses."[22]

Certain entire buildings on Main Street were gambling casinos. Others were located above stores, such as the casino at Twelfth and Main, across the street from the Eagle Hotel and above John Graeme's grocery store. Some casinos were on streets just off Main or in dark dirt alleys. Some were run by rough-looking gamblers, but most were owned by well-dressed, amiable men who made a fortune off gambling, such as the tall, thin Henry Street, who always dressed in black linen suits and who ran a casino next door to Graeme's Grocery. In an alley behind Main Street stood a gambling house known as "The Profile," run by well-known gambler and sportsman Nat Rives. Brothers ran some of the casinos, including the one that sat next to Henry Street's near the Eagle Hotel.[23]

The casinos offered every type of card game and game of chance that was available in the country. Faro was probably the most popular. Roulette tables were in most gaming houses, as was the infamous wheel of fortune. Dice were exceedingly popular. Men spent countless hours, day and night, playing billiards. Players addicted to the game found themselves gambling for hundreds of dollars a game.

The cheaters soon arrived. Card dealers dealt from the bottom of the deck, the roulette managers jiggled the wheel, and the men who ran the dice games loaded dice with quicksilver to make them bounce a certain way. The loudest complaints were filed in the billiards parlor, where the ancestors of pool hall sharks such as Minnesota Fats lured young men into games, let them win, and then hustled them for thousands of dollars later.

Gambling losses caused great personal problems. Men who lost money wound up in ongoing arguments with their wives, who needed the money for household costs. Men with large losses were unable to pay their bills. Some committed suicide and others contemplated it.

And gamblers such as George Wythe Sweeney had to pay their debts. There was no way that losses to gamblers could be kept private; news of a man's debts would be learned quickly by his family, neighbors, friends, and employer. Many sold their horses. One man paid off his debts with a new watch he had purchased for his wife that afternoon. Others, fearful of losing, brought a variety of goods with them in their saddlebags or in wagons to pay debts if they incurred them.[24] Some longtime customers who lost at the tables were loaned money by the casino managers, even though they were certain they would lose the funds they had just advanced to the customers. One major lender in Richmond during that era was not a gambling impresario but Nancy Farrar, the madam who ran the city's most prosperous brothel. She loaned gamblers who were good customers several hundred dollars to pay off their debts so that they could continue to gamble. Perhaps their luck would change, and they could continue to come back to her brothel to be entertained by her young ladies.[25]

A gambler whose hometown was Staunton, Virginia, remarked of his gaming debts in Richmond, "If I did not pay them, the news would be spread not only in [Richmond], but it would be carried to Staunton and I should be ruined."[26]

That was George Wythe Sweeney's problem. He constantly lost at the tables, the track, and wherever else he bet, and to keep the news quiet he stole extremely valuable, one-of-a-kind books in several languages from his uncle's prized library, along with other goods, and forged numerous checks using his uncle's name.

Virginians had tried to do away with gambling for nearly a century. The state legislature had passed bills making it illegal since 1727 and had even made it illegal for gamblers to collect losers' debts. At the start of the Revolution, even the Continental Congress tried to bar casino gambling, while charging that it was unpatriotic.[27] No one paid much attention.

One problem in getting law enforcement officials and legislators to enforce the antigambling laws was that those very legislators and other respectable community leaders were themselves often found playing cards and rolling dice in the emporiums. On walking into one casino, a man wrote, "To my surprise there I saw gentlemen of the first characters and of all professions, members of the assembly, lawyers, merchants and others. In the multitude I saw two old gentlemen belonging to the assembly, whom I knew at home, who were reputed pious and were members of churches. I was a good deal surprised."[28]

By 1806, gambling had become a way of life in Richmond. Thousands participated. Few won, and one gambler described his rush to gamble: "I hurry to my ruin."

Dice and cards could always be seen in Richmond's taverns and gambling houses, amid entertainment that consisted of happy fiddlers, lively bands, pretty singers, and, from time to time, colorful circus acts. Professional gamblers from all over the United States flocked to Richmond, with its wealthy planters, merchants, and drunken sailors who were flush with wages from a year at sea.

Gamblers prospered in taverns because, in addition to their bars, dining rooms, and card rooms, most taverns had rooms upstairs and downstairs for sleeping. Some were single rooms, but others were large dormitory-style rooms. On any given night, a single tavern could hold twenty or more men. Taverns could accommodate several hundred men throughout town. They were cheaper than the few hotels in the city and certainly offered more entertainment. The men who stayed overnight in the upstairs rooms of the tavern provided a ready-made clientele for the gamblers downstairs.[29]

Among the busier taverns in the center of the city at that time were the Bird in Hand, on the northwest corner of Main and Twenty-Fifth streets; Hogg's, at Fifteenth and Main; Galt's, at Nineteenth and Main; Cowley's, at Twenty-Third and Main; Fornicola's, at Main and Fifteenth streets; Bowler's, later named Bell's, at Fifteenth and Main, which was run by the colorful, rotund Major Bowler, who always dressed in a bright green coat with gold buttons and wore a carrot-colored wig; and the Swan, between Eighth and Ninth streets on the northern side of Broad Street. It was at the two-story Swan, with its large wooden veranda and brightly painted sign in front, where most of the city leaders, state legislators, and judges congregated for drinks at the end of the business day.[30] In addition, there were the popular City Tavern, the Rising Sun, Virginia Inn, Major Davis's Tavern, the Union, Indian Queen, and the Globe. There were more bars at Rockett's Landing, at the wharves, that catered to thirsty shipyard laborers and sailors, and on the outskirts of town. In addition to the large taverns, the city was home to nearly two hundred smaller, illegal drinking establishments that contributed to the drunkenness of the population. The drinking problem was so bad that from 1800 to 1810, a city grand jury handed down 184 indictments of bartenders at the illegal drinking houses.[31] The taverns in most U.S. cities had to import beer from large breweries in New York and Philadelphia, but there were so many taverns in Richmond, and so many thirsty patrons, that the Hay and Forrester Company opened a brewery right in town. Any bartender who ran low on beer knew that a wagon full of kegs was just a few blocks away.[32]

All gamblers, teenager George Wythe Sweeney included, feared sitting down at the gaming tables of Richmond with the traveling card sharps. "Shield yourselves against the insidious and fawning smiles of men whose faces beam with conciliation and courtesy, but whose hearts are a spring of malevolence and artifice," lamented one after he himself had lost $2,000.[33]

The men and the women who did not lose their money at the gaming tables in the casinos or taverns or through the purchase of lottery tickets could always bet on the horses at the well-maintained Jockey

Club racetrack outside of Richmond. Two racing meets lasting a month each were held every year, in the fall and the spring, as they were in other cities, such as Philadelphia and Annapolis. Crowds of thousands attended. The Jockey Club races were the highlight of the season for the city's socialites. Men wore their finest suits and hats and women their most elegant gowns to attend the parties and the balls that were held to celebrate each racing season. Hundreds of rich visitors from out of town came to Richmond in their coaches, in buggies, or on horseback, many with groups of slaves to attend them. "The Race Week was a perfect carnival," wrote Sam Mordecai, a child in Richmond at the time, who recalled that the working classes filled the hotels, the boardinghouses, and the taverns.[34]

Horse racing had always been a favorite sport in Richmond and throughout Virginia. "The assemblies [are] remarkably numerous, beyond my expectation," remarked one schoolteacher who attended many. A Richmond doctor wrote that the sport was such a part of cultural life that all he ever heard state legislators talking about were "horse races."[35]

The highlight of the racing meets in Richmond, one of twelve communities with racetracks in the state, was the Race Ball in the ballroom of the Eagle Hotel. There, a large orchestra played for a hundred or more wealthy Virginians. The partygoers danced everything from the minuet to the Irish jig, with some of the new French dances added in, and highlighted by a rousing version of the Virginia reel, all amid an atmosphere of laughter and much drinking.

Numerous moral organizations were relentless in their drive to end gambling. They were so driven that they targeted any game of chance, such as billiards, ninepin bowling, and harmless clothing-store raffles. The city's moral guardians assured any and all participants in these games that they were condemned to eternal damnation. This angered most residents of the city, who thought that the moralists' contentions about sports like ninepins were absurd. The organizations, the forerunners of the mammoth national antigaming and temperance groups that would be born in the 1830s, also painted a vile picture of the casinos and the taverns. This did not close them but merely caused their attendance to grow, fueled by all of the men who were now intrigued by the dissipated life described by the crusaders. "It has greatly increased the numbers of votaries who join the midnight orgies," wrote a state assemblyman.[36]

Thomas Macon, a store clerk, agreed. "Gambling is an important part of the city's life," he said, fondly remembering the "scrumptious suppers" served in the gaming houses.[37]

The first law forbidding gaming in Virginia was passed in 1727. It barred all games of chance and required any managers of gaming contests to return any monies or goods lost by the participants. People paid so little attention to it that another law was passed in 1740, which added betting on horse racing and cockfights to the list. It, too, was ignored. Two more statutes were passed, in 1744 and 1748, and they were also useless. Believing that little attention was paid to the statutes because many of the gamblers were public figures, the legislature passed a law in 1799 stating that any public official caught gaming at a public casino or tavern or in private, at a party, would be henceforth ineligible to hold office. No one paid any attention to that law, either, especially the public officials it targeted.

Other laws that banned gaming, and billiards as well, were passed in 1779, 1787, and 1792. One law even authorized any justice of the peace to burn down casinos or taverns where gambling took place; none did. Another law, passed in 1798 and generally ignored, urged local constables to burn down billiard parlors. In 1803, around the time that George Wythe Sweeney began to live with Judge Wythe for several months a year, yet another law was passed that provided for the arrests of not only tavern keepers and casino operators, but anyone who worked in these establishments. This law was just as ineffective as all the rest.

From 1800 to 1810, police handed out eighty-four summonses for illegal gaming, which were all ignored.

Hovering over these debates, which lasted fifty years without any resolution, was the common knowledge that many state legislators and city councilmen gambled in the Richmond casinos or in their own homes with friends. "There were generals, colonels, captains, senators, assemblymen, judges, doctors, clerks and crowds of gentlemen of every weight and caliber . . . sat all together about the fire, drinking, smoking, singing and talking ribaldry," remarked one surprised doctor, Johann Schoepf, after he arrived in Richmond. Did the legislature really want to arrest dozens of its own members?[38]

The numerous antigaming laws that did pass were not effective because they were never enforced. The poorly paid city constables who were charged with carrying them out and the county sheriff's deputies were usually bribed by the gamblers or the gaming house owners to ignore their duty. The police did so happily. The overt corruption of the constable force was common in all cities with crime problems and would be until professional police departments were established in the 1840s. One exasperated newspaper editor in Philadelphia later wrote, "It amounts in fact to this—keeping a set of rogues in pay for the benefit of police officers."[39] The situation was the same in Richmond. When Dr. Foushee was mayor in 1782, he wrote that the guards in the Richmond jail were "either principals or accessories to almost every robbery which has of late been committed among us."[40]

City politicians railed that the type of men who became constables were from the "lower classes" and were eager to accept bribes. They lamented over the "unlimited command of money possessed by these individuals and the influence upon society which they are enabled to exert by such means."

Even if a gambling emporium czar was arrested, who would testify against him? Regular customers would be reluctant to take the stand because they would not be allowed to gamble there, or anywhere else in Richmond, again. Their testimony in court would also mark them as gamblers, something that many who gambled in secret had no desire to make public. Would minors such as George Wythe Sweeney take the stand and let everyone know, especially their parents, that they were sneaking out of their homes at night to visit the tawdry gambling houses—and were losing their families' savings?

Later, in 1833, the state legislature discussed the licensing of casinos. Lawmakers were hopeful that regulating casinos would not only cut down on fighting, cheating, drinking, and gambling addiction, but would provide tax money to the state. The licensing proponents also believed that if casinos were public, attendance would drop because the secret gambler would not visit. Legislators envisioned an early nineteenth-century Las Vegas. They foresaw licensing for only certain cities, such as Richmond, so that gamblers would flock there and not operate in their hometowns. The number of casinos would be limited, and all would be regulated by a state gaming commission. The casinos would be remodeled to look elegant, and entertainment would be added to gambling. The bill was soundly defeated.[41]

The single loudest complaint of the various committees that studied gambling in the 1833 legislative session was the negative effect it had on the young men of Richmond. Referring to the early years of the 1800s, when George Wythe Sweeney lived in Richmond with his granduncle, a committee report stated, "The most essential benefit of licensing would . . . be found in its effects in deterring the younger class of society from being enticed into these resorts. No opportunities would then offer to enable a gang of black legs to entrap the youth in possession of the funds of his employer (or family) and, we are convinced that hundreds who now frequent the faro table would refrain from doing so."[42]

Many in Richmond agreed with their conclusion about youth and the lure of gaming. One man wrote, "Nearly every young man in the city . . . think[s] no more of being seen in a faro bank than in a bar room."[43]

Teenage gambling and drinking had been problems for Richmond since the 1790s. Teens wandered into the taverns and the casinos so often that even the professional gamblers warned families to keep them away. George Wythe Sweeney was one of the most well-known visitors. He frequented the casinos and the racetrack and might have purchased lottery tickets, too. For Sweeney, slipping away at night to visit the gaming houses was easy. All he had to do was walk downhill three blocks to Main Street and then east for a few blocks more to reach Brick Row and the casinos, a stroll of less than ten minutes. One professional gambler, Robert Bailey, was appalled at the proliferation of teenagers in the card rooms and warned their families that the card sharps and the beer would be their end. He said, "Parents, never suffer your children to gamble, youth is the time to suppress a disposition to vice[,] then how important is the duty you owe your offspring at this tender period of their lives."[44]

Drinking and gambling went hand in hand in the taverns. Alcoholism became such a problem in Richmond during that era that a few years later, the city was the target of some of the largest temperance organizations in the country. Alcoholism was so widespread that factories in town, such as the Tredegar Iron Works, formed their own temperance societies.[45]

The difficulty in curbing gambling was that Richmonders simply loved it. In the 1833 report on city gambling, the authors admitted that "Gambling is a vice which must always exist in this community. A fondness for games of chance evidently arises from the combined operation of two powerful passions—the love of gain and the love of ease, or, in other words, an unwillingness to labor. These features are to be recognized in the character of a large portion of the people of this state. There is no race of men more desirous of obtaining the means of procuring the luxuries and elegances of life, or more averse to the tedious process of acquiring them by laborious pursuits [than Virginians]," wrote the authors of the report.[46]

The epidemic of sex, alcohol, and gambling was so overwhelming by 1806 that a local historian wrote that Richmond was "more famous for its amusements in racing, drinking and frolicking . . . than for those of a higher character." A short time later, a pious Northern visitor to the South complained about Southerners in general, saying "that no business is so important at any time as to prevent them from attending the horserace, the cockfight or any other kind of sport." [47]

THE MURDER OF GEORGE WYTHE was merely the latest gory episode in the life of the violent and deadly city that Richmond had become. It did not shake the people of the capital only because Wythe was such a respected judge and a venerated historical figure. The slaying made all of Richmond tremble because it was the highest-profile murder yet in a city that had been torn apart by assaults, robberies, burglaries, and murders. Richmond's ever-climbing crime rate was among the highest in America.

The number of crimes in the city grew in almost direction propor-tion to the town's increasing population, the inability of city fathers to regulate that growth, expansive opportunities for criminals in a chaotic community, and the lack of any effective law enforcement. The crime rate really surged during the period from 1804 to 1806, just prior to Judge Wythe's murder. The increase to 900 felonies, including 180 physical assaults, which was quadruple the number of crimes in 1802, alarmed the whole city. The 900 crimes commit-ted in 1806 meant that there was a crime committed against one in every eleven residents of the community. On average, a violent assault occurred in Richmond every other day; this news sent residents reeling. Many assault-and battery cases involving one person against another, such as a bar fight and most domestic assaults, were never reported. Violent disputes, duels, or both between members of the gentry were never recorded. Very few single women who killed their newborn babies, being victims of abandonment by the fathers and suffering from postpartum depression, were ever charged with a crime, either. So, the actual crime rate was much higher than the already frightening 11.3 percent. Even the reported crime rate in the city, not the actual rate, was just as high as the crime rate of Richmond two hundred years later, in 2006, and as high as that of almost every major city in the United States in 2006. If all of the crimes in Richmond had been counted, as they would be today, the crime rate would have been nearly twice as high as those in the most crime-ridden U.S. cities today.[48]

In fact, Richmond, like all cities in the United States and Europe, had large, malevolent subcultures of poor whites and blacks who earned little money or were unemployed and preyed on others, making up a brand new "criminal class." These criminals, who were made famous in the penny press and the novels of Charles Dickens, were, by the early nineteenth century, a permanent fixture in urban America. "It is a fact against which we ought no longer to shut our eyes," complained one newspaper editor of the era, "that we have in the very midst of us a population of the most abandoned kind."[49]

Most of the crimes in Richmond were committed by white males (56 percent), with black freedmen in second place and slaves third. Murders rose from 1784 until 1800 and then climbed at an even brisker rate from 1800 to 1806. White men committed 62 percent of the murders; black men, 21 percent; and white women, 14 percent. Slaves committed 32 percent of all robberies and 21 percent of assaults. Eleven percent of all robberies were committed by female slaves.

Burglaries, horse theft, robberies, and other crimes against property were consistently high in the years after Richmond became the capital, but they soared in 1805 and 1806, on the eve of the judge's murder, with an average of 800 crimes per year, or nearly 3 each day, a rate that alarmed residents of the city.

Larceny increased, too, especially in the taverns, where pickpockets thrived and found drunken men and women easy targets. It was rampant in the large new stores, where there was no security and the theft of goods was common. Records showed that male slaves committed 52 percent of the burglaries and 34 percent of the larcenies in town. Freed male blacks committed 10 percent of the burglaries and 17 percent of the larcenies.

During that period and up until the Civil War, one of the strongest arguments that slaveholders and Southern politicians used against freedom for slaves was the premise that freed black men would rape white women and taint the race. That was a lie. Virginia court records showed that in the nearly forty years between 1784 and 1820, in the capital city of a large Southern state filled with black slaves and white women, there was not a single rape of any kind reported.[50]

Surprisingly, the all-white male juries of Richmond showed no favoritism between whites and blacks in dispensing justice. Throughout the 1790s and in the first six years of the 1800s, the same number of whites (43 percent) as blacks (44 percent) were found guilty of charges filed against them. The same number of black women (32 percent) as white women (29 percent) were convicted.[51]

The only advantage whites had was that their cases were permitted to be appealed to a higher court (95 percent); none of the black people's cases were appealed.

The true source of crime in Richmond, however, as court records showed, was the vast, unregulated army of lower-class white workers that arrived throughout the 1790s and the early part of the nineteenth century to work in the bustling shipyards, mills, tobacco warehouses, and growing businesses. Eighty-four percent of all crimes by white people were committed by this floating, shiftless population of itinerant men who owned no property, paid no taxes, and reported no addresses. Most of them lived in large converted warehouses or in the town's ever-growing neighborhoods of overcrowded wooden boardinghouses. Forty-six boardinghouses rented to blacks only, and it was not uncommon to find several men living in a single spartan room. This substratum of itinerant men also made up most of the population in the taverns and the gambling houses that George Wythe Sweeney and many others frequented.[52]

It was their advice that Sweeney listened to when he panicked over his financial problems and sought means to obtain large sums of cash to pay off his gambling debts.

Criminal punishment for blacks and whites was substantially different. Whites who were convicted of minor crimes were sentenced to short terms in the city jail or lengthier terms in the state penitentiary. Blacks who were guilty of crimes (or who were runaways) were either lashed at a public whipping post or had the palms of their hands burned by hot pokers. Sometimes the convicted felon had his hand burned and was whipped as well. A convicted black might have also had an ear cut off, but few were put in prison, because they were needed for work.[53]

A growing number of murders occurred in the city, the county, and on nearby plantations, as well as in villages and other communities throughout the state. This surprised no one, because Virginia had a history of violence that extended back to the settling of the Jamestown plantation. The first recorded murder in the colony's history was in 1619. There were so many homicides during the early years that in 1684, a woman wrote in her diary, "So many horrid murders and duels were committed about this time as were never before heard of in England." Most of the men and the women sentenced to death for murder were brought to Richmond for hanging because it was the state capital. Most of them were white. In Richmond itself, only 6 black slaves and freedmen were arrested for murder during those years; all were acquitted. Half of the 18 white men charged with murder were convicted and later executed. Another 52 white men had been hanged for murders committed between 1706 and 1784 in other communities, prior to Richmond's designation as the state capital. During that eighty-year period, in local communities, authorities had executed 567 slaves, 300 of them for the murder or the attempted murder of whites (slave murders of whites increased during Wythe's last years, with 34 slaves hanged for this crime from 1795 through 1806). There were 20 slaves hanged from the public gallows in Richmond, but not for murder. They were hanged on capital charges such as horse thievery and multiple burglaries or larcenies (slave punishments were not reduced by the legal codes written by Wythe in 1779).[54]

White judges and juries in Richmond held black freedmen in a special class distinct from slaves, however, when it came to sentencing. Although freed blacks were convicted of major crimes more often than whites or slaves were, their punishment was more in line with that of whites than of slaves. As an example, although 80 percent of all convicted slaves were whipped and had their palms burned, only 18 percent of freed blacks suffered those fates. No freed blacks were ever hanged, and in 79 percent of the cases in which a freed black, man or woman, was convicted, that person was allowed to appeal to a higher court.

To house the growing number of criminals convicted of minor crimes, Richmond built a large city jail in 1800. The three-story-high brick-and-stone building had a dome and was located at the corner of Main and Seventeenth streets. It was open on three sides, with iron cagelike gratings, so that passersby could watch the inmates in a zoo-like atmosphere. The combination of confinement and embarrassment was meant to serve as a deterrent to future crime. To house those convicted of more serious crimes, the state built a penitentiary on a cow pasture overlooking the James River. The population in the correctional facility soared soon after it opened. By the winter of 1806, just before the judge was killed, it held 118 inmates: 113 men and 5 women, 80 percent of them white. As an example of how high the crime rate was in 1806, the state penitentiary held only 155 prisoners twenty-six years later, in 1832, a 24 percent increase in inmates, even though the population of the city had grown by some 175 percent during that time period. The Richmond penitentiary would serve as a state prison until 1928.[55]

The growing number of aggravated assaults, robberies, and murders and the corresponding need for a large city jail and state penitentiary alarmed the population of Richmond even more than did the pernicious spread of gambling, drinking, and prostitution. All agreed with a harsh grand jury presentment in 1799 that found that a large number of "vagrants, beggars, free Negroes and runaway slaves . . . daily infest the streets and by night plunder the inhabitants."[56]

Perhaps no one summed up the violence and the degeneracy of Richmond better than an appalled Quaker, Tom Scattergood, who visited the city in 1793. "O! The wickedness and abomination of the little city," he said.[57]

It was in this cesspool of crime, sin, gambling, drinking, and sex that George Wythe Sweeney spent his nights.

7

The Dying George Wythe
Changes His Will

GEORGE SWEENEY must have been surprised at how rapidly events moved as the court went about its work. Sweeney had lived all of his life in the shadows, protected by his family. He was a loner who did not keep any diary or journal. There were no letters found that people had written to him and none written by him. He lived in solitude until he was seventeen. Then he seemingly came out of nowhere to allegedly murder his granduncle and Michael Brown. No one knew much about him; they never would.

Sweeney must have been even more astonished when he learned that his granduncle, who was certain he was going to die, summoned Edmund Randolph to help him change his will and cut Sweeney out of it.

That was accomplished on June 1, the day that the teenager Michael Brown died. The feeble Wythe was certain that he was going to die, too. Dr. Foushee informed him of Michael's death and told him that Lydia Broadnax had survived her illness, barely, and would live, although the poisoning had significantly affected her eyesight.

"I shall not be far behind," the judge said to those in the room, when he was told of Brown's passing. He insisted that an autopsy be performed on the teenager and on himself. He looked straight into the eyes of his friends, pointed at his chest, and told them, "Cut me!"

The two ministers who had been visiting him decided to leave. As they rose, one said, "We shall see you again. God be with you."

"Not in this world," Wythe replied glumly.

When Randolph arrived with Sam Greenhow, William Price, and Samuel McCraw as legal witnesses, the judge sat up in bed and dictated his new will, eliminating Sweeney. "I do hereby devise and bequeath all the estate which I have devised or bequeathed to the said George Wythe Sweeney, or for his use, in the said will and codicils, and all the interest and estate which I have therein devised or bequeathed in trust for or to the use of the said Michael Brown, to the brothers and sisters of the said George Wythe Sweeney, to be equally divided among them," the judge wrote and then made certain that the will specified a number of prized personal items to be given to Thomas Jefferson.[1]

Wythe and Jefferson had remained friends all of their lives, even as Wythe's age kept him closer to home and Jefferson's success propelled him onto the world stage as a diplomat, secretary of state, vice president, and president. Jefferson often wrote to Wythe about the events in his life, personal and political, and Wythe was an eager correspondent. The pair exchanged letters on just about every imaginable topic. When the judge opened an envelope from Jefferson, he never knew whether the enclosed letter contained the thoughts of his friend on European politics, the function of American government, new telescopes, Greek literature, or growing corn at Monticello.

As an example, Jefferson wrote to Wythe from Paris in 1783 that the French people were "the most benevolent, the most gay, and amiable character of which the human form is susceptible."[2] In the fall of 1794, just after Jefferson had resigned as secretary of state, Wythe tore open a letter to discover that his brilliant young friend was not spending his time analyzing the financial structure of the Russian government but was grappling with making bricks for his new home at Monticello. Jefferson wrote blissfully of his work as a rookie mason, "now living in a brick-kiln, for my house, in its present state, is nothing more."[3]

Jefferson often sought Wythe's advice on important constitutional matters. He was uncertain what parliamentary rules he had to adopt in overseeing the U.S. Senate when he was elected vice president in 1797, so he asked Wythe. He wrote to his mentor, "I know that [parliamentary rules] have been more studied and are better known by you than by any man in America, perhaps by any man living."[4]

Jefferson heard the news that the Virginia bill on religious freedom had passed from Wythe. Pleased, he wrote from Paris to his friend that America had now moved centuries ahead of Europe on religion. "If all the sovereigns of Europe were to set themselves to work to emancipate the minds of their subjects from their present ignorance and prejudices, a thousand years would not place them on the high ground on which our common people are now setting out. . . . If anybody thinks that Kings, nobles or priests are good conservators of the public happiness, send them here."[5]

Both men were proud of their religion bill. It not only protected religious freedom, but also made it possible for people of all faiths to worship unimpeded in Virginia. This brought about even more growth to the state and to Richmond, attracting an influx of Jews and Europeans, who helped to make the growing city more cosmopolitan in nature.[6]

The friendship between the two men was so long and so close that Jefferson even had his grandson named after George Wythe.

Physically drained, yet thinking of his friend Jefferson, George Wythe reclined on his pillows as Randolph read the will back to him and had the witnesses in the bedroom sign it. Wythe muttered something to Randolph about the investigation of Sweeney for forgery, and he predicted his own death. The old man lay there, his body wasting away after a week of vomiting and diarrhea attacks and his skin cold and clammy. Randolph, looking down at him with sad eyes, must have remembered how long he had known the judge. They had first met more than forty years ago, back in the 1760s, when, as a boy, young Randolph was enrolled in the grammar school of the College of William and Mary. They had been friends there, during the early years of the judge's life, and friends in Richmond in the later years.

Wythe had gained fame in Williamsburg, but he had history in Richmond, too. He had achieved great success in Richmond, first as the chairman of the Constitutional Convention, then as the high chancellor, and later as one of the most respected members of the community. He had been just as beloved in the new capital as he had been in the old.

8

Moving Day: A Second Life in Richmond and the Return of George Wythe

GEORGE WYTHE arrived in the busy river town of Richmond in the autumn of 1791 with very mixed emotions. The eminent jurist was happy to be in Richmond because the capital city was booming. The community was home to many of the judge's political friends and former students. There were wonderful gathering places, such as Lynch's Coffee House, where he stopped from time to time and where many politicians congregated. Lynch's garrulous proprietor read political stories from newspapers out loud as his customers sipped the latest piping-hot aromatic coffees that had just arrived from exotic countries in South America. There were newly opened bakeries, where Wythe could purchase treats for his legendary sweet tooth. The city had recently installed torches on all the streets so that he and others could take leisurely evening walks.

But he was melancholy, too. Wythe continued to mourn the death of his second wife, Elizabeth, who had given him so much love and joy throughout his life. He knew he would miss Williamsburg, with its quaint lanes, warm summer evenings, village green, and numerous ponds that glimmered in the fall when the leaves of the trees that surrounded them turned colors. He would miss his spacious brick home and the quiet solitude of Bruton Parish Church, where he had served as a vestryman for many years. Wythe had lived in Williamsburg for forty years, and, despite the deterioration of the community, he had left behind many friends.

Physically, the judge, now sixty-six, felt worn out. He did not want to travel great distances. Advanced arthritis and gout had crippled his right hand; he had to teach himself to print letters using his left hand, and each letter took much time to write. One of the reasons he hired clerks when he arrived at the capital was to have someone to do most of his writing. His other ailments included the beginnings of a slight stoop that would become more pronounced as he aged. He now required the use of a gold-tipped cane to walk around the streets. His hair began to thin even more, and he would soon be nearly bald. He purchased a home close to the capitol building so that he had only a short walk to work in the mornings; he had given up most horseback riding.[1]

As he approached his seventies, the judge developed certain eccentricities. For example, he often sank into silent moods, walking about the streets or the court house with a smile but saying little. The employees in his favorite bakery reported that he would enter the store, point toward pastries that he desired, pay for them, and leave, never saying a word.[2]

He seemed demoralized. People who knew him or worked with him noted great sadness and sometimes tears when he heard of the passing of a personal friend or of someone he had worked with during the Revolution.

In 1791, Wythe made a clean break with Williamsburg and his plantation at Chesterville. He packed everything he could think of, from his precious books to some small pieces of furniture, into a small caravan of wagons and left. One of his last acts in Williamsburg, which gave him a deep sense of pleasure, was to emancipate several of his most trusted house slaves, (he had freed the cook Lydia Broadnax earlier, and she remained with him as a paid servant). He did not free all fifteen of his house slaves, because he was legally bound to turn them back to the Taliaferro family, but he did free three of them. The judge made certain that all of the others were returned to the Taliaferros so that the slave families could stay together. He sold his plantation at Chesterville and the two dozen slaves who lived there with it. When he left for Richmond, he had removed slavery from his life, once and for all.[3]

Throughout his life, Wythe had been uncomfortable owning slaves. He had inherited slaves at the Chesterville plantation and purchased several during his years in Williamsburg to help his wife with the care of their home, as did many other Virginians. But as time passed, he turned against the system.

No one knew Wythe's views on slavery better than Jefferson did. He had discussed slavery with Wythe for years as a student and as his law clerk. Jefferson wrote to a British abolitionist in 1785 that as a teacher, Wythe had greatly influenced Jefferson against slavery and had also swayed all of his other students.[4] Wythe had talked Jefferson into introducing a bill to free all of the slaves in Virginia (it went nowhere), and later, perhaps under Wythe's direction, Jefferson added a clause in the Declaration of Independence to free slaves (it was killed by delegates). Jefferson had endlessly discussed his own hatred of slavery, hoping it would be eliminated and calling it "a great political and moral evil." He understood Wythe's fury at the slave system. "[His] sentiments on slavery are unequivocal," Jefferson wrote in 1785.[5]

While there was agreement on theory, there was none on execution between Jefferson and Wythe. Wythe advocated freedom for slaves, he freed some of his, and he rid himself of the rest. Jefferson, who was famous for writing about slavery—"Indeed, I tremble for my country when I reflected that God is just, that his justice cannot sleep forever"—never freed any.

Wythe was convinced that blacks were as intelligent as whites and, given the same opportunities, would be just as successful. He had tutored both black and white students to prove his point. Jefferson always believed that slaves were inferior to whites. He wrote that blacks smelled, were overly sexual, had little intelligence, had no appreciation of art, did not speak well, could not write poetry, and were far less intelligent than everyone, even Indians. He wrote, "The blacks, whether originally a distant race, or made distinct by time or circumstances, are inferior to the whites in the endowments both of body and mind."[6]

Jefferson's solution was the same as that of every other antislavery advocate in the South who did not release his slaves: responsible care. Jefferson wrote in later life, "My opinion has ever been that until more can be done for them, we should endeavor, with those whom fortune has thrown on our hands, to feed and clothe them well."[7]

Wythe began to rule against slavery in cases, such as the 1798 *Pleasants v. Pleasants*, that came before him in Richmond's Chancery Court or as a justice when he sat on the State Supreme Court (which was made up of the judges of the appeals courts). John Pleasants had died in 1771 and in his will offered his slaves freedom if Virginia ever permitted that. His children were given his slaves. They refused to release the slaves when Virginia passed its short-lived manumission act in 1782. Years later, one of his sons sued the others, claming that they had to free their slaves. Wythe ruled that not only should the slaves be freed, but that they were owed hundreds of thousands of dollars in back wages by the Pleasants brothers. On appeal, with John Marshall representing the slaves, the Court of Appeals upheld Wythe's decision to free the slaves but denied them back wages. In 1806, Wythe championed slaves again in *Hudgins v. Wrights*. The Wrights were slaves belonging to Hudgins, who wanted to send them out of Virginia as his chattel. The Wrights sued, claming that they were not black but descendants of an Indian chief. They had some paperwork to prove their ancestry, but they were mulattos. Wythe ruled in their favor, noting their claim but going much further. He shocked Virginians by stating in his ruling that slavery of any kind was wrong. "Freedom is the birthright of every human being, which sentiment is strongly inculcated by the first article of our 'political catechism,' the bill of rights . . . and that whenever one person claims to hold another in slavery, the *onus probandi* lies on the claimant."[8]

Wythe's radical ruling that slaveholders had to prove their ownership of a slave, and not the other way around, set a precedent in the judicial world of Virginia. The state Court of Appeals upheld his decision, but on the Indian heritage grounds, not because of his bold statement that slaves should be as free as whites. Wythe's ruling in the Pleasants case permitted one of the largest manumissions of slaves in U.S. history.

With his plantation sold, his home returned to his wife's family, and his ties to his slaves ended, George Wythe headed west to Richmond.

His cook, Lydia Broadnax, traveled with him (in Richmond, after a few years, Wythe helped Lydia buy a small wooden home on a half-acre of land).[9]

The judge was an impressive-looking man as he continued his duties as the high chancellor after moving to Richmond. Some people, however, chuckled behind his back that his old-fashioned gray-broadcloth coats, silver-buckled shoes, and long buttoned vests made him look like a Quaker and that he seemed very out of place in Richmond. There, an influx of French men and women had changed all the rules of fashion for the gentry in the city. Now stockings and boots were out and shoes were in. The tricornered hats that had adorned men's heads since the early days of the Revolution were no more. Women's dresses had undergone a dramatic change. Wealthy women now wore dresses of silk, silk stockings, satin and calimanco shoes, colored kid gloves, and brand-new riding hats with colorful feathers tucked into them. The dresses featured rather daring cleavage, causing one state legislator to remark to another that in Richmond there was now "a sect of naked ladies."[10]

The judge received a warm welcome back to the capital by both old and new friends. His former students and political colleagues were especially glad to have him around. One nineteenth-century historian, Hugh Grigsby, wrote, "Many . . . had been his scholars and loved him with an affection that neither time nor distrust could weaken."[11]

Richmond had become a city of great hospitality, for rich and poor. The residents embraced new arrivals, whether residents or travelers, and went out of their way to make the newcomers feel comfortable. Everyone took an interest in the working class and the poor, too. The Amicable Society was formed from among the gentry to help recently arrived individuals and families in distress; several almshouses were established to assist the poor.[12]

Judge Wythe carried himself with great dignity, despite his physical stoop and his cane. He was gracious to all, especially small children whom he met on the streets or at Capitol Square. He hailed friends and neighbors and returned the greetings of anyone who waved to him. The judge always made, Henry Clay remembered, "the most graceful bow that I ever witnessed." In 1851, Clay wrote, "Even at this moment, after the lapse of more than half a century since I last saw him, his image is distinctly engraved on my mind."[13]

Clay, like others, remembered many things about Judge Wythe (like Wythe, Clay lives forever in Richmond; the town erected a statue of him there in 1860). He told friends that the judge made him include Greek phrases in his opinions and letters that Clay did not understand. Clay never did learn to read Greek, but he loved to listen to the judge speak it. "I was often highly gratified in listening to his readings in Homer's *Iliad* and other Greek authors, so beautifully did he pronounce the language," wrote Clay. In order to impress important world figures later in life, Clay often quoted lines from Homer. Wythe had read these to him so often when he was Wythe's teenage clerk that they were always fresh in his memory.[14]

The home Wythe purchased in Richmond afforded him a majestic view of the James River that he enjoyed, as did everyone who visited the town or lived there. One traveler from England wrote, "The city of Richmond deserved to have a song written about it."[15]

In Richmond, Wythe continued his lifelong role as a teacher, spending innumerable hours with his law clerks, Clay being the first, in order to provide them with the same kind of advanced, personal, one-on-one education he had given to Thomas Jefferson and others. They all appreciated the chance to learn from him. "To no man was I more indebted, by his instruction, his advice and his example, for the little intellectual improvement which I made," Clay wrote.[16]

Wythe's courtroom in 1806 was on the ground floor of the gorgeous white marble capitol building designed by Jefferson. During that time, it sat alone in the middle of a large and uneven lawn that was cut by several ravines, and the square surrounding it contained only a few homes. Still, the building itself was majestic and could be seen for miles, an alabaster-white architectural beacon. Jefferson was proud of the capitol building. He wrote, "[It] improves the taste of my country-men, to increase their reputations, to reconcile to them the respect of the world and procure them its praise." The landscape architect Frederick Law Olmstead, who designed New York's Central Park, said that the capitol building was "an imposing Grecian edifice, standing alone, and finely placed on open and elevated ground in the center of town."

There, the lawyers of Virginia argued their cases before Wythe, certain that they would receive an impartial hearing. Munford wrote that attorneys "knew he held the even scales of justice well balanced in his hands and that nothing but undoubted equity and law could turn those scales to the right or left."[17]

By 1806, the Wythe household had grown to four pretty much full-time residents: Lydia Broadnax, Wythe's cook and former slave, lived nearby but spent most of the week in the home. His latest protégé, Michael Brown, a freed black teenager, had a room there. The final member of the quartet was George Wythe Sweeney, Wythe's impulsive grandnephew, who had lived with him for weeks and months at a time over the last few years.

The city was still primitive in 1791 when Wythe arrived, and throughout the remainder of the decade not much progress was made, despite considerable growth. Except for the homes of the rich on Shockoe Hill, where the judge and his friends lived, most residential homes were small wooden structures with only a few rooms. The large, bustling warehouses along the river wharves, which serviced hundreds of oceangoing sailing vessels that moved in and out of the city each year, were always overcrowded with cargo and workers. The noise from the docks was loud and incessant, and the roar of the river's rapids and waterfalls could be heard throughout the city, all day and all night. The streets, like those in most Southern cities, were unpaved and turned to mud in rainstorms, making transportation difficult. The streets became dust bowls in the summer, and people who walked a single block had to brush from their clothes the dirt that was kicked up by horses, buggies, and wagons in the streets. There were no sidewalks yet, and everyone walked in the street with the horses and the carriages. The streets flooded with water whenever the James River overflowed.

There were several churches, a handful of bookstores, musical entertainment from time to time, and the Society for the Advancement of Useful Knowledge, which Wythe joined to show off his electrical machines. Small poetry groups gathered at the homes of the better-educated residents in town, with one meeting regularly at Wythe's.[18] These cultural institutions were few. The state capital had no library, no university, and few schools of any kind. Men and women from the upper crust had to develop their own private schools and clubs to educate their children and entertain themselves.

The view of Richmond that the rich and the powerful, such as
Judge Wythe, had from the top of the hill was quite different from
the view shared by just about everyone else in town. They all lived
at the bottom of the hill in overcrowded, noisy neighborhoods that
had sprung up over the previous fifteen years with little or no planning. To these residents, Richmond was a miserable place. One visitor
to the town called it "one of the dirtiest holes of a place I was ever in."
A refined woman who moved there in 1780 wrote that although it
might be "a great city" one day, at that time "This little town is made
up of Scotch [tobacco] factors, who inhabit small tenements scattered
here and there from the river to the hill."

Richmond was so unrefined that the governor's mansion was only a
small, unpainted wooden house, where goats grazed in the front yard.[19]

It was a violent town in which many men carried guns and knives
and where bar fights and street brawls were routine. "They fight like
wild bears," wrote one man, "biting, kicking, and endeavoring to tear
each other's eyes out with their nails."

Street attacks were provoked for the most minor of reasons.
Dr. William Foushee, one of Wythe's physicians, nearly had his eye torn
out when during the Revolution he was attacked on the street by a man
who accused him of being overly friendly to paroled British officers.[20]

Richmond suffered from repeated fires, as did most cities, because
the majority of its buildings were made of wood. Flames that consumed
one building easily leaped to the wooden frames of buildings nearby and
caused considerable damage. The worst conflagration was in January
1787. A fire fanned by high winds destroyed six entire blocks of the
business district on the southern side of Main Street, several blocks on
the northern side, and a large tobacco warehouse. The uncontrollable
fire, which was fought unsuccessfully by the town's tiny volunteer fire
company, also burned down more than fifty private homes.[21]

There were so many fires and so much damage that in 1794,
Frederick Ast formed the Mutual Assurance Society, the South's first
insurance company, to write policies on businesses and residences.
Ast's first two policy holders were George Washington and Thomas
Jefferson.[22]

Although it was the capital of the largest state in the nation and
home to some of America's most brilliant and sophisticated men,

Richmond was, from 1791 until the judge's death, a wild, bulging frontier town with all of its attendant problems.[23]

One of the most unsettling issues was the ever-growing population
of immigrants from countries around the world. The town welcomed
hundreds of arrivals from England, usually bright young men who
saw business opportunities for themselves. Every day the river port
also greeted more and more inhabitants from Caribbean islands and
South American nations, in addition to traditional immigrants from
Germany, Ireland, Scotland, Spain, and France. There was an influx of
Brazilians, who came with their coffee ships and stayed. The immigrant
population continued to grow until, within a few decades, foreign-born
residents in the city made up 13 percent of its total.

The city population also had 31 percent slaves and 7 percent freed
blacks, making the nonwhite, non–American born population 51
percent, a majority. The mixing of black and white Americans and
immigrants from so many countries worried Richmonders, who feared
clashes of nationalities as much as they did revolts by slaves. They
were unhappy that they were being overwhelmed by foreigners and
blacks.[24]

The immigrant populations of many towns doubled and tripled
every few years; more than ten thousand immigrants arrived in New
York each month. A former mayor of New York, Philip Hone, expressed
the exasperation of all city dwellers, in Richmond and elsewhere, with
the waves of immigrants who arrived without jobs and homes. "All
Europe is coming across the ocean," he said, "all that part, at least, who
cannot make a living at home, and what shall we do with them? They
increase our taxes, eat our bread, and encumber our streets and not one
in twenty is competent to keep himself."[25]

It was the immigrants, as well as the blacks, whom Richmonders
blamed for many of their problems, especially crime. Two early historians wrote that the residents believed that "Too many new faces in the
area fostered an atmosphere in which disorderly houses and thievery
thrived."[26]

In 1782, just as Richmond started to grow, Jefferson worried that
America welcomed too many immigrants. "The growing population of
foreigners," he wrote, could lead to "unbounded licentiousness passing,
as is usual, from one extreme to another. They will infuse into it

[society] their spirit, warp and bias its direction and render it a hetero-geneous, incoherent, distracted mass."[27]

The number of immigrants flooding the streets of Richmond and other American metropolises was so high that in 1798, Congress passed the Alien Act. It was in effect for only two years, but it limited the amount of time that any recent immigrant could live in America. The Alien Act was debated heatedly throughout the country and often served to set newly arrived ethnic groups against Americans and against one another.

It was one of the many jurisdictional and political topics that Wythe discussed with his new clerk in Richmond, Henry Clay. The fifteen-year-old Clay had been left in Henrico County to fend for himself when his mother and stepfather moved to Versailles, Kentucky, to open a tavern. His stepfather knew Peter Tinsley, the clerk of Virginia's High Court of Chancery, and had asked him to give Henry a job as a secretary in the winter of 1792, just after Wythe arrived. Wythe took the bright teenager under his wing and made Clay his personal clerk. Clay's formal duties were to copy all of the judge's decisions, inter-spersed with his famous Greek phrases, and organize his office work. Wythe looked upon Clay as he did his protégés in Williamsburg and gave him the same intense legal, historical, and philosophical educa-tion that they had received. Wythe was convinced, as he had been with Jefferson, Marshall, and Monroe, that the brilliant Clay had a great future. He taught Clay how to conduct legal research and how to work with lawyers and judges and helped him become a better speaker. The teenager, who worked for Wythe for four years, had undergone little formal education prior to that and suddenly found himself being tutored by one of the most brilliant men in America. Wythe also con-vinced Clay that slavery was wrong and urged him to do all that he could to end the practice in Virginia or in Kentucky if he ever joined his parents there.[28]

After leaving Wythe, Clay became a lawyer and moved to Kentucky. The rise of Wythe's protégé in Kentucky politics was meteoric. He was soon elected to Congress and became the speaker of the House of Representatives, ran for president three times, and won everlasting respect as one of the most important political leaders in the history of the United States.[29]

Jefferson was happy that Wythe was in Richmond. "I shall forever cherish the remembrance of the many agreeable and useful days I have spent with you," he wrote to Wythe in 1799, "and the infinite obligations I owe you for what good has fallen to me through life. May your remaining years be as many as you would wish them, and filled with the enjoyment of all your faculties."[30]

IN RICHMOND, Wythe continued to assert the power of the U.S. Constitution over state matters and state constitutions over legislative matters. In 1783, Wythe, representing Chancery on the State Supreme Court, was reported to have said in the matter of the *Commonwealth v. Caton* that no state legislature, even though it represented the people, could pass a bill that overrode the U.S. Constitution. "Nay more," said the judge, "if the whole legislature . . . should attempt to overlap its bounds, prescribed to them by the people, I, in administering the public justice of the country, will meet the united powers at my seat in this tribunal; and, pointing to the Constitution, will say to them, here is the limit of your authority; and hither, shall you go, but no further."

Sitting in Wythe's jammed courtroom that day to see how the judicial panel would rule was his former student and friend John Marshall. A decade later, using that same judicial philosophy, Marshall, as chief justice of the United States, would rule in *Marbury v. Madison* that the federal Constitution superseded all state and local laws, thus giving enormous powers to the federal government.[31]

What made Chancellor Wythe so special, though, was the delightful way that he wove into his judicial opinions various digressions and elaborations, such as algebraic equations, geometric progressions, astronomical calculations, and commentaries from Greek and Latin philosophers, European poets, theorists, and even popular novelists. In one eight-page opinion, he discussed Bracton and Justinian, Juvenal's *Satires*, Quintilian, Euclid, Archimedes, Hiero, Littleton, the novels *Tristram Shandy* and *Don Quixote*, Petronius, Halley, Prometheus, Locke's *Essay on Human Understanding*, and, if those were not enough, the novelist Jonathan Swift's *Tale of a Tub* and newspaper stories about Turkish travelers. People throughout the courthouse and the capitol building jammed Wythe's courtroom to listen to him read decisions laced with these marvelous tales and references; one of those who listened to his decisions most often was Marshall.[32]

Through Wythe's judicial rulings, renowned gentility, friendships, and participation in numerous civic organizations, poetry clubs, and political alliances, he had become, by the summer of 1806, one of the most prominent members of Richmond and Virginia government and society, as well as an unusually well-liked old man. Everyone shuddered when they heard the news that he had been poisoned and would probably die.

PART TWO

The Investigation

9

The Arrest

GEORGE WYTHE SWEENEY's brazenness was his undoing. On May 27, a Tuesday, two days after his granduncle had fallen desperately ill, Sweeney forged Wythe's signature on a check for $100. This was a large amount of money at the time. Sweeney tried to cash the check at the Bank of Richmond. A teller there, William Dandridge, aware that Wythe was very ill, as was just about everyone else in the city, was startled when Sweeney handed him the check. The teller took the check into another room and examined it carefully. He returned, gave Sweeney the $100, and watched the young man leave. Dandridge then went to the bank president, who was as stunned as the teller that Sweeney had come in with a forged check so soon after what everybody said was his poisoning of the judge. They looked for a constable.

It was not the first time Sweeney had forged a check. The bank knew that on at least six other occasions, Sweeney had forged Wythe's name on checks. Bank officials had taken each of the checks to the judge, who acknowledged that his nephew had stolen them. The judge would not press charges, each time assuring bank officials that he would reprimand Sweeney and that it would not happen again.

Each time, it was learned, Wythe had confronted Sweeney about the forgeries and argued with him. Sweeney's defense was always the same: he had lost considerable sums gambling and needed the money to pay his debts. He had forged two checks just a few weeks earlier, one for $50 and another for $100, to pay debts. He had also stolen boxes full of rare books from the judge and sold them for the same reason.

Wythe had exploded at Sweeney after the previous week's forgeries. He told Sweeney that the forgeries and the thefts were a direct result of gambling. Wythe was disappointed that his nephew had chosen to ignore the refined life that the judge provided him, had shunned the judge's sophisticated and influential friends, and had chosen instead to spend his time at the racetrack, the gaming houses, and the raucous taverns of Richmond. Sweeney was leading a dissipated life. Wythe had done everything he could for Sweeney. He had spent a great deal of time with him when he was a child at the Chesterville plantation and on the numerous lengthy visits the boy had made to Wythe's Williamsburg home, when his parents and his grandmother, the judge's sister Ann, brought him there. Exasperated, Wythe warned Sweeney that if he stole anything else or forged any more checks, Wythe would cut the youth out of his will.[1]

And now Sweeney had forged his dying granduncle's signature to pay gamblers. The bank president alerted the authorities. On June 2, Sweeney was arrested and brought before the Court of Hustings, a grand jury, where it was determined that there was enough evidence to try him on violating Virginia's forgery laws. Sweeney, who appeared distraught at the hearing, was bound over to the District Court for trial.

Bail was set at $1,000, a substantial sum in that day. Sweeney then had the audacity to request that Wythe be asked to post the bond for him. The judge, who must have been flabbergasted by the request, refused. Sweeney was taken to the Henrico County jail to await trial in the District Court.[2]

While Sweeney sat in his cell, all of Richmond kept watch as the frail judge slowly slipped away. He died on June 8. On June 18, Sweeney was taken back to court for a hearing on murder charges for the deaths of the judge and Michael Brown.[3] Several city alderman conducted the hearing, which lasted five hours and included considerable testimony. They determined that there was enough evidence to suggest that young Sweeney had poisoned his uncle and Michael Brown, and they ordered the Hustings Court to consider murder charges against him. On June 23, following a hearing, the Hustings Court ordered Sweeney to stand trial for the murder of the pair. The trial would open on September 1. During the summer, the incarcerated Sweeney became so depressed about the upcoming trial that he asked one of his jailers to procure ratsbane so that Sweeney could kill himself. Sweeney then asked the astonished jailer whether he wanted to kill himself with the ratsbane, too.

Sweeney should have been depressed. He soon learned that the prosecutor of his case would be none other than the state's aggressive attorney general, Phillip Norborne Nicholas. Sweeney learned, too, that he had no lawyer and that one would have to be appointed to represent him. No attorney in Richmond would aid the man accused of murdering the popular judge. Attorneys throughout the city all agreed that no lawyer in his right mind would defend the teenager.

There was no way that Sweeney could be acquitted. The state would have an autopsy showing arsenic poisoning as the cause of death; a motive in the forged checks, the gambling debts, and the inheritance; plus a reliable and respected eyewitness to the poisoning in the testimony of Lydia Broadnax. Sweeney would hang.

10

The Investigation, Part II

NEWS OF YOUNG SWEENEY's arrest on forgery charges, on top of
the rumor that he had poisoned Chancellor Wythe, spread
quickly. On hearing of the forgery arrest, several people
then went to the authorities with information that deeply implicated
Sweeney in the poisoning of his granduncle, Lydia Broadnax, and
Michael Brown.

For convenience, the Richmond jailer, William Rose, lived in a
small wood-frame home next to the jail. He maintained a garden there,
which was adjacent to the outer wall of the jail yard. His black servant
girl Phoebe told him that she had found pieces of paper and clumps of
white powder in the garden just a few feet from the jail wall the morning after Sweeney was incarcerated there. Rose summoned Samuel
McCraw, who accompanied him to the garden with the slave girl. They
found two pieces of paper with some arsenic powder inside them lying
on top of the soil. Two small plants had been damaged nearby, and the
men assumed that the paper had been part of a package containing
arsenic that had been thrown over the wall, had hit the plants, and
had then broken apart.

William Rose told McCraw that it had to have been thrown by
Sweeney. The previous day, when Sweeney was brought to the jail,
Rose had patted him down, looking for weapons, and felt a package in

his pocket. Sweeney had told him it was a packet of pennies. Rose said that because he had assumed someone would bail out Sweeney within hours, he did not take his money. He had thought nothing of the packet then but now was certain it was the arsenic and that the teenager had thrown it over the wall during his exercise time to dispose of the evidence.

The case against Sweeney, already potent, grew even stronger a few days later when a friend of his, Taylor Williams, said that in a casual conversation, Sweeney had gone into great detail in explaining to him how poison was produced by mixing copper and water. A week later, Sweeney had engaged Williams in another conversation, indicating that he wanted to procure some poison. Williams had thought that Sweeney wanted to kill rats, which ran amok throughout the city and were cursed by everyone. Williams had told him that he could buy ratsbane at any store. Since ratsbane was a poison, it was technically illegal to purchase it over the counter; however, druggists usually sold it to anyone who produced a written note stating that it was needed. Everybody used ratsbane laced with arsenic, the most effective rat poisoning in the world, Williams had told his friend.

Mayor DuVal told authorities that he had inspected the outbuildings and the grounds of Wythe's home and found what he believed to be arsenic powder in the outhouse and on a wheelbarrow in the smokehouse. DuVal said that he used a pin to spread the powder on the wheelbarrow and looked at it closely; he was certain it was arsenic. A man named Nelson Abbott said that the week before the judge was poisoned, he had let Abbott use his workshop. Abbott returned on the twenty-seventh and found what he said was arsenic powder on an axe and a yellowish sulfuric coloring on the hammer. Both were later cleaned. Two slaves who worked for Abbott said they had actually seen Sweeney use the hammer to crush a white substance into powder on the side of the axe. When the substance was crushed into fine powder, Sweeney had brushed it into a piece of white paper, folded it, and put it in his pocket.

"Do you know what I am doing?" Sweeney had asked the slaves. They told him they assumed that he was making ratsbane because there was a rat problem at the judge's house. Sweeney then walked away, leaving the axe and the hammer stained. The slaves had thought nothing of it and did not mention the incident to anyone until after the chancellor died and the investigation heated up.[1]

The macabre circumstances of the crime itself, a nephew poisoning his own uncle, were enough to make the upcoming murder trial one of the most talked about in the history of Virginia and the country. But what made the trial such a sensation, talked about throughout the state for weeks and at times the sole topic of conversation, was the fact that the judge's murder followed the trial of the Virginia mass murderer Abel Clements by only a few weeks.

The coverage of the Clements trial had filled up the columns of most of Virginia's newspapers. His crimes were so heinous that ministers delivered sermons about them, which were reprinted in several of the state's newspapers. Clergymen lamented that mankind had fallen so far as to produce a bloody fiend such as Abel Clements.

Clements, a farmer who lived near Morgantown in the western part of Virginia, had decided to move to the Ohio territory. He had sold all of his corn crop to a neighbor, George Nicely, and loaded his wagons for the journey. Neighbors said that Clements had been melancholy for several weeks.

Then, the night before departing for Ohio, Clements, who had been known as a quiet individual and a family man, took two short-handled axes and butchered his wife and eight children. He struck his wife in the head with two savage blows and killed each of his children with a single strike to the head that split open the child's skull. He then methodically laid his children and his wife in their beds, with their hands at their sides, faces up, and eyelids closed. He piled clothing on top of them.

The next morning, Nicely and one of Clements's relatives, Isaac Clements, arrived to ask whether the corn crop could be moved to a different floor of his barn to make it easier to load the corn onto wagons. They found a distraught Clements sitting in a chair near his fireplace, nervously whittling a stick. His eight-year-old niece was sitting next to him. Nicely asked what was wrong, and Clements began to talk in a disoriented way. He rose and unbuttoned his pants, letting them drop to the floor and then pulled them back up. He then took his shoes off and put them back on. Isaac Clements noticed some blood on Clements's clothing and asked where the family was. Receiving no answer from Clements or the girl, he walked upstairs and went into one of the little girls' rooms. He found her dead, with her head smashed in, under a pile of clothes. Isaac went back downstairs and asked the niece whether she knew that her cousin was dead and she said she did not. Clements then told Nicely that he had murdered his family because he was afraid that an illness might befall them and that they would suffer. Despite his attorneys' plea that the farmer was insane at the time of the killings, Clements would be hanged.

The Clements case jolted Virginians because although many people worried about murders and other crimes committed by angry slaves or the surging army of foreigners and itinerant laborers that had been moving to Virginia for decades, no one expected to be murdered by a member of his or her own family. The mass murder of the Clements family had shocked Virginians, and now, coming on the heels of the Clements trial, was the murder of George Wythe by a member of his family.[2]

At the end of June 1806, all of the gossip in Richmond centered on who, if anyone, would defend George Wythe Sweeney in his murder trial. The case was argued at the rowdiest taverns in town, such as Bell's, Bowler's, Union, and the Eagle, as well as in the bars jammed with men and women at the City Hotel and the St. Charles Hotel. It was the primary topic of conversation as Samuel Pleasants' Book Store and in the Cash Store.[3] The customers who sat for hours at Lynch's Coffee House, sipping exotic Brazilian coffee, seemed to talk of nothing else. People discussed the murder and the prospective lawyers at the racetracks, the gambling houses, the churches and the synagogue, the overcrowded county jail, and the noisy James River wharf. It was debated in the corridors of the state House and in the homes of the South's top attorneys and judges. Who would defend such a dastardly murderer, the man who had killed the most beloved old man in Virginia?

Who would walk into the courtroom in Richmond, or any courtroom, and commence legal combat with Philip Norborne Nicholas, the tenacious thirty-one-year-old state attorney general? Nicholas was not only one of the most talented prosecutors in Virginia, but the head of the Republican Party in the city and the state. His brother George became the attorney general of Kentucky, his brother John was a congressman, and his brother-in-law Wilson Cary would become a governor of Virginia. Later, Nicholas would be made a director of the Bank of Richmond, then president of the Farmer's Bank, and next a director of the Bank of the United States. Nicholas had known and admired the chancellor and was a close friend of President Jefferson, along with all of the members of his influential family. The Nicholas-Carter family had worked hard for decades to help Jefferson become governor and then president. Philip Norborne Nicholas was one of the five members of the Virginia committee who had been named to help run Jefferson's 1800 presidential campaign. No Virginia family had contributed more to Jefferson's success than the Nicholases had. More than anyone, Nicholas would be relentless in prosecuting Wythe's accused murderer.

And so, the lawyers of Virginia debated, who would take on Nicholas?

Everyone denounced Sweeney, from newspaper editors to shipyard stevedores to the governor of Virginia. The editor of the *Petersburg Republican* minced no words when he wrote, "It is generally believed that this patriot has been brought to the grave by means, 'the most, base and unnatural.'" Mayor DuVal wrote to President Jefferson that "The conduct of Sweeney has excited the most lively sympathy for the deceased and detestation against the supposed culprit." The state's last governor, John Page, a lifelong friend of Judge Wythe's, wrote, "I shudder when I think of [his murder]. . . . It shocked my soul." The current governor, William Cabell, exhibited the opinion of all when he wrote, "There was but little doubt of his guilt in the minds of most persons." A minister, M. L. Weems, prayed that Wythe would be received in heaven as a great man and not as a man who arrived covered in "the blood of murdered patriots."[4]

Someone had to defend Sweeney; the court would have to appoint an unskilled novice attorney to take on the odious task.

Everyone in Virginia and throughout the country was shocked, then, when not only one lawyer, but two, stepped forward to represent the defendant. They were not young pro bono attorneys, bumbling public defenders, or minimally trained rookie lawyers, either. The men who defended George Wythe's alleged killer were the two best attorneys in Virginia and perhaps the entire country: former attorney general of the United States and ex-governor of Virginia Edmund Randolph and former High Chancellor William Wirt, who would, eleven years later, go on to become the U.S. attorney general himself in the Monroe administration. They were both titanic personalities, two of the most unique characters in U.S. legal history. It was especially shocking that Randolph had taken on the case; the prosecutor Nicholas was his own son-in-law.

Each man had a legal portfolio that any hundred lawyers combined could not put together in a lifetime. Each had accumulated an impressive string of courtroom victories at the highest levels not merely in civil cases, but in criminal cases as well. Why on earth would two of the most prominent men in the nation lower themselves to defend the culprit awaiting trial in the city jail, near a permanent gallows that had been constructed several years earlier for people like him?

Each attorney took the case because he believed that Sweeney, like anyone, was entitled to a competent legal defense, but each man also defended the accused because he saw the case as a milestone in his career and a chance, through the enormous publicity an acquittal would bring, to establish himself as a lawyer of not only national, but legendary, status.

And each defense lawyer sought the personal redemption that only an impossible acquittal could bring.

11

For the Defense: William Wirt

WILLIAM WIRT was one of the most physically impressive men in Virginia. The attorney was just over six feet in height, but he stood very erect, making himself appear even taller, and when he moved it was with a grace that everyone remembered. Wirt had a large Roman nose, thin lips, and a square, defiant chin. Thick, arching eyebrows that he liked to raise to show surprise accentuated his stunning cerulean blue eyes, which always attracted attention, especially from women, who could often be found in the audience at his trials. He had a wide, high forehead and a head full of thick, curly brown hair that tumbled casually over his forehead and ears. He always dressed well, favoring expensive, finely tailored suits and white silk cravats.[1]

Those who knew him admired him. Wrote one man, "[I] had never met any man so highly engaging and prepossessing. His figure was strikingly elegant and commanding. . . . He was a most fascinating companion, irresistibly and universally winning." Another gushed that in his elegant clothes and confident manner, Wirt was "a continual letter of recommendation."[2]

Wirt was also one of the best lawyers in the country; few could match him in courtroom oratory. "He possessed rare powers of description, raciness of wit and humor and an elocution at once graceful and powerful," wrote one historian. "He could charm and persuade an audience, touch their hearts by his pathos, delight them by beauties of style and sentiment and bear them on with him in the rapid flow of his eloquence." Another said that his great skill in the courtroom was to build up his own argument, step by step, with great logic and then, having finished that task, destroy his opponents'. The two-tiered approach never failed to impress juries.[3]

Wirt had known George Wythe well. He had first met Wythe when he moved to Richmond the first time, in 1796. He got to know him even better when he served as the clerk to the State Legislature for three terms, from 1800 to 1803, and then during the year that he joined Wythe as one of the state's three judges on the Chancery Court. Wirt served in the eastern district, however, residing in Norfolk, and Wythe remained in Richmond.

Wirt admired Wythe's long career as a lawyer and a judge who was willing to serve for a salary of only $1,165 a year, a small sum compared to the money the old man might have made as a private attorney in his later years. Wirt was impressed by Wythe's service in politics and his extraordinary success as a law professor. Like many other attorneys in Virginia, Wirt had matured in the courtroom during an era when Wythe was growing in importance as a judge. It was Wythe, with Jefferson and Pendleton, who had rewritten the laws of Virginia that were legal canon by the time Wirt became a lawyer. Many of the case law precedents that Wirt studied for his own trials had been decided by Judge Wythe.

How, then, could Wirt defend the young man who was charged with murdering Wythe? After all, even Wirt was appalled and thought that Sweeney was guilty; he wrote to his wife, "I had hoped no one would undertake the defense of Sweeney."[4]

Sweeney's right to an attorney was not Wirt's primary motivation. The thirty-four-year-old lawyer from Norfolk was intensely ambitious, a man who sought fame and who wanted to make a lot of money. He had moved to Norfolk for that reason. The town, at the convergence of the Chesapeake Bay and the Atlantic Ocean, was a seaport with a harbor deep enough to accommodate any of the large European merchant ships that arrived regularly. It was a town of four hundred homes, ample wharves, warehouses, inns, taverns, and churches.

William Wirt was one of George Wythe Sweeney's two defense attorneys, who stepped forward after no one would take the case. Wirt later went on to become the longest-serving attorney general in the history of the United States.

Surrounding the town were gently rolling lowlands and forests full of tulips, honeysuckle, and dogwood trees, whose white flowers gave the entire region a marvelous appearance when they bloomed in April. The shipping business in Norfolk and nearby Yorktown provided substantial legal business for Wirt.[5]

Then why defend the unpopular Sweeney?

Trials like Sweeney's were high-profile judicial showcases, which were discussed in courthouses, general stores, and taverns throughout Virginia, and, far more important, debated extensively in the newspapers. Winning the cases of men who were seen as villains by the public, and to whom no one gave much of a chance of acquittal, would not only establish Wirt's reputation as a skilled lawyer, he believed, but would also bring him enormous publicity—publicity that he wanted to use not merely to establish a lucrative law practice, but to win high office of some kind for himself in Virginia or on the national stage, either by election or appointment.

He had left the highly prestigious post of chancellor after a single year because it paid little money, only $1,500; he could make more in private practice. Wirt, whose first wife had died in 1799, had remarried on September 7, 1802, and by the winter of 1803, he and his second wife, Elizabeth, had two children to rear and he needed money. He could not earn it as chancellor. He wrote to his friend Dabney Carr, "The honor of being Chancellor is a very empty thing. . . . Honor will not go to market and buy a peck of potatoes. On fifteen hundred dollars I can live, but if death comes, how will my wife and family live?"

Ironically, Wirt always mentioned George Wythe when he complained to friends that he needed funds, and not importance, to make ends meet; he referred to the judge as the paragon of prestige in America. He told Carr, "It is possible that I may, like Mr. Wythe, grow old in judicial honors and Roman poverty. I may die beloved, reverenced almost to canonization by my country, and my wife and children, as they beg for bread, may have to boast that they were mine."[6]

Wirt often toyed with the idea of moving to Kentucky because he had heard that the few lawyers there were making handsome salaries—five times the annual earnings of top Virginia lawyers—in what was a booming region. He knew of only two lawyers in Virginia who made "a fortune" and the rest made very little money, although they had other businesses. He wrote to Carr, "With the exception of these two, there is not another individual who has hitherto done this at the bar of these courts or who is now in the way of doing so. Baker, Innes, Pendleton, Wythe, Marshall, [Bushrod] Washington and others—what have they made *by the profession?*"[7] Wirt, lamenting to friends that he was already thirty years old and well on in his life, also added that even if he did resume his private practice in his hometown of Norfolk, he could not possibly make enough to pay for his house, food, taxes, entertainment, and the care of his children.

And this income shortage was despite Wirt's wide reputation as a workaholic. In the summer of 1805, when the heat was unbearable in Norfolk and malaria prevalent, as always in the summer months, Wirt refused to spend the season inland, where it was cooler, with his brother-in-law, as his wife did. He couldn't, he explained, because he had clients to attend to and needed the revenue.

Elizabeth Wirt, raised in comfort in Richmond, was in no hurry to move to the desolate frontier of Kentucky. She did not want to remain in Norfolk, either. The town itself had undergone years of reconstruction following its bombardment by the British in 1776. Its architecture was

erratic, with long blocks of dreary-looking wooden buildings inter-
spersed with a few brick structures. The wooden buildings frequently
caught fire. In 1799, a fire destroyed half of the main square in town,
and in 1804, another leveled more than three hundred warehouses,
stores, and homes. Sparks set fire to several ships docked at the wharf.
Yet another fire in 1805 burned down a dozen major buildings in the
business district. Women there complained that the volume of sailors in
port had led to an excess of bars and dance halls and that drunkenness
and prostitution had become the leading hobbies of the men in town.
Drunken sailors rioted in 1803, injuring many residents with stones. A
yellow fever epidemic hit Norfolk in the summer of 1806.[8]

Visitors to the seaport detested it. A Frenchman, François
La Rochefoucauld-Liancourt, wrote that "It is one of the ugliest, most
irregular, dirtiest towns that I have ever seen," and an American,
Thomas More, wrote, "It abounds in dogs, Negroes and Democrats."[9]

Wirt was not happy in Norfolk. He found it very expensive and
complained to friends that everything he had to purchase was over-
priced. "Wood is four to eight dollars per cord, Indian meal is nine
shillings per bushel, [stables] $40 per month, flour eleven and twelve
dollars per barrel . . . and so on."[10]

He also discovered that although much legal help was needed in
the shipping industry, he had no training in it, and learning the laws of
the sea required a lot of hard work. "I have fallen into a business new to
me and every case calls for elaborate examination," he complained.[11]

Elizabeth Wirt sometimes burst into tears when trying to convince her
husband to move to Richmond. She enlisted her father in the cause, who
bluntly said that he would not lend Wirt any money for the trip or the
purchase of land or a home if Wirt moved to Kentucky. The father would
also refuse to cosign any loans Wirt might need in the future. Dissuaded
from a life in Kentucky, Wirt turned back to Richmond; that was where
the real money could be made by an enterprising lawyer like himself.[12]

His life revolved around his wife. He missed her every time he left
their home in Norfolk to argue cases in Williamsburg or other communities. He was also missed in their Norfolk home. The Wirts had
created a unique marriage, in which he assisted her with household
work and she aided him in his legal enterprises. He gave her money to
spend on the house and on herself as she saw fit, which was an unusual

procedure in an era when men controlled the family finances. His legal office was in their home, and he hired several law clerks, who also lived in the home. When he was away, his wife oversaw his legal business, sorted out his papers, and supervised the work done by the clerks. At the same time, she had to run the household and raise their two small children. The Wirts also owned five adult slaves and their children; Elizabeth supervised them as well. Her husband's absence, then, created more work and responsibility for her.[13]

Elizabeth was not well, either. She had nearly died after giving birth to their second child in 1803, and Wirt lamented that his legal business carried him to Williamsburg and away from her while she recovered. She became pregnant right away after the birth and had a very difficult third pregnancy—the child died soon after birth. Her three pregnancies in three years had nearly ruined her health. Wirt, again, after the child's funeral, was on the road with his legal practice and far away from a wife who needed him. He always hated to leave her and wrote to her that both of them needed a "firm trust that brighter and sweeter hours are at hand."

Elizabeth was furious with him for abandoning them yet again in the summer of 1805. In one verbal blast in a letter, she wrote, "You say your clients expect it of you, but, my husband, will they provide for your children—guide, instruct and raise them to happiness and virtue?" And in another letter she scolded him for preferring money over her and reminded him that his actions were causing her "misery." She wrote, "I am and must continue to be, exceedingly unhappy."

He knew she was right and worried that the children's mother and not their father was raising them. He wrote to her, "Kiss my dear children for me half a dozen times apiece and don't let Laura forget that she has a father."[14]

If they lived in Richmond, of course, Wirt could remain at home and practice law in the city and state courts there. Elizabeth's family would be nearby, she could rekindle friendships with the men and women she had grown up with in the city and once again enjoy the entertainment of the town that had given her so much joy as a teenager. Her father, eager to have his daughter back home, told Wirt that if they moved to Richmond, he would buy Wirt a plot of land and pay for the construction of a home there.

But something more than money drove Wirt: a raw lust for fame, position, and power. That spring he wrote of his dreams in life that "Hope . . . sketches some most brilliant and ravishing scenes to my waking as well as sleeping fancy. Wealth, fame, respect, the love of my fellow citizens, she designs with the boldness and grandeur of an angel."[15]

To gain that fame and power and earn the money he desperately wanted through a very lucrative law practice, William Wirt needed a big case that would bring him national attention. Sweeney was it.

And William Wirt wanted—absolutely needed—legal redemption from his last major trial in Richmond. This debacle was the sedition trial of the journalist James Callender in 1800. Wirt had been made to look like a fool in that trial. It had ended in chaos and disgrace for himself, his fellow attorneys, and the defendant, a newspaper man who had been critical of the administration of President John Adams.

James Callender, who had been given a job at a Richmond newspaper through the intercession of Thomas Jefferson, had published numerous articles that derided the Adams administration. Then he began work on a book, *The Prospect before Us*, that was even more critical of the president. Adams's supporters were threatening to drive Callender from town, even forming a public society dedicated to that goal. In the summer of 1799, the journalist wrote to Jefferson that he was even afraid someone would murder him.[16]

Callender excoriated Adams in the book, writing that the president possessed "a hideous hermaprodatical character which has neither the force and firmness of a man, nor the gentleness and sensibility of a woman."[17]

The federal government arrested the writer under the controversial Sedition Act, which had been passed in 1798 and which made it a crime to criticize the government. The writer argued that all press criticism was protected under the First Amendment. Wirt, working for the State Legislature at the time, leaped to the defense of Callender. Wirt had no great love for the testy journalist but saw the case as a means to restore freedom of the press and a chance to gain substantial attention for himself. Ironically, Wirt was joined at the defense table by Philip Norborne Nicholas and George Hay.

The key to their defense was to convince the jury to rule the Sedition Act unconstitutional. They never had a chance to mount much of a defense, however, because the government sent Samuel Chase, an associate justice of the U.S. Supreme Court and a notorious enemy of journalists, to Richmond to hear the case. He told the jury that all of the charges in the indictment were true. He continually interrupted the attorneys whenever they attempted to examine a witness or make a legal point in his courtroom.[18] Chase also prevented some of their key witnesses from testifying.

Justice Chase told the jury that all of Wirt's arguments were false and that the jurors should ignore anything he said about unconstitutionality. Nicholas, too, was cut off several times by the judge and was told at one point that whatever argument he would make would be wrong. All three attorneys then rose and marched out of the courtroom, to the astonishment of all.

The angry judge dismissed the three men and told Callender that he could not hire any other lawyers. The jury, which was made up of pro-Adams federalists, found Callender guilty in two hours.[19] He was sentenced to nine months in prison (He asked Jefferson for a government job when he was released but was turned down. In revenge, he exposed Jefferson's ongoing sexual relationship with his slave at Monticello, Sally Hemings, which caused a scandal).[20]

IT WAS in the criminal cases in which Wirt worked for defendants whom all considered guilty that he established his reputation as a trial lawyer. Wirt never wavered from his public stand that everyone, no matter how unpopular, deserved a defense. Privately, though, his view was very different. He put his conflicted feelings best in a bitter letter to his wife that he had written a year earlier, in 1805, while traveling the judicial circuit to defend his tawdry clients. "This indiscriminate defense of right and wrong—this zealous advocation of causes at which my soul revolts—this playing of the nurse to villains, and occupying myself continually in cleansing them—it is sickening, even to death," he told her. He also referred to much of his legal work as "groping through the dark and disgusting mazes of human fraud and villainy."[21]

But he was certain that the notoriety he would achieve with the Sweeney case would enable him to move permanently to Richmond, where he would flourish as the state's most famous lawyer. He frequently daydreamed about that. "I amuse myself in planning fairy visions of futurity," he told his wife. "I imagine that we have laid by money enough to build a house in Richmond—and that we are living there, and I practicing in the Superior Courts, in the van of the procession, making my [income] a year without once leaving the town."

In another letter to Mrs. Wirt, written on May 19, 1805, the lawyer again pledged to her, "We will go to Richmond to live as soon as prudence will permit."[22]

His desire to move to Richmond and become a famous lawyer had burned in him for years. In 1803, he had written a series of popular newspaper essays about life in Virginia, called *Letters of a British Spy*, which were published as a book a year later and were well received. In the essays, he composed colorful and sometimes biting sketches of people and places in the state. These essays made up the first of four books that he would author in his lifetime. The book brought him some attention in literary circles, but not the wide public recognition he had anticipated. "It has been the means of making me extensively known, and known to my advantage, except perhaps, with such men as Jefferson and Jay, whose just minds readily ascertain the difference between bullion and chaff." Wirt's need for fame was now consuming him.[23]

As luck would have it, the ambitious Wirt finally made up his mind to go to Richmond just after the murder of Judge Wythe. No sooner had he signed a five-year lease on a home in the state capital and begun to wrap up his cases in Williamsburg than he had a visitor.

The stranger was George Sweeney's uncle, who was exhausted from the lengthy stagecoach ride from Richmond. The uncle pleaded with Wirt to defend his nephew.

The notorious murder immediately intrigued Wirt. For weeks, playing devil's advocate, he had casually discussed it with students, lawyers, merchants in Williamsburg, and members of the College of William and Mary faculty. He heard not only their opinions, but, through the gossipy legal profession, the viewpoints of people throughout the state.

And Wirt had learned in a highly improper way, from a very knowledgeable source, that there might be evidence in the trial that had never been made public and that would be a legal bombshell.

Wirt remained open-minded. He listened with great intensity to everything Sweeney's uncle had to say. The uncle told Wirt that

Sweeney had not put any arsenic in the food or the coffee consumed by the Wythe household that morning; anyone who said he did not only was speculating, but had no proof. No paper containing arsenic had been found in the kitchen. If the food and the coffee had been poisoned, wouldn't Sweeney have died, too? What motive did Sweeney have to kill Wythe? The old man had left the youth much of his estate in his will; Sweeney had not been shortchanged. The old man had had confidence in Sweeney, which was why he had loaned the teenager money to pay his debts. If the old man was so suspicious of his nephew, why had he continued to permit the boy to live in his home? Ratsbane poisoning? All of the residents of Richmond used ratsbane to protect themselves from vermin. Anyone could have poisoned the old man with ratsbane. And was it ratsbane? Why hadn't the judge died right away if he had been poisoned with a lethal dose of arsenic? If it was arsenic, and arsenic was so lethal, why hadn't Lydia Broadnax died? The uncle turned personal, reminding Wirt that the accusations against Sweeney threatened to ruin the reputations of his large family, a family that had been respected throughout Virginia for generations.

Wirt had apparently conducted an investigation of his own to ascertain whether Sweeney was guilty of the murder and forgery charges. By the time Wythe died, Wirt was convinced not only that Sweeney was guilty of the forgeries and the homicide, but that he had been robbing his uncle for quite some time. There was no doubt in Wirt's mind, he told his friend James Monroe, that Sweeney was guilty. "The young villain [only sixteen or seventeen] had been in the habit of robbing his uncle [i.e., his granduncle, George Wythe] with a false key, had sold three trunks of his most valuable law books, had forged his checks on the bank to a considerable amount and wound up his villainies by this act [murder]."[24]

Members of Wirt's family and all of their friends believed that Sweeney was guilty, too. His brother-in-law, Littleton Tazewell, wrote, "It was generally believed [Wythe's death] was produced by poison, administered in his office, by a reprobate boy, a relation of his who he had undertaken to educate and who was afterwards convicted of having committed many forgeries of checks in his patron's name."[25]

Wirt was so convinced of Sweeney's guilt that he had told other lawyers in Williamsburg that the young man would hang for the murder and that he hoped no lawyer would step forward to take the youth's case, which would assure Sweeney a trip to the gallows.[26]

Even so, the ambitious Wirt was attracted to the case. He had not even bought his stagecoach tickets for Richmond and here was a chance to show his legal skills by getting a man who appeared guilty to every single citizen of the country off the hook in a coup de théâtre of jurisprudence. It was high profile, it was front-page newspaper coverage throughout the country, and it was Richmond. It would, Wirt told his wife, "give me a splendid *debut* in the metropolis."

Just three years earlier, in front of a packed courtroom in Williamsburg, Wirt and two other lawyers had defended a man named Shannon against whom the prosecution seemed to have an air-tight case. Shannon's father-in-law, standing in his parlor, had been killed by a shotgun-type musket blast fired from outside the window. A piece of wadding paper with a scrawled letter "M" on it, which appeared to have been ripped from a letter, was found where the shot must have been fired. Shannon, who had been in Williamsburg that night, was found asleep in a tavern thirty miles away. A Williamsburg blacksmith said that he had been asked by Shannon to repair Shannon's shotgun on the day of the murder. Shannon had taken the gun with him when the repair could not be made that same day. Shannon had the shotgun, with extra buckshot, in his possession when arrested, as well as a torn letter with a missing scrap of paper the same size as the piece found at the scene of the crime.

Wirt, dismissing all of the incriminating circumstantial evidence against Shannon, had delivered a soaring summation to the jury that convinced at least one juror that Shannon might have been innocent. The jury acquitted him in front of a pleased and smiling defense attorney.[27]

Wirt's representation of Sweeney might not bother him or many in the legal fraternity, but it could bring a lifetime of shame upon his family. He wrote to his wife, "My conduct through life is more important to you and your children than even to myself; for to my own heart I mean to stand justified by doing nothing that I think wrong. But, for your sakes, I wish to do nothing that the *world* shall think wrong. I would not have you or them subject to one reproach because of me."[28]

The much-anticipated return letter from his wife at Norfolk arrived a few days later; she told him to defend Sweeney, regardless of what anyone said. She said that the children and her entire family would stand behind him no matter what happened—and that his wife desperately wanted to move back to Richmond.

William Wirt had wanted to establish himself in Richmond with a case that would bring him some publicity and help him start his practice in the state capital. He was now involved in the trial of the young century. He packed his bags and moved to Richmond as quickly as he could to see young Sweeney in jail—and for the chance to get him out of jail.

Sweeney appeared guilty to all? So had Shannon, the shotgun killer of Williamsburg.

THIS TRIAL WAS a chance, too, for Wirt to continue a lifelong crusade to overcome his pronounced stuttering. This severe, damaging stammer had bothered him since childhood and had threatened to end his legal career and curtail his personal life. It was an affliction for which there was no cure in that era. Almost all of the men and the women who stuttered were mocked by other children as they grew up or were hidden away in their parents' homes to avoid public embarrassment from their forced, halting speech and the verbal difficulties that stammering brought about. Wirt had a pronounced stutter, one of the worst that his contemporaries had seen, which at times had even prevented him from speaking at all. Yet he wanted to become a lawyer and argue cases in a courtroom, the most public of all venues and the one area where clear and forceful speech was necessary. No one thought that Wirt could conquer this disability. When he married for the first time in 1795, his in-laws were so concerned about his stammer that they encouraged him to remain inside the house and to avoid venturing into any public areas to avoid embarrassment. They suggested that Wirt work as a legal researcher so that he would never have to speak in a courtroom. They, like others, saw no hope for him to overcome his stammering.

"His utterance was thick—his tongue clumsy, and apparently too large—his pronunciation of words clipping—and, when excited by feeling, his voice unmanageable; sometimes burst out in loud, harsh, indistinct and imperfect articulation," wrote one man who knew him.[29]

The lawyer himself did not see much hope at first and at times found himself verbally paralyzed, unable to speak. He wrote, "My pronunciation and gesture at this time were terribly vehement. I used, sometimes, to find myself literally stopped, by too great rapidity of utterance. And if any poor mortal was ever forced to struggle against a difficulty, it was I, in that matter."[30]

Sometime in his early twenties, Wirt began a self-directed campaign to end his stutter. He knew that, surprisingly, people who stutter are able to sing without difficulty. Wirt loved to sing and had done so all of his life; he enjoyed the sound of his voice. He did not stutter when he sang, and the knowledge that he could at least overcome it with song drove him to devise other ways to end the stammer. He worked on it for years through self-designed vocal exercises and the development of a strong speech pattern, one that overcame any excitement that might bring back the stutter.

By 1806, Wirt not only seemed to have brought his stuttering under control, but had worked so hard at enunciation that he became a powerful public speaker. According to one acquaintance, "His reputation for eloquence was high." A man who had known Wirt most of his life said that people who first met him in his later years were shocked to learn that stuttering troubles had once beset him in childhood and during his early adulthood. Wrote a friend, "They who have since been familiar with the clearness, music and flexibility of his voice in conversation and his distinct, emphatic and unembarrassed pronunciation in public speaking [were surprised]."[31]

Wirt not only was gratified that his hard work had just about cured his stutter, but was enormously pleased that he'd had the inner strength to do so. His victory over his stammer showed him that he also had the ability to do many other things in life. He wrote, "But my stammering became at last a martyr to perseverance, and, except when I get some of my youthful fires lighted, I can manage to be pretty intelligible now."[32]

Reining in his stammer permitted Wirt to succeed both inside and outside the courtroom. Now in control of his voice and his temperament, he plunged into civil and criminal court cases, working either with other lawyers or alone. He always offered impressive oral arguments to judges and juries, backed up by solid research, in cases that took him throughout the northern part of Virginia. The conquering of his stutter, those in the legal profession said, had enabled him not only to work as a lawyer, but also to become a very good one.

His control of the stutter, which still occasionally surfaced for brief moments throughout his life, also helped him to enjoy a rich and often-times wild social life with other young men. Wirt, like so many single men, went to taverns; attended balls, receptions, and dances; and visited the homes of friends and neighbors for weekend and weeklong festivities, such as weddings and anniversaries. His merriment some-times got out of hand, and he nursed many a hangover the following day, but, overall, Wirt could now take advantage of the flourishing social activities in northern Virginia. At these parties and through his legal work, Wirt became friendly with the most influential men and the most powerful families in the state.

Wirt was a changed man. His stammer-free speech had given him enormous self-confidence as he moved through the social world. He became a much-sought-after guest. A friend who knew him during those years wrote, "[I] have never met any man so highly engaging and prepossessing. His figure was strikingly elegant and commanding, with a face of the first order of masculine beauty, animated, and expressing high intellect. His manners took the tone of his heart: they were frank, open and cordial, and his conversation, to which his reading and early pursuits had given a classic tinge, was very polished, gay and witty. Altogether, he was a most fascinating companion, and to those of his own age, irresistibly and universally winning."[33]

In fact, his social skills grew so quickly after he mastered his stutter, and he was so successful in his interactions with others, that he some-times purposefully showed up late for receptions and dinner parties. He was secure in the knowledge that his charm and wit, now without the debilitating stammer, would be so engaging that he himself could keep the party going far past the time planned by the host. He once deliberately arrived at a dinner party as it was ending and extended it until dawn, to the delight of everyone present.

WILLIAM WIRT was born in Bladensburg, Maryland, in 1772. His parents were immigrants; his father was Swiss and his mother German. Both died before Wirt was seven years old, and he was raised by an uncle who sent him to a boarding school. There he met Ninian Edwards, later the governor of Illinois and a close friend of Abraham

Lincoln. Edwards's father, a Maryland congressman, liked Wirt and let the youth live in his home for two years while Wirt studied to be a lawyer. Wirt started his law practice representing clients in Culpepper, Orange, and Albemarle counties in the northern part of Virginia, where, over seven years, he met and befriended numerous important men, such as Thomas Jefferson, John Marshall, James Monroe, and James Madison. His practice grew and he earned some renown as one of the state's up-and-coming attorneys. He also acquired a deep love of music that remained with him all of his life. He attended every musical concert that he could in the northern region of the state and later in Williamsburg. The attorney even learned to play several instruments to add to his enjoyment. He accompanied his playing with singing, and those who heard him sing over the years agreed that he possessed a rather melodic voice. Wirt embraced the classics and carried a pocket edition of the writings of Horace and Seneca with him wherever he went on the legal circuit. Wirt also became a lifelong devotee of novels and short stories.

He met Dr. George Gilmer of Albemarle County in 1794 and married his daughter Mildred a year later, while he still stuttered. Wirt lived with her in the home of the doctor, who was a physician and a member of Virginia's gentry.

Sometime during that period Wirt made a critical decision: he would not hide from his affliction but would conquer it. Excessive conversation was part of the cure. He engaged anyone he could in discussions about whatever they brought up. He seemed to find it easy to talk to everyone. He engaged in discourses on geography, history, politics, and the legal profession. He talked about his travels and delighted in describing in great detail the beauty of the areas of Virginia where he had visited. He had a ready audience in the friends of the Gilmer family. These sophisticated, educated planters and merchants became fascinated by Wirt's discussions.

Wirt found that lengthy anecdotes interested people, so he told as many as he could. He soon began to regale friends and acquaintances with stories of all kinds, especially humorous ones. For each tale, he led his listeners through a labyrinth of twisting plots until he brought them to a rousing finale. His best stories involved ghosts and witchcraft. Wirt not only told these to delighted listeners, but also listened to as many similarly frightening stories as he could wherever he traveled. They seemed to be favorites at mountain vacation resorts, where he spent time over the years. Wirt remembered every story and every episode of each one and expanded on them to create his own verbal theater of horror and fright. He usually recounted the stories after blowing out most of the candles in the room to create a foreboding atmosphere. People who listened to his horror stories over the years found themselves genuinely scared and often shrieked at the dramatic conclusions.[34]

Slowly, his speaking became clearer. He made great efforts to slow down his voice, pronounce words correctly, pause for effect in telling stories, and control the embarrassing verbal outbursts that had plagued him since childhood. Through enormous effort, he became an able conversationalist and, over the years, a brilliant one.

He did the same in his public life. Wirt shunned Gilmer's advice to remain at his home and took on as many legal cases as he could. He defended clients who ranged from wealthy merchants to itinerant farmers. Wirt often sought out defendants who had little chance for success, in order to make himself a better courtroom lawyer. Powerful oral arguments would be needed to win acquittals for these clients, and those arguments would make Wirt a better speaker and lawyer. Over the years, people who observed him in the courtroom said that he developed an elegant but deliberate style, avoiding any wild theatrics that might cause him to lose control of his voice. An unintended consequence of his lifelong battle to control his stammer was a highly effective courtroom manner that impressed judges and juries alike.[35]

News of Wirt's decision to defend George Sweeney traveled through Richmond's gossip networks in mere hours. Many residents were startled that Wirt had taken the case, but others were not. After all, Wirt was young and ambitious. He always seemed pleased at the opportunity to have a jury exonerate a defendant whom everyone believed was guilty—and murder cases had become his specialty.

What really surprised Virginians was not Wirt, but the man who suddenly decided to volunteer as his co-counsel, Edmund Randolph, the former governor of Virginia and a U.S. attorney general, who had been forced to resign from George Washington's cabinet in disgrace.

12

For the Defense:
Edmund Randolph

I F THERE WAS ANY FIGURE in Virginia who approached George
Wythe in judicial experience and skills, in the estimation of the
upper echelons of the legal community, it was Edmund Randolph.
A descendant of the prestigious and financially comfortable
Randolph family, who married into the even wealthier Carter family, Edmund Randolph had succeeded at everything he had attempted
in his life, especially in his legal career. The educated, sophisticated
Randolph, a graduate of the College of William and Mary, had served
in the Revolution in 1775 at age twenty-two as a staff aide to General
Washington in Cambridge, Massachusetts, and was a delegate to the
Virginia State Convention the following year. At twenty-five, he was
elected mayor of Williamsburg, his hometown, and a few years later was
named the attorney general for the state of Virginia. In 1779, Randolph
was elected to the Continental Congress and in 1787 was a delegate
to the Constitutional Convention. There, with James Madison, he
introduced the Virginia Plan, which called for three branches of government and a set of legislative checks and balances.

Randolph was elected governor of Virginia in 1786, at the age
of thirty-three. The celebrated attorney, politician, and governor

crowned his career in 1789 by serving as the first attorney general of the United States in President Washington's administration and then, when Jefferson resigned, as the secretary of state. Randolph had fame, position, universal respect, wealth, and one of the most cherished reputations in the entire country.

The tall, wavy-haired Randolph, whose large eyes and thick eyebrows highlighted his round face, had accomplished all of that despite being disgraced in the early days of the Revolution by his father, who became a Loyalist. His parents were so strongly against the war that in the summer of 1776, they had packed all of their belongings and sailed for England, never to return. At that same time, an embittered Edmund had joined the army.

Edmund Randolph had been close to his father, who had given him all of the finer things in life, from a stately home in Williamsburg to his handsome horses, fine clothing, and a position in Virginia's social circles. There were private tutors and even a dancing instructor. When Edmund was a teenager, John Randolph had introduced his son to all of the important people in Williamsburg, such as George Wythe, Patrick Henry, and Thomas Jefferson, and helped him enroll at the College of William and Mary. His father's departure for England not only disgraced him but left him without an adult male to turn to for advice. He had his respected uncle Peyton, but Peyton died in Philadelphia that summer as the Continental Congress was readying itself for war. Young Randolph was on his own. He not only had to establish a legal career and serve first as the mayor of Williamsburg and then as a congressman, but was also saddled with the time-consuming work of cleaning up his parents' legal and real estate affairs. Despite those obstacles, Randolph managed to become a highly successful lawyer, perhaps the best in the state, and he served Virginia and the federal government in key positions throughout his life.[1]

All of that fell apart in 1795.

Randolph, then secretary of state, had been regularly corresponding with the French minister Jean Antoine Joseph Fauchet about American politics and international affairs. There was speculation in Europe that the 1794 Whiskey Rebellion, in which hundreds of Pennsylvanians refused to pay their taxes and fought off a state militia company before surrendering to a U.S. force led by President Washington himself, was

Edmund Randolph, a former
attorney general of the United
States, hoped to enhance
his legal career by defending
George Wythe Sweeney, even
if it meant working with his
enemy, William Wirt, and
against his friend Wythe.

orchestrated by political factions in America to undermine the federal
government. In 1795, someone gave U.S. officials copies of several dispatches from Fauchet to Randolph in which Fauchet appeared to state
that Randolph had tried to extort thousands of dollars from the French
in order to assure stability in the administration, which would help to
protect French trade interests in the United States. These dispatches
then went to Secretary of War Thomas Pickering and Oliver Wolcott
Jr., the treasury secretary, both of whom had been enemies of Randolph's
for years. Furious, they brought the dispatches to the president.

Randolph was called into Washington's office at his mansion in
Philadelphia. There Randolph met with the stern-looking president,
along with Pickering and Wolcott, and was asked to explain himself.
Randolph felt unfairly pressured and a little nervous; he resigned on the
spot, believing that it was the proper thing to do. He told the president
that he would obtain documents from Fauchet that would clear him.
Randolph then traveled to Newport, Rhode Island, and gained assur-
ances from the French minister, who was about to sail home to France,
that he would provide letters that would exonerate Randolph.

The president could have told Randolph to remain in office while he conducted a quiet investigation, but Washington was angry with Randolph and let him quit, knowing that the resignation would start a scandal. Washington was angry because Randolph, whom the president had known since the early 1770s, had worked strenuously against him in resolving the Whiskey Rebellion the previous year. Washington had ordered the Pennsylvania distillers to pay their taxes or face dire consequences. They refused. Hamilton then urged Washington to assume his constitutional role of commander in chief and attack the whiskey rebels. The president agreed. He had suffered several serious mutinies during the war that threatened to wreck the army and knew that if the whiskey mavericks got away without paying their taxes, others would try to do the same thing. The government's ability to tax would collapse.

Randolph, though, as the attorney general, insisted that Washington did not have legal grounds to assume control of the federal army for the purpose of going into a state to collect taxes. Not only did Randolph disagree with the president, but he argued for weeks against the idea. Washington and Hamilton reminded him that as he had been an aide in the Revolution, he knew how dangerous insurrections were and also knew that, constitutionally, the president was the commander of the army and had the right to put down revolts. The president and Hamilton ignored Randolph and took an army into Pennsylvania. The tax rebels surrendered without a shot being fired. The entire episode strengthened Washington's position as president and brought him added respect from the people for acting tough against the obstinate Pennsylvanians.

Fauchet's letter came to Washington at the same time that he learned about another series of Randolph's letters to French diplomats during and after the Whiskey Rebellion. In these letters, Randolph had not only been critical of the president, but had also written that Washington was becoming unpopular with the people, which was not true. Washington never forgave Randolph for everything that happened during the Whiskey Rebellion.

The three most influential men in the country, after President Washington, who could have convinced the president to conduct a quiet investigation or perhaps even dismiss the charge against Randolph were Thomas Jefferson, James Madison, and Vice President John Adams. None desired to help Randolph, for different reasons.

Madison had been a longtime colleague of Randolph's in Virginia state politics and was furious when Randolph, as governor, went with him to the Constitutional Convention in Philadelphia but then refused to sign the Constitution and publicly denounced it.

Jefferson had never liked Randolph, and his disdain for his fellow Virginian grew when both men served in the cabinet. Jefferson was unwavering in his political beliefs, which centered on states' rights, even when these beliefs seemed unpopular in the cabinet. Other cabinet members, such as Jefferson's enemy Hamilton, had not vacillated either. Randolph, though, constantly waffled in his beliefs, depending on which policies seemed popular at the time. This angered Jefferson. "[He is] the purest chameleon I ever saw, having no color of his own and reflecting that nearest him. When he is with me he is a Whig. When with Hamilton, a Tory. When with the President, he is that which he thinks will please him."[2]

Vice President Adams disliked most of the Virginians, and none irritated him more than Randolph, whom he saw as a classic wealthy, egotistical slave owner. He was ecstatic when Randolph resigned. "Happy is the country to be rid of Randolph," Adams said.[3]

Randolph found no friends in Congress, either. Playing Jefferson's "chameleon," he had moved back and forth between political positions, siding with the Federalists in some sessions of Congress and then switching allegiance to the anti-Federalists in others. By 1795, he had earned the enmity of both groups.

Members of the diplomatic corps were also glad to see him go. "Every man of that party [Federalists] seems willing to let this ruined Bark [Randolph] sink of itself and to shape the vortex which hurries it to the bottom," said one British diplomat.[4]

What followed was a lengthy series of missteps by the increasingly unpopular Randolph. Rumors swirled about the Fauchet letters, and within weeks the incident became a full-blown scandal. Instead of quietly obtaining his documents and pleading his case to Washington, Randolph pleaded his defense in the newspapers. In private, he told anyone who would listen that Washington had been predisposed against him, only listened to his critics, and treated him coldly. Randolph also charged that Wolcott and Pickering were conspiring with British ministers to have him removed from office.

Not satisfied with all of that, Randolph sent a letter to the president, who was then on his way to Mount Vernon. The letter requested some documents that Randolph assumed Pickering was withholding from him. Instead of waiting for Washington's reply, Randolph had a copy of the letter published in the *Philadelphia Gazette*. In it, he assured the president and readers of the newspaper that he was innocent. He wrote, "I am in possession of such materials, not only from Mr. Fauchet, but also from other sources, as will convince every unprejudiced mind that my resignation was dictated by considerations which ought not to have been resisted for a moment and that everything connected with it stands upon a footing perfectly honourable to myself."[5]

The problem that arose, though, was that the newspaper published the copy of the letter before the president received it. Washington learned of it from friends who read it in the *Philadelphia Gazette*. The president then heard stories about Randolph's criticism of him back in Philadelphia.

President Washington had given Randolph time to gather information and produce a defense, travel to Newport to see Fauchet, interview whoever else he felt could help him, and search for whatever documents he thought necessary for his exoneration. The president had even provided a copy of the missing letter for Randolph's files. And this was Randolph's thanks?

Now, Washington learned that Randolph was offering a wild defense that involved a British plot, had besmirched Wolcott's and Pickering's reputations, and had been unfairly critical of him. He coldly wrote to Randolph that he had no desire for Randolph to mail him the much-promised vindication pamphlet. Washington wrote that he would simply read about it in the newspapers, as he had just read Randolph's letter there.

Washington felt betrayed. After the publication of the pamphlet, he told Pickering that he had promised Peyton Randolph, Edmund's uncle and a friend, that he would always look out for Edmund after the young man's father fled to England. The president had told Peyton that he would "be to him as a father," and he had been. Washington had made Randolph an aide in the war, helped him in his political life back in Virginia, and then put him in the cabinet. "While at the head of my cabinet he has been secretly, but actively, plotting with the opponents of my administration, consulting and contriving with them for the defeat of its measures . . . conducting intrigue with the ambassador of a foreign government, receiving from the ambassador money to aid in accomplishing that object."

Washington's voice rose in anger as he went on. He slammed the pamphlet against a tabletop. "All this time I have had entire faith in him and been led by that faith to pay deference to his representations, to delay the ratification of the British treaty, thereby exposing myself to imputation of having been intimidated by party clamor from the discharge of a public duty and imputation contrary to the truth, a thought abhorrent to my feelings and my nature and now he has written and published this."[6]

The incident ended the longtime friendship between the two prominent Virginians. The men who had known and admired each other for nearly thirty years never spoke to each other again.

Fauchet's statement was included as part of Randolph's published *Vindications*, but it was a poorly written document in which the minister explained very little. He did exonerate Randolph of trying to bribe him and insisted that Randolph's language had been misinterpreted; there was no illegal soliciting of money.

But Fauchet's rambling statement did damn Randolph in another way. Fauchet asserted that Randolph had held a secret meeting with him to discuss a treaty, without the knowledge of the president or any member of the cabinet, which Randolph should not have done. Furthermore, Faucet charged that Randolph wanted the French government to lend money to merchants who were his friends so that they could pay their debts to English creditors. Fauchet said that Randolph assured him that these merchants would be instrumental in averting civil war in America, thus protecting French trade interests.

Randolph was never able to refute that final charge. He had not benefited personally from the sordid series of meetings and transactions, but he had obviously used his cabinet post and influence to perhaps improperly obtain loans for friends. He should not have been involved in this sort of unethical conduct.

Washington's dismissal of Randolph's friendship, Randolph's resignation, his murky defense of the charges against him, and Fauchet's charge of misuse of office all combined to end Randolph's political career.[7]

When Randolph moved back to Richmond, he was finished with government service and politics, which had consumed his entire adult life. His lofty reputation was ruined. He was only forty-two years old and in generally good health, but he faced spending the rest of his days under a cloud of suspicion. He needed something to keep himself busy to avoid falling into a deep depression. He needed to earn money and restore his reputation. So he went back to his old law practice, took on as many cases as he could, and earned as much money as possible.

Randolph was quite successful. He wrote to friends that he had at least one case in court each day and sometimes two. He handled so many cases that when he was ill or had to travel, the entire court calendar was changed to accommodate his absences.

He enjoyed considerable legal accomplishments, earned large amounts of money, and at the same time worked hard to improve his civic image by organizing various committees to improve life in Richmond. For example, Randolph was the head of a citizens' committee that convinced the city to hire more constables for its tiny police force and more guards for the county jail.

This combination of courtroom mastery and civic responsibility helped rebuild his image in the city and the state and brought in needed revenue. He was so prosperous following his return home that he moved into one of Richmond's grandest homes, the Octagon. It was so named for its eight sides, and the house stood on Capitol Square, directly opposite the capitol building itself.

Randolph's image suffered a shattering blow in 1797, however, when yet another federal investigation showed that as attorney general, he had somehow misplaced more than $49,000. A Treasury Department probe was started and it continued for five years, being repeatedly extended by Randolph's pleas for more time to mount a defense.

His Richmond friends supported him in the highly damaging case. "I knew more of his affairs than any other man," wrote one of his secretaries. "I cannot conceive any possible way in which he could have dispersed of [money]."[8]

Finally, the federal government appointed an arbitrator. He ruled against Randolph. The arbitrator did not accuse Randolph of theft, but of malfeasance in not accounting for the money. In 1804, the government insisted that the former attorney general repay the entire amount over a four-year period. Randolph had little cash, and most of his family's wealth was tied up in land and slaves. Early in September 1805, his brother-in-law William Cary Nicholas stepped forward and agreed to pay the money through bonds that he would back. Randolph, in turn, said that he would turn over all of his assets to Nicholas and repay the rest of the money whenever he could.

The arbitrator's ruling was a severe blow to Randolph's pocketbook, as well as to his reputation and pride. Despite his insistence that he had no knowledge of how the $49,000 had been lost and his pledges that he had never profited from the incident, the former attorney general was once again under a cloud of suspicion. The federal government tenaciously pursued the money from the Randolphs and the Carters, too, and it was not until 1856, seventy years after the transgressions, that all of the money was finally paid back.[9]

The next year, 1806, Randolph took on as many appellate cases as he could to earn the money he owed to William Nicholas. Earning money was not enough, though. Randolph needed to restore his own confidence and to show the city, the state, and the country yet again that although he might have failed in public life, he was still a great lawyer. He needed a single highly publicized case to redeem himself. None of the appellate cases received much publicity because they were dry legal dealings involving money, land, and wealthy but unknown people. Few cases gave him a chance to exhibit any legal skills beyond filing sheaves of papers and making cold arguments in empty courtrooms.

And then his old friend George Wythe was poisoned, along with others in his household.

Randolph was one of the first people summoned to the bedside of the emaciated and dying Wythe. The two had been longtime friends in the Virginia courts and in national and state politics.

When Wythe went to the Continental Congress in 1776, it was Randolph who took his place as a delegate at the Virginia Convention. Randolph had argued cases in front of Wythe when the latter sat as a judge on the State Court of Appeals. Randolph, like Wythe, had been considered for the U.S. Supreme Court, before the offer went to Wythe, who turned it down. The pair were elected as delegates to the Constitutional Convention in 1787 while Randolph was governor of Virginia.

Wythe was certain that he was dying after being poisoned on May 25, 1806. He asked Randolph to revise his will so that he could cut his nephew out of it.

Despite his fondness for Wythe, Randolph took the clearly unwinnable case because he needed a legal comeback. Getting an acquittal for Sweeney against seemingly insurmountable odds would be the lift he needed to put this latest financial scandal behind him and resume his place as one of the state's finest attorneys and most famous citizens. The publicity generated by a courtroom victory would bring him many clients—wealthy clients, whose fees he desperately needed to pay back the millions that he now owed to the Carter family.

Sweeney probably could not believe his good fortune as he sat in the Henrico County jail, awaiting trial. One day he was the most despised man in all of the South, shunned by everyone, and the next he was being represented by two of the best lawyers in the United States.

Most people were furious that Randolph had decided to defend his close friend's killer and that he would attempt to exonerate Sweeney by outmaneuvering his own son-in-law, Philip Norborne Nicholas, in the courtroom.

James Monroe was one. The former governor and future president was an important member of Thomas Jefferson's brain trust. Monroe had been a protégé of Wythe's at the College of William and Mary and, like Jefferson, venerated the old man. Monroe was in mourning for Wythe, his teacher, and here was Randolph defending Wythe's murderer.[10]

Monroe had disliked Randolph for nearly twenty years. When the Constitutional Convention had been called in 1787, Monroe had wanted to be one of Virginia's delegates but was not among the seven selected by the legislature, which included then Governor Randolph. Unexpectedly, one of the seven, Patrick Henry, an opponent of the Constitution, had dropped out in order to attack it publicly. Randolph and the state's executive council then overlooked Monroe, who had every right to go and who let it be known that he desired to be in Philadelphia. The council had instead named Richard Henry Lee. When Lee turned the council members down, they again snubbed Monroe and picked a Richmond doctor, Dr. James McClurg, who had little national political experience. Ironically, McClurg would perform Wythe's autopsy. Randolph had cast the deciding vote in the selection of each alternate. Monroe had been angry that Randolph had ignored him and had even chosen an unknown physician over him. He never forgot the slight. Monroe, like many others, wanted a Constitution with a Bill of Rights to protect the individual and was unhappy that his voice was not heard to ensure one.

Enraged, Monroe wrote Jefferson a curt letter after his snub, saying, "The Governor [Randolph], I have reason to believe, is unfriendly to me and hath shown a disposition to thwart me. . . . [This] hath given me much uneasiness."[11]

THE TWO LAWYERS' eagerness to defend Sweeney was greeted with disdain throughout the state. While all agreed that every defendant needed an attorney, they did not think that Sweeney deserved two of the very best in the country. Virginians quickly saw through the motives of both attorneys. The scandal-plagued Randolph was trying to redeem himself, and Wirt was attempting to jump-start what he hoped would be a brilliant career with a triumph in what seemed to be an unwinnable case. Both men were vilified from one end of the state to the other.

The Reverend M. L. Weems, one of many who were enraged that the two had taken Sweeney's case, wrote in a newspaper eulogy that Virginians should not shed tears for the slain Wythe, because he was heaven-bound. "No," wrote Weems, "give them to the *vile attorney*, who, for a fee, supported the villain's claims, and tore from the little weeping orphan, his cake and homely robe—give them to the infatuated miser, who, darkened at the sight of a creditor, curses his own signature if it compelled payment of a dollar—and, unmoved by the calls of honor, still hugged to himself his precious self, content to live a scoundrel, provided he might but die rich—'guilt's blunder and the loudest laugh of hell.'"[12]

And many felt that it was unfair for the two lawyers to obtain any kind of justice for the accused killer. They echoed a harsh line that Wythe himself had often used about those who tried to cheat the law: "He, therefore, who knowingly acts against justice, is a rebel against God and a premeditated murderer of mankind."[13]

Another reason that many people were shocked at the actions of Wirt and Randolph was that there was such universal esteem for Wythe as a lawyer. Robert Alexander, a merchant, summed up the feelings of numerous individuals when he said that Wythe was "the only honest law-yer I ever knew."[14] How could two other lawyers work to free his killer?

Yet what truly amazed people throughout Richmond was that Wirt and Randolph would work together on *anything*. The two men hated each other.

Wirt had often used Randolph as an example of the greedy lawyer when explaining to others that lawyers did not make enough money in legal cases. He juxtaposed his arguments that lawyers needed higher fees by writing that even money-hungry Randolph did not make a lot of money. Wirt always pointed out that Randolph was the best-paid lawyer in the state.

Wirt had seemed relentless in his pillorying of Randolph. In one of his initial newspaper essays that were later published as *The Letters of a British Spy*, Wirt was critical of several prominent Virginians, such as John Wickham, but saved his most savage lines for Randolph. "R" (and everybody knew that he meant Randolph) was physically "large and portly. . . . His mind, as is often but not invariably the case, cor-responds with his personal appearance; this is, that it is turned rather for ornament than for severe use."[15]

As soon as the essay was in print, Wirt knew he had made a griev-ous mistake. It was too late. "The die is cast," he wrote, adding, "I had made enemies of the gentlemen themselves, with all their connections and dependencies."

Randolph was livid. Pointing at a table where lawyers sat, an angry Randolph told George Wythe in court one day that he wanted to get his hands on Wirt. Randolph said, "I wish the 'British Spy' was practic-ing at that bar."

Most of the other men and women whom Wirt scrutinized in *British Spy* forgave the author for his curt remarks about them because they under-stood that the book's style was satire—but not Randolph. He despised Wirt for portraying him as arrogant and sarcastic in newspapers that all of Randolph's professional peers, personal friends, and relatives read.

"He was wounded past all power of forgiving," Wirt wrote of Randolph's reaction. "If he had never been my enemy before, that one adventure would have made him so."

Randolph was so upset with Wirt that no one believed they could work as colleagues in a legal trial. They had met once before following the publication of the essay, on opposite sides of a case, and Randolph's irritation with Wirt was such that he could barely make an argument to the judge and had thus lost the case.

"He was so confounded that in his argument he manifested nothing of the orator, nor even of himself. . . . His arguments were the very weakest his cause furnished; his order was all confusion and he is said to have made the very worst speech that he ever did make. He disappointed everybody," said Wirt.[16]

If Randolph was disoriented when his opposing council was standing halfway across the courtroom, how could he get along with Wirt sitting in the chair next to him?

13

Mourning at the Executive Mansion

BEFORE WYTHE DIED, Mayor DuVal sent off a hastily written note to President Jefferson at the Executive Mansion (the White House) to tell the chief executive that Wythe was near the end. DuVal, like everyone, knew how close the two men had been throughout their lives; Jefferson had to be informed. Unfortunately, due to the slow mail delivery of the day, the letter about Wythe's imminent death did not reach the Executive Mansion until a day after Wythe's funeral, making it impossible for Jefferson to ride to Richmond for the service and lead the mourners in the enormous funeral procession.[1]

In a touching note, DuVal wrote to Jefferson, "I believe that the great and good Mr. Wythe loved you as sincerely as if you had been his son; his attachment was founded on his thorough knowledge of you, personally. Some years ago, he mentioned that if there was an honest man in America, Thomas Jefferson was that person; everything that he said has been verified." In another note, DuVal told the president, "I know from what Mr. Wythe often said, that you were dearer to him than any relationship he had—that his attachment arose from that impulse that unites great minds, the sincere love of virtue."[2]

William DuVal was the mayor of Richmond in 1806. He was also a neighbor and a close friend of Judge Wythe's. DuVal was one of the first to suspect that the judge had been poisoned.

In one letter, DuVal enclosed a copy of Wythe's will, in which Wythe left some of his silver cups, his gold-headed cane, and his library and its entire contents to his friend the president, a fellow lover of books (Mayor DuVal sent Jefferson a miniature portrait of Wythe that had been painted in 1804). Wythe wrote in the will, "I give my books and small philosophical apparatus to Thomas Jefferson, President of the United States of America, a legacy considered abstractly perhaps not deserving a place in his museum. But, estimated by my good will to him, the most valuable to him of anything which I have power to bestow."[3]

Of course, Jefferson never did receive some of the rare books and the valuable globe of the earth in Wythe's library—Sweeney had stolen and sold them and had spent the money gambling.[4]

The president was despondent over the death of his friend. Throughout his life, Jefferson had always marveled that while the nature of politics and the judiciary seemed to be that all of the men involved in those careers had opponents, his friend Wythe never seemed to be a target of venom. "He never had an enemy," wrote the president.[5]

Jefferson was also upset about the death of Michael Brown. No one in the country understood more than Jefferson the great love and attachment that Judge Wythe had over the years toward his protégés. And Jefferson was his most accomplished protégé. The others included some of the most successful men in America, such as John Marshall, Henry Clay, and James Monroe. The president, then, mourned the end of the life of the very promising Michael Brown, whom he had agreed to house and tutor in the Executive Mansion if his friend the judge died while Michael was still in Wythe's care. The president wrote, "I sincerely regret the loss of Michael not only for the affliction it must have cost Mr. Wythe in his last moments, but also as it has deprived me of an object for attention which would have gratified me unceasingly with the constant recollection and execution of the wishes of my friend."[6]

Jefferson told DuVal to let him know what happened at the trial. The president was not the only person interested in the outcome of the case. The entire country awaited the verdict with great eagerness. And then the nation would await the hanging of Sweeney on the public gallows in Richmond, which everyone expected to draw an even larger crowd than the one thousand Virginians who had watched the slave Gabriel Prosser be hanged for the 1800 slave insurrection. Swarms of people from all over Virginia would attend the hanging of a famous man's murderer. They would arrive on horseback and in carriages and boats, dressed in their finest dresses and coats, and would pack the hotels and boardinghouses of the city. Crowds of twelve thousand and more had witnessed public hangings in cities such as Providence, New York, and Philadelphia. Ten thousand people had attended a hanging in tiny New London, Connecticut. The hanging of Katharine Garret in Portsmouth, New Hampshire, had attracted more people than any other public event in the history of the state. The Sweeney hanging might even set a record.[7]

The courthouse was packed with spectators for the trial, which began on September 2, 1806. Sweeney was brought over from the jail early in the morning. The lineup of damning witnesses was expected to include the three doctors who had performed the autopsies on the judge and Michael Brown; Mayor Duval and other friends who were with the judge in his last days; and a lengthy parade of witnesses. They would tell the court about Sweeney's suspicious actions in the days prior to the poisoning, his conversations with friends about how to buy poison, his making of arsenic powder, his allegedly tossing a package of the powder over the jailhouse wall, the discovery of arsenic in his room, the forged checks, the will, Sweeney's animosity for Michael Brown, and his disputes with the judge, who had done so much to help the young man after he moved into Wythe's house. And, of course, there was Lydia Broadnax and her eyewitness account of the poisoning of the coffee. Sweeney would hang.

PART THREE

The Trial

14

The Forensics Nightmare, Part I:
Arsenic, the Poison of Choice

Trioxide Arsenic: an oxidized form of arsenic, with a sweet-
ish taste and erythropoietic effect; used in weed killers,
sheep dips and rodenticides.

—*Dorland's Illustrated Medical Dictionary*

ARSENIC would have easily entered George Wythe's body, after
it dissolved in the cups of steamy coffee he sipped while reading the newspapers on the morning of May 25, 1806. The
colorless substance, hidden in the coffee, would have surged into his
mouth, cascaded over his tongue, and then plunged rapidly down
his throat and into his stomach. There, some particles of the arsenic
that had been assimilated into the food he ate for breakfast would have
stuck to the lining of his stomach. Other particles would have moved
down the alimentary canal into his large and small intestines and his
rectum. The rest of the poison would have filtered into his bloodstream
and surged through his system like a river, pumped through his capil-
laries and veins by his aging eighty-year-old heart. Eventually, the

arsenic would have found its way into his liver, lungs, bones, hair, and fingernails.

There were immediate cries for an autopsy to be performed on George Wythe. In bedside conversations with authorities, the judge insisted that he, along with his maid and his protégé, had been poisoned on the day he fell so desperately ill. His friends in Richmond and throughout Virginia were certain of it. In Washington, President Thomas Jefferson feared it, too. One friend said that a weakened Wythe had asked him in a barely audible voice to have an autopsy done as soon as Wythe expired. With heavy eyes, the judge had tried to speak in his rapidly worsening state. He pointed to his chest with the bony and emaciated fingers of his right hand and blurted out, "Cut me!"

The autopsy on the eminent jurist, conducted just hours after his death on June 6, was not only pivotal to the criminal prosecution in the high-profile case, but was one of the few that had been ordered in Virginia in some time. Consequently, it attracted enormous public attention.

By 1806, the postmortem autopsy had been a part of medical procedure for nearly two thousand years. The first known official, state-mandated autopsy to determine the cause of death in a publicized murder investigation was performed on Julius Caesar in 44 BC. Caesar, who for five years had been the iron-fisted dictator of Rome, was assassinated on March 15 in the Forum by friends and allies, led by Brutus. The autopsy was ordered by the Senate to close the case (physicians determined that Caesar had been stabbed twenty-three times that day and died from one fatal wound through the heart).

The first general body dissections were conducted in ancient Egypt, during the reign of Pharaoh Ptolemy I. He not only ordered autopsies so that doctors could study the inner workings of the body, but was so fascinated by dissection that he assisted in the operations himself.[1]

A Greek doctor, Galen (131–200 AD), was one of the first physicians to treat gladiators. To study diseases in the body, he conducted numerous dissections of the limbs, the organs, and the tissues of people who died in the arena and those who expired from natural, as well as violent, means. He performed similar dissections on apes, being certain that the physiology of gorillas was similar to that of humans. There were few autopsies during the next thirteen hundred years because many religions, especially Catholicism, forbade them. The church made an exception to its autopsy ban in 1410, however, when it ordered one for Pope Alexander V. Church officials suspected that he had been poisoned, perhaps with arsenic. Leaders of the Holy See were determined to bring the pontiff's killer to justice, but the autopsy showed no foul play. The church changed its policy shortly afterward, when Pope Sixtus IV allowed autopsies in Italian medical schools so that students could dissect bodies and study vital organs. At about the same time, members of a powerful family in Bologna claimed that a member had been poisoned. A professor at the University of Bologna performed that city's first autopsy to find out.[2] Autopsies were performed in China even earlier and were chronicled in a five-volume book set, *Instructions to the Coroner*, which was published in the thirteenth century.[3] By the Middle Ages, autopsies were performed frequently, sometimes outdoors. They drew large crowds of spectators, and doctors were happy to have the public in attendance as witnesses. Sometimes members of the audience—those who appeared to have strong stomachs—were asked to participate in the autopsy by examining the opened body close up.

The first forensic autopsy performed by medical professors specifically to find out whether poison had been an agent of death was conducted in 1590 at Freiburg University, Germany, to learn how twenty-eight-year-old Count Jacob III of Baden, Austria, had died. The two professors quickly determined that he had been murdered by the administration of arsenic powder.[4] By the mid-seventeenth century, autopsies on sections of the brain were being performed by doctors such as Thomas Willis, who wrote several books on his work. The French doctor Antoine Serres, practicing in the early eighteenth century, autopsied 370 brains during his career.

Unlike many European courts, American judicial tribunals were reluctant to order an autopsy for any cause of death, even poisoning, if the deceased's family objected. British courts maintained a similar aversion to ordering an autopsy if the family objected.[5]

In the eighteenth century, autopsies to show the cause of death, whether violent or natural, and for the general purpose of human anatomical study were quite popular in the world's medical schools. Almost every school had anatomical classes in which a professor opened up a cadaver and then dissected it as students observed. The professor carefully explained how to look for and remove vital organs and study tissues to determine death. The dissection was performed on a large wooden table on the ground level of a room in which students sat above the professor in tiers of chairs and peered down into the open cadaver, like a medical theater-in-the-round. Similar classes were offered in nearby city hospitals in most European cities in which the local medical schools did not have anatomical classes with autopsies. Everyone considered Scotland's University of Edinburgh to be the world's premier school for anatomical studies. All of the anatomy classes and autopsy workshops in American universities were based on Edinburgh's practices, and most of America's anatomical professors had trained at that university. (Of the nearly four hundred American physicians who had gone to medical schools in Europe or the United States in 1806, 35 percent had been educated at Edinburgh; more than half of Virginia's physicians had trained there.)[6]

The University of Edinburgh's medical school was founded in 1726 and within thirty years was considered the premier school of its kind in the world. The school's specialty was anatomy, and by the time James McClurg arrived in 1762, it boasted an academic chair for anatomy, with several courses on the subject that featured autopsies and dissections.[7]

The popularity of anatomical study and dissections caused numerous scandals throughout Europe and America in the eighteenth and nineteenth centuries because there were too few bodies available for study. The infamous "body snatchers," later the subject of numerous movies, appeared to find cadavers by stealing them from graveyards and selling them to medical schools. The public was so appalled at the number of bodies stolen from graves in New York City during this era that in 1788, two thousand people rioted and attacked the dwellings of doctors who had paid the body snatchers for their corpses. The mob ransacked the doctors' homes in a hunt for the cadavers (some homeless people were even murdered and their corpses sold to schools).[8]

Now amply supplied with stolen cadavers, professors in medical schools conducted thousands of autopsies for students. One doctor-author traced more than three thousand autopsies in Great Britain in the late seventeenth century alone. The first internal dissection in the United States, the first true autopsy, was performed in 1662 on Elizabeth Kelly. On her deathbed, she accused her nurse, Goody Ayres, of murdering her (Ayres, who had loudly proclaimed her innocence, abruptly left town when she heard of the court order to open up Kelly's body). Hundreds of autopsies were performed in the United States during the remainder of the seventeenth century and throughout the eighteenth century, as the number of medical schools grew.[9]

Overall, autopsies often proved the prosecutor right, but on some occasions they revealed that the prosecutor was wrong, and the results caused a public uproar. One of the most macabre cases of such forensics involved the hanging of a beautiful twenty-eight-year-old Worcester, Massachusetts, woman, Bathsheba Spooner. She was found guilty of paying three men to murder her husband, Jonathan, in 1778.

Bathsheba, who told anyone in Worcester who would listen that she was trapped in a sexless marriage, began an illicit sexual affair with a local sixteen-year-old, Ezra Ross, and tried to talk him into murdering her husband, but he refused. A short time later, the flirtatious Bathsheba befriended James Buchanan and William Brooks, British soldiers who had escaped from an American prisoner-of-war camp. She convinced them to kill Jonathan. She talked young Ross into helping them and promised all three men $1,000 apiece and, it was assumed, sexual favors.

The three men beat Spooner to death near his home one night during a thick snowfall and dumped his body into a nearby well. They were soon caught, tried, convicted, and sentenced to hang, along with the young widow. It did not help Bathsheba's cause that she was a fiery Tory in patriotic Massachusetts in the middle of the American Revolution and that for years her father had been one of the state's leading British sympathizers. Bathsheba then dropped a bombshell into the court proceedings: she claimed that she was pregnant and, under state law, should receive a stay of execution until the baby was born.

The judge asked three Worcester midwives to examine her; they claimed that she was barren. Her lawyer demanded an examination by other midwives, and they said she was pregnant. The judge ignored the results of the second examination and condemned her to die. On July 2, 1778, Bathsheba, with her hair neatly combed and attired in her finest dress, was taken to the Worcester gallows. After being denounced for her extramarital sex life in a savage gallows sermon by a local minister, she was hanged.[10]

Right to the end, when her neck snapped, Bathsheba insisted that she was pregnant. Her angry lawyer demanded an autopsy following the execution, and, sure enough, doctors found that she was carrying a tiny five-month-old fetus in her womb. This delayed verdict did the late Bathsheba Spooner little good.

The Richmond court had no trouble finding doctors to conduct the autopsy of George Wythe—many physicians wanted to participate. To make certain that justice was carried out, a magistrate selected Doctors James McClurg, James McCaw, and William Foushee. The three doctors were a colonial era "dream team" of forensic skills, and all had been trained at the University of Edinburgh. They not only were among the best doctors in the state, but were acknowledged to be three of the leading physicians in the country. McClurg was considered among the world's most accomplished physicians.

Well-trained doctors were treasured in early eighteenth-century America because there were so few of them. Only six medical

Dr. James McCaw, one of Wythe's doctors, helped perform the autopsy that was crucial to determining whether the judge had been poisoned. McCaw went on to a long and distinguished career as a physician in Virginia.

Dr. James McClurg, one of the most renowned doctors in the world and a delegate to the Constitutional Convention, led the team of three doctors who performed the autopsy on Judge Wythe.

The dapper Dr. William Foushee was a former mayor of Richmond and one of its most popular doctors in 1806. He was one of the three doctors who performed the autopsy on Wythe. Richmonders thought so highly of Foushee that they even named a street after him.

colleges existed in the United States at that time. The University of Pennsylvania's medical school in Philadelphia opened its doors in 1765, followed by King's College in New York, which later became Columbia University; Harvard; Dartmouth; Transylvania University in Kentucky; and Yale. They did not have large student bodies and produced few graduates. Most Americans who wanted to become doctors studied at the dozens of highly regarded medical schools in Europe. That number was small, too, because tuition was expensive, and their families would have had to pay for their housing and food for the duration of their education.[11] Many independent, smaller medical schools in the United States were founded by groups of doctors to make money. These schools formed a second tier in terms of quality. They required only fourteen weeks of study and offered a curriculum dominated by lectures, with no laboratory work or hands-on treatment. The doctors who ran them maintained very low standards for graduation to ensure high enrollment and substantial tuition revenue. Their graduates learned little.[12]

The other route to becoming a physician was to apprentice to doctor for five to seven years, which was an inferior education. Prior to the 1770s, when several colonies insisted that aspiring doctors pass a medical exam, anyone could become a doctor. Numerous village ministers served as doctors, as did public officials. One doctor's slave, who had had no training, took over the doctor's practice and ran it for years. Pharmacists who ran apothecary shops also served as doctors. Every village had at least one untrained housewife who was the physician for the community. Midwives delivered babies in most towns and also worked as the community doctors. School principals took it upon themselves not only to educate their students, but to act as their physicians, and in that capacity prescribed herbs and medicines that they knew nothing about. The governor of Connecticut, John Winthrop Jr., served as a physician and even made house calls. One New York City shoemaker worked as a doctor. In 1806, only 13 percent of all U.S. doctors had been trained at a formal medical school in either America or Europe.[13]

The public had a dim view of the apprentice doctors and even of those who had gone to U.S. medical schools. At best, they had little or no knowledge of medicine and relied on odd diets and herbs. One study of seven thousand patients treated by five apprentice-trained doctors in New England during that era showed that in nearly 90 percent of their cases, they merely advised sick patients to rest, eat bland foods, and consume snakeroot and other plants, plus laxatives.[14] At worst, they were bunglers. In 1785, one man wrote to a newspaper that doctors "daily intrude themselves upon the public as proficient in the healing art, totally unqualified for their important task." Others were less kind. A colonial newspaper editor said that the doctors were a worse plague than the plagues they tried to cure. Another said that medicine was "dismal havoc made by quacks." One army general wrote in the middle of the Revolution that since surgeons were highly paid and useless, the army should hire barbers for surgery because they had the same skills and worked more cheaply. Even doctors abhorred these unqualified doctors. Dr. Benjamin Rush, the chief surgeon in the Continental Army and later a professor at the University of Pennsylvania, said famously of army doctors that the worst thing a sick soldier could do was go to the hospital. Dr. John Douglass, of Massachusetts, warned patients that there "was more danger from the physician than from the distemper." A doctor in New York snarled, "Quacks abound like locusts in Egypt."[15]

One historian wrote that during the Revolutionary period, only one hundred of the thirty-five hundred listed physicians in the United States were considered reliable. In Philadelphia, which was home to eighty-five physicians, one of the highest numbers of doctors in any American city, only one-third had attended a medical school of any kind.[16]

The remedies that Americans could purchase for their ailments, many of which were prescribed by these armies of untrained physicians, consisted of fraudulent concoctions that accomplished little. Colonial newspapers were full of ads for medicines that promised to cure every sickness known to man. People believed them. One ad offered a solution of freshly made tar mixed with water that was guaranteed to cure everything from an upset stomach to smallpox and asthma. Victims of diphtheria were told to take corns from a horse's feet, dry them, grate them, and mix them into a bottle of French wine that had to be left standing for two days before drinking it once each morning and evening for a week. A person afflicted with a toothache was advised to continually jab the tooth with a magnet. Victims of rabies were told to consume large quantities of ground-up liverwort and black pepper mixed in warm cow's milk. Friends of people who collapsed from drinking large quantities of cold water on hot summer days were advised to insert a blacksmith's bellows into their anuses and blow fresh air into them to clear the lungs.[17]

Americans were also angry that their doctors, who did such a poor job, charged them excessive fees. Newspaper editors and clergymen argued that people were dying because they could not afford the care of physicians, even of quacks. This uproar caused most states to regulate the fees that doctors could charge.[18]

Public anger at badly educated doctors was particularly livid in Virginia, where the mortality rate had been high for two hundred years. During the first eighteen years of the Jamestown settlement, from 1607 to 1625, shabby medical care resulted in the deaths of nearly 85 percent of the inhabitants. One man who survived the early days in Jamestown, George Percy, wrote, "There were never Englishmen left in a foreign country in such misery as we were in this new discovered Virginia." John Smith, one of the legendary leaders of the settlement, lamented, "God plagued us with such famine and sickness that the living were scarce able to bury the dead."

That historic death rate had remained in the minds of Virginians ever since, and they always feared that their physicians did not have enough training to care for them properly or were, to put it simply, bunglers. The son of a prominent Virginian asked his father, who lay dying, whether he wanted a doctor to be summoned. The dying man told his son not to do so, that he had a better chance of living without one.[19]

These were the same reasons, however, that the public had such a high opinion of McClurg, McCaw, and Foushee. They had, over the years, proven their skills in crisis after crisis. And, most important, they had graduated from Edinburgh. The Scottish university was so esteemed worldwide that when the first ten U.S. medical schools were created, they copied their entire curriculums and all of their autopsy procedures from Edinburgh. The medical profession's admiration for Edinburgh was so great that American medical professors obtained the lecture notes of Edinburgh teachers and used them to teach their own students. Edinburgh was the apex of medical education, and McClurg, McCaw, and Foushee were its grandest alumni in America.[20]

They were also leaders of the city's political community, well-known on the social circuit, and envied for their neatly tailored suits and the well-appointed carriages in which they were driven about town. The men lived in the most elegant homes in the city. James McClurg lived in a mansion on Capitol Square itself, opposite the capitol building.

Dr. McClurg, who had just turned sixty and lived near George Wythe on Grace Street, was born in Hampton, Virginia, in 1746. He was educated at the College of William and Mary and graduated in 1762. He sailed to Scotland and spent eight years training as a physician at Edinburgh University, where the administrators considered him one of their best students. Following his graduation, armed with laudatory letters of recommendation from the deans at Edinburgh, McClurg set up a practice in London and then Paris, and he wrote numerous articles for European medical journals.

The young surgeon returned to America in 1773 and set up a lucrative surgical practice, which was interrupted by several years of service as a doctor in the Virginia State Navy during the Revolution. The brilliant McClurg was acknowledged as one of the best surgeons in America and at only thirty-three years of age was named to the faculty of the College of William and Mary as its professor of anatomy and medicine when the school was reorganized in 1779 by Thomas Jefferson. (There, McClurg was a faculty colleague, a neighbor, and a close friend of the law professor George Wythe.) McClurg taught full time and also worked as a physician and a surgeon. He was so prominent throughout Virginia that people from all over the state brought sickly family members to Williamsburg for him to diagnose and treat.

His patriotic fervor did not end after his stint as a navy doctor. McClurg became deeply involved in Revolutionary activities. He was so passionate about politics and worked so hard in government that in 1782, fellow Virginian James Madison nominated him as the U.S. secretary for foreign affairs (secretary of state), but McClurg was not selected by Congress. He always saw public service as a life's calling, along with medicine. He wrote that he wished he could "gratify at the same time my passion for improvement in the profession I am destined to and my zeal to do my country some service. In this time of general activity, I do not like to be an idle spectator."[21]

McClurg, with Wythe, was sent to Philadelphia in 1787 as one of Virginia's seven representatives to the Constitutional Convention, thus becoming one of the Founding Fathers. He was so highly regarded as a political figure that in 1793, George Washington seriously considered naming him secretary of state when Jefferson resigned.[22] A few years later, in 1797, McClurg became Richmond's mayor and stayed in office for three one-year terms, while he continued his flourishing medical practice. Having Dr. McClurg as the mayor helped the city avoid an outbreak of yellow fever in 1798. In addition to his three terms as mayor, Dr. McClurg served for more than a dozen years as a city councilman.[23]

But it was as a doctor that McClurg achieved his greatest fame. In Richmond, he treated patients who came to his office from all over the state, seeking the care of Virginia's foremost physician. He ministered to rich landowners, planters who had earned fortunes through tobacco sales, wealthy ship owners who thrived in the import-export business, and the town's leading merchants and their families. Like other doctors in town, he frequently offered his medical services to the poor.

He was respected across the United States. Virginia had no medical journals in that era. There were only a handful in the country, with the *Philadelphia Journal of Medical and Physical Sciences* being one of the most prestigious. It was considered the capstone of any doctor's medical career to be asked to write an article for any of the medical journals. McClurg was published in the *Philadelphia Journal of Medical and Physical Sciences,* and his article, on reasoning in medical diagnosis and doctors' pitiable lack of success in diagnosing most patients, was widely read and discussed throughout the nation. He was even better known as a medical author. Only a handful of American doctors had ever published an article in a medical journal, much less written a book. McClurg wrote *Experiments upon the Human Bile and Reflections on the Biliary Secretions.* The book was not published by some backwater publisher, either, but by the noted T. Cadell, in London in 1772. The book was a study of stomach bile and how it could cause everything from discomfort to death; it was reprinted in several languages. All of the top surgeons in Europe were familiar with it. It made McClurg one of the world's leading authorities on stomach bile. When the *Philadelphia Journal of Medical and Physical Sciences* began to publish, its editors decided to dedicate each of its volumes to a leading doctor in the United States as a tribute. McClurg was the very first to be so honored. The journal referred to him as the "elegant scholar and accomplished physician," a testament to his international fame.[24]

McClurg found himself reunited with his old college classmate Wythe when the judge moved to Richmond and bought a house in the same neighborhood where McClurg later built one of his homes. The two reestablished their friendship as Wythe continued in his judicial profession and McClurg flourished in his dual career of politics and medicine.

Dr. James Drew McCaw was not only one of the many doctors in the South who admired McClurg, but he was also McClurg's nephew. McClurg did not have a son, so he had decided to take his nephew under his wing. He helped raise the youth, paid for his tuition at the University of Edinburgh, and then allowed the young man to live in his home for several years until James McCaw had built up his medical practice. McCaw, who had returned to Richmond from Scotland in 1792, began a family medical dynasty in Virginia that continued for five generations. The well-dressed McCaw was the personal physician of many prominent Richmonders and Virginia planters, including Wythe. McCaw and the judge were neighbors during the years that McCaw lived with his uncle at Sixth and Grace streets, before McClurg moved to prestigious Capitol Square. McCaw was among the many doctors who were kept busy in 1794 when a smallpox epidemic hit the city.

The weary McCaw, who had gained the thanks of the city for his work in curbing the epidemic, was ready to confront more of them and insisted to friends that swift inoculations were the only solution. He had his chance a few years later, in 1802, when smallpox again engulfed the community. This time Dr. McCaw led a team of doctors in immediately inoculating as many people as possible. He insisted that the doctors inoculate the poor, at no charge, and they did, under his direction. McCaw and his fellow doctors not only saved the lives of thousands, including hundreds of poor families, but allowed them, via the inoculations, to develop an immunity against several smallpox outbreaks that swept across the South over the next few decades. The doctors were hailed as heroes.[25]

The dapper Dr. William Foushee was born in Northern Neck, Virginia, in 1749. He, too, was sent to Edinburgh to study medicine by his wealthy family. He returned to Richmond after graduation and soon became a prominent physician in the capital. Like McClurg, he became involved in local and state politics early and, in addition to being one of Richmond's most reliable doctors, was a highly honored public figure. He was elected Richmond's first mayor in 1782 and then, when he left office after one term, served as the city's part-time post-master for several years and on the city council for ten. He was elected to the State Legislature for numerous terms and held several appointed state offices. During the 1800 smallpox epidemic, Foushee and his brother John, another doctor, opened up their office and homes for a massive smallpox inoculation campaign that reportedly saved the lives of thousands of people who had not been inoculated three years earlier during a similar epidemic.[26]

The likable Foushee was the most popular doctor in town, especially with women. He had, everyone agreed, the most charming bedside manner of any physician in the state. He enjoyed the finer things in life and had common areas of interest with female patients, such as theater, art, interior decorating, and gardening. Dr. Foushee's amiable disposition and medical skills also made him a favorite for Richmonders whose slaves became ill. He cared for them with the same proficiency that he did their owners.[27]

He oversaw the cultivation of a vast, well-tended garden behind his home that covered three city blocks and was a tourist attraction. No one doubted his medical skills, which had become legendary. "He had the best medical education which Edinburgh can impart to her students—the experience of half century over his head—a coolness in studying the symptoms of a case, a firmness in applying the most effective remedies and a delicacy in the treatment of his patients which few physicians ever possessed," reported the *Richmond Enquirer* in its 1824 obituary of Foushee (he was so admired that the city named a street after him).[28]

Who better to perform an autopsy on Judge Wythe than these three nationally renowned physicians and community leaders? And especially McClurg, who had written a medical textbook and contributed to and wrote for the prestigious *Philadelphia Journal of Medical and Physical Sciences?*

What most people did not know, however, was that the esteemed McClurg's medical analyses were no more advanced than the primitive diagnoses of most doctors of the era. In fact, McClurg had made many bombastic and simply untrue statements about medicine and treatment, orally and in print, which should have astonished anyone connected to the Wythe murder case.

Among his insistent and wrong beliefs:

- Fresh air and good eating are better remedies for illness than any medicine.
- Only old people, not young, go into convulsions.
- Residents of very hot regions, such as the Southern states, are more sober in their living than those from colder, Northern states (their exemplary demeanor is caused by the oppressive heat).
- Anyone suffering from a high fever and near death can be cured by consuming several bottles of wine each day.
- Breathing in foul air, such as that in a ship's hold where hundreds of sailors live, can cure most diseases.
- Anyone who drinks tea, beer, or wine runs the risk of developing a fatal bile buildup.
- People who are immoral become victims of epidemics; God-fearing Christians never do.[29]

McClurg also believed that any and all diseases could be cured by bleeding the patients to drain out "tainted" blood, by purging the system, or by using the purgatives calomel and castor oil. He was roundly criticized later for assuming that epidemic diseases he had treated were responsible for everything. Experienced doctors wrote in national medical journals to berate him for misdiagnosing victims of the mysterious "cold plague" that took the lives of hundreds of Virginians, many of whom were McClurg's patients, in recurrent outbreaks between 1812 and 1820. He was wrong, they charged, to assume that all of them were victims of yellow fever and to bleed them; the bleeding might have weakened them, drained their bodily defenses against the plague, and ultimately killed them.[30]

McClurg's immediate targeting of bile as the cause of many disorders was debunked by hundreds of patients and their families, for whom the treatment failed badly. Also proven to be misguided was his advocacy of calomel and castor oil to purge the system, a practice used by many patients who followed his advice. One of the most vociferous critics of the theory that bile was a general cause of illness and calomel the cure was President James Monroe, an old friend of McClurg's. The president's doctors treated Mrs. Monroe for a stomach disorder in 1823, suspecting bile, and giving her calomel, among other treatments, to purge her body. She wound up sicker than when the treatment started. The president complained, "Still her nerves are very much affected, she has lost appetite, has frequent fevers and is very weak, so that we cannot say with any confidence that she is convalescent."[31]

McClurg's biggest problem, though, was his soaring ego. He had convinced himself, through his books and journal articles, and others had convinced him via their fawning praise, that he was not only one of the world's greatest medical experts, but one of its finest human beings. Perhaps McClurg described himself best in his tombstone inscription: "Here lies interred the body of James McClurg, M.D. In life, admired and honoured for learning, taste and genius and venerated for virtue; of studious and retired habits—yet of the most easy and polished manners; of the readiest and happiest wit, tempered with modesty and benignity; with a native dignity of character and deportment, always sustained without effort, united with unaffected simplicity and softened with the utmost suavity of temper; formed to delight, instruct and adorn society."[32]

McClurg chided doctors who were not willing to listen to criticism and learn from experience. He insisted that all experts should be challenged and every theory contested. He said of any doctor who stuck with a poor diagnosis, "We are astonished at his unwearied industry whose curious eye seeks everywhere to support for a favorite doctrine." McClurg also said that the notion of medical infallibility had to be banished and all diagnoses scrutinized. "The attempts of the medical system will frequently miscarry," he wrote. Describing the doctor with an incorrect diagnosis, he continued, "His errors are readily detected. His course is regular, and may easily be traced."[33]

This did not apply to him, however. The supremely confident McClurg routinely sneered at anyone who disagreed with his own decisions. He was the great Dr. McClurg; how dare anyone challenge his diagnosis? He thought so little of doctors who disagreed with him that in one article he wrote that those physicians were "no better than mere yahoos."[34]

Regarding cases such as that of George Wythe, in which many people had different opinions than McClurg's, he wrote that the "doctors who see symptoms and presume the disease" were "absurd" and "vulgar." In his book on bile he went further, insisting that everyone had to agree with the experts, such as he, and there could be no dissent. "There is no art . . . which requires in its professors such a perfect harmony opinion as the art of medicine."[35]

He brought this combination of primitive beliefs and haughtiness wherever he went, including to the autopsy room to spend his final minutes with his friend of forty years, George Wythe.

The fabled trio, assisted by two younger doctors, assembled together in their brilliant white surgical aprons to open up the bodies of Judge Wythe and young Michael Brown on the days that they died in early June.

Standard procedure would have been for doctors to first examine Wythe's skin, face, eyes, and hair for any signs of disorder, then his trunk and limbs, and finally his interior organs. One doctor would use a sharp scalpel to make a large "Y" incision in the judge's body, cutting straight lines down from each shoulder to his sternum and then a single line down to his pelvis. The deceased's skin would slowly be peeled back and secured to reveal his skeletal frame and inner systems. The surgeons would then wield a heavy saw to cut through his rib cage and remove it from the body cavity to clear the way for their investigation of his internal organs. Since cartilage turns into a white bone in older people, that same saw would probably be used to cut through cartilage that connected the breastbone to the rib cage of the eighty-year-old jurist, in order to lift the breastbone to examine the chest cavity and the heart.

In autopsies in that era, the chest cavity and the lungs were examined next. The lungs were observed for pneumonia and other abnormalities. Doctors chose which organs to extract, depending on what they were looking for. An arsenic investigation would call for removing the liver and parts of the intestines, plus examining the entire stomach, especially its inner walls, and the fluid in it.

The three doctors knew that they were looking for arsenic. Wythe claimed that he had been poisoned, and his servant had told police that she saw what looked like a powder of some kind being put in the coffee. Witnesses told authorities that Sweeney had asked several people in Richmond where he could procure ratsbane poison. A slave told investigators that he had seen Sweeney pounding a white substance with the flat side of an axe, and that the substance appeared to be sugary crystals that resembled arsenic grains. Sweeney had told a friend that he had arsenic and wanted to kill himself. Finally, a servant girl told investigators that she had found two pieces of wrapped-up paper containing an arseniclike powder in a garden only a few short steps from the jail yard where Sweeney was held. A friend of the three doctors, Samuel McCraw, visited the garden with the authorities, and he said that the papers the girl found not only appeared to have arsenic on them, but they seemed to be the same blotting paper that McCraw had seen in Sweeney's room. Authorities then went to Sweeney's room and found more arsenic there, plus paper identical to that found outside the jail yard wall.

The way that Wythe and Brown had died had all the hallmarks of arsenic poisoning. There was an obvious motive, too. One of Wythe's friends, William DuVal, told the doctors that he was absolutely convinced that Wythe had been poisoned, probably by arsenic, so that Sweeney could gain control of Wythe's estate, pay his gambling debts, and cover up his check forgeries. DuVal told them, and also wrote to Thomas Jefferson, that the case bore an uncanny resemblance to a well-publicized 1780 British murder. In that incident, a twenty-year-old baron, Sir Theodosius Boughton, was poisoned. The suspect was Captain John Donellan, who had been dishonorably cashiered out of the British army. English authorities charged that Donellan had poisoned the baron because Boughton would gain a sizable monetary inheritance on his twenty-first birthday, but if he died before that age, the inheritance would be passed on to Boughton's sister. And to whom was the sister married? None other than Captain Donellan. DuVal argued that Sweeney had done the same thing to get Wythe's money.[36]

THE THREE DOCTORS knew all about arsenic. All doctors did. Arsenic, or, technically, arsenic trioxide, had been employed as an easy-to-use, fast-acting, highly effective, and nearly undetectable poison for almost two thousand years. Arsenic was a favorite of killers because victims could be finished off in a neat, clean fashion. There were no bloody gashes in the body caused by knives or swords and no hideous gunshot wounds. A person could surreptitiously administer a small amount of arsenic into a cup of coffee, for example, where it would dissolve. There was none of the emotional trauma that came with physically murdering someone with a pistol, an axe, or a knife. Since the clear poison was practically undetectable, the killer, if he or she was smart, stood a very good chance of getting away with murder.

A murderer would need only a few grains of arsenic, about 125 mg, to accomplish his or her goal. Arsenic traumatizes enzymes in the body, paralyzes essential body systems, and causes a horrific death. It shocks the body and triggers violent diarrhea or vomiting in anywhere from thirty minutes to several hours (anyone who has had food poisoning knows the frightening initial feeling). The toxic substance is not completely purged by vomiting or diarrhea, though. The arsenic works so quickly that by the time vomiting or diarrhea begins, the poison has already been absorbed. Incessant and painful vomiting or diarrhea that renders the victim helpless continues long after the initial purging and goes on for hours.[37] The victim also experiences sharp pains in the joints, cramps, a dry tongue, a bad sore throat, and continuous pains in the mouth. The person finds swallowing anything to be difficult, suffers severe stomach pains, and feels debilitated. He or she soon runs a high fever, up to 104 degrees. The victim's skin becomes cool, damp, and pale. The blood pressure drops. Traditionally, the individual usually dies within twelve to thirty-six hours or, in terrible deaths, lingers up to four or five days, sometimes longer.

POISONING WAS certainly not new in 1806. Poisons, either arsenic or others, such as hemlock, root of mandrake, wild mushrooms, aconite ("wolf's bane"), and mercury, were mentioned in the writings of the Sumerians as early as 4500 BC. The ancient Greeks used tiny amounts of an arsenic derived from red ore realgar (As_4S_4) and another sulfide mineral, orpiment (As_2S_3), in 200 BC. The Greeks took copper ore with realgar or orpiment and smelted it in vats that they placed in large fires. The arsenic by-product of the ore clung to the sides of the vats as a white film that could be scraped off with a knife and dried into a poisonous powder, arsenic trioxide. The powder dissolved easily in food and even more swiftly in liquid.

The Chinese used an arsenic derivative as a pesticide in 200 BC. At the same time, the Egyptians were using poison found in plants on the banks of the Nile for medicine.

Arsenic and other toxic substances were used in warfare long before the birth of Christ. Soldiers in ancient Greece, Persia, China, and South America put tiny traces of plant poison on the tips of their arrows in order to kill enemy warriors. Poisons were discussed in the Chinese writer Shen Nung's forty-volume work *Chinese Materia Medica* (2735 BC).[38] The Greek Diocles (375–300 BC) wrote about poisons in his works on physical fitness and hygiene. (In addition to warning readers to avoid poison, he also reminded them to brush their teeth every day and to take a nap in the middle of the afternoon.)[39]

The Bible often mentions poison, such as in Deuteronomy 32:33, "poisonous are their grapes and bitter their clusters," and in Jeremiah 08:14, "he has given us poison to drink." Some recent medical scholars have spent a considerable amount of time studying the Bible because they are certain that Job was poisoned with arsenic.[40]

The Roman Empire was riddled with arsenic homicides. Early malevolent powerbrokers who needed to depose an emperor, a king, or a dictator, or men and women who found it necessary to get rid of a wife or a husband rather quickly, found that they could commit murder and get away with it by using arsenic. There were no reliable tests for arsenic then, and defendants could argue that their victims died of long-standing physical maladies. Undetectable arsenic was a perfect murder weapon.

The Greeks and the Romans also used poisons to execute people who were found guilty of crimes. The most famous case was the Greek philosopher Socrates, who was sentenced to death in 399 BC. His friends were permitted to join him in his last hours. The philosopher and writer was then given large goblets full of the poisonous plant hemlock, the official state poison. Socrates died within hours. In Rome, in 200 BC, authorities charged some two hundred unhappy women with conspiring to murder hundreds of men in the city by slipping arsenic into their drinks. An investigation began after several prominent city officials died suddenly after downing goblets of wine. The women were rounded up, but they vehemently insisted that the men's drinks were filled with medicine, not poison. Since the drinks were supposedly harmless, authorities ordered the ladies to drink glasses of their "medicine." They all died.[41]

One of the early Roman practitioners of arsenic murder was Agrippina, who reportedly poisoned her husband with arsenic to free her to marry her uncle, Emperor Claudius, one of Rome's most respected early rulers, in order to promote the fortunes of her emotionally unbalanced son, Nero. She poisoned Claudius's wife, Valeria, and several of his advisers, in order to become the emperor's new bride. Her last step was to murder Claudius, too, with a poisonous mushroom, which allowed her incompetent and power-mad son to become emperor in 54 AD at the age of sixteen. She did not enjoy too much time as the emperor's mother, however, because Nero had her murdered five years later, after his arsenic poisoning of a political rival, Brittanicus. The deranged Nero, of course, gained everlasting fame as the man who "fiddled" while Rome burned in a catastrophic fire that many people accused him of setting.[42]

Murder by poison in the Roman Empire had been practiced long before the ambitious, single-minded Agrippina arrived. It was prolific enough to cause the dictator Sulla to issue a law in 82 BC that made poisoning a crime. Punishment was either loss of property and exile or being ripped apart by beasts. Few murderers were charged, however, because poisoning was hard to prove.[43] In the third century, Emperor Diocletian was so afraid of poisons and of his own murder in politically volatile Rome that he ordered soldiers to burn all of the books about the transmutations of metals and poison derivatives—precious works of science—that he had confiscated in his defeat of the Egyptians.[44]

In the 1500s and the 1600s, politically motivated members of the Italian nobility again turned to arsenic to advance their careers. The two most famous were Cesare Borgia and his sister Lucrezia, a busy woman who, in addition to murdering several people with arsenic, found time to have a baby with her own father, the pope. The Borgias developed a white arsenic trioxide powder that they fondly named "La Cantarella." They dissolved it in wines to get rid of troublesome political foes. Catherine de Medici, from another prominent Italian family, reportedly poisoned both Dauphin François of France and the Cardinal of Lorraine. Nearly a hundred years later a Sicilian woman, known as Toffana, manufactured large amounts of arsenic that she dubbed "Manna of St. Nicholas." Publicly, she sold it as a woman's facial cosmetic, but everyone knew that it would result in an early burial for an unloved husband. Worse, the arsenic solution was made in such a way that a cruel killer could administer it to a victim in very small doses, making him or her sick for months before the killer increased the dose to kill the person. Some victims were poisoned over a year's time span. The lengthy illnesses were also a cover for the poisonings. Toffana's arsenic was reportedly used to kill five hundred people.[45]

European noblemen were poisoned in the fourteenth, fifteenth, and sixteenth centuries. In 1534, Pope Clement VII was poisoned in public as he participated in a somber religious procession through the streets of Rome, which teemed with pilgrims. Someone put arsenic in the base of a torch that an acolyte held while walking directly in front of His Holiness. The pontiff continually breathed in the arsenic in the smoke as he walked, and he eventually collapsed and died. At that same time in Venice, over a number of decades, dozens of politicians were poisoned, usually with arsenic, and records were kept of each murder in the city archives. There were several failed attempts to poison England's Queen Elizabeth I. Prince Alexander, the son of Tsar Peter the Great of Russia, was poisoned by political foes in 1782.[46]

No one made murder by poison more a part of the literary landscape of that era than the British playwright William Shakespeare. Numerous characters in Shakespeare's plays met their dreadful end via poison, such as Hamlet's father, poisoned by Claudius, and Regan, poisoned by her sister Goneril in King Lear. And, of course, there were Romeo and Juliet.

Poison, especially arsenic, became so feared in those years that noblemen and political figures in various European nations employed "tasters" to sample their meals and drinks. If the taster was still healthy after fifteen minutes or so, the public figure happily devoured his meal.

One of the more notorious killers who was brought to justice was the beautiful Marie D'Aubray, the Marquise de Brinvilliers of France, whose father was the mayor of Paris. She coveted the family fortune and murdered her father with an arsenic produced by a boyfriend, only to realize too late that her father's fortune went to her two brothers. She and her lover soon murdered them, too, employing minuscule amounts of arsenic that were not detected. Several years later, her boyfriend's letters were discovered, implicating her in the slayings, and she was beheaded. A Frenchwoman named Catherine Deshayes, nicknamed "La Voisin," sold a homemade brand of arsenic to the mothers of unwanted children; more than two thousand of them were murdered.[47]

Another famous victim was the noted British poet Sir Thomas Overbury. The poet was a friend of King James I's minister Robert Carr, but the two had a falling out, and Carr had Overbury imprisoned in the cold, damp, dreaded Tower of London. There, Carr tried to kill him with poison mixed into his food and drink by prison personnel, but the poet's system somehow rejected it. Three attempts at arsenic poisoning failed but finally, in September 1613, a fourth attempt succeeded and the poet died. The warden of the tower, at the direction of Carr, convened a jury of six jailers and six specially selected prisoners. The men examined the yellowed, emaciated body and found it full of ulcers, sores, and large blisters, all of which had been caused by the four poisonings. The men, aware of the politics involved, agreed that the poet had died of natural causes. To prevent further inquiries, the warden had the body cremated only nine hours later.[48]

In the early 1750s, the Englishwoman Mary Blandy tried to poison her father by mixing arsenic into his food four times. He survived each of the first three attempts but finally died on the fourth. At her trial, a doctor ran four different tests on powder confiscated from Mary's home and showed that the results were identical to tests he then ran on pure arsenic. They put Mary to death in April 1752, after she asked the executioner not to hang her too high because she did not want men in the crowd to look up under her dress.

Love triangles produced a number of poisonings with arsenic and other chemicals throughout the seventeenth and eighteenth centuries, particularly in England and America. Most often, a husband used poison to murder his wife in order to marry another woman with whom he had enjoyed sexual trysts. Similarly, wives with ardent boyfriends employed either arsenic or mercury to dispatch their husbands. Joseph Sager, a farmer in Augusta, Maine, poisoned his wife, Phoebe, in the

MISS BLANDY at the place of Execution near Oxford, attended by the Revd. Mr. Swinton.

Great Britain's Mary Blandy finally killed her husband with arsenic on a fourth attempt, after waiting an agonizing nine days for him to die. Just before she was hanged, she asked the executioner not to hoist her high enough for the men in the audience to look up her skirts.

early 1790s, and the case received so much publicity that more than a thousand people attended his hanging.[49]

Many unsuspecting victims were poisoned for inherited land and money, and arsenic had long ago been nicknamed "inheritance powder."

Some love triangle poisonings took odd turns, such as the case of England's John Cupper of Shrewsbury. Cupper was having a torrid affair with his servant girl Judith Brown, who was eager to become the second Mrs. Cupper. The problem was that the first Mrs. Cupper was very much alive and well. The two conspired to poison Mrs. Cupper in 1684. They were both convicted. Cupper was hanged, and Brown was burned at the stake.[50]

Family feuds were also solved with arsenic. In 1676, the townspeople of Plymouth, England, were shocked when members of a family were found guilty of using arsenic to poison the entire household. In 1677, a sixteen-year-old girl in St. Martin's, England, used ratsbane arsenic to murder her mother, whom she detested. Perhaps to eliminate any witnesses, she poisoned their servant girl as well. She got away with it. Since she was a minor, a local magistrate felt sorry for her and sent the teenager to live with two women who shared a home in a nearby village. The girl was unhappy there and used ratsbane to kill both of them, too.[51]

Records show that arsenic was often employed as a poison around the time of George Wythe's murder, so frequently that forensics specialists called the era the "Age of Arsenic." For example, between 1819 and 1829 in France, there were 221 known cases of murder by poison; two-thirds of them were by arsenic. From 1850 to 1871, 1,000 cases of successful or failed poisonings occurred in that country, and arsenic was used in 331 of them (strychnine accounted for 14 and cyanide for only 5). England had another 1,000 cases of arsenic poisoning in the 1830s, or 100 per year.[52]

Around the same time that Wythe died, a couple in Yorkshire, England, was poisoned in a case that drew much attention in the British press. Mary Bateman, a fortune-teller, whom the British press immediately dubbed the "Yorkshire Witch," decided that two of her clients, William Perrigo and his wife, Rebecca, were ripe for a financial fleecing. In 1806, Bateman explained to the Perrigos that for a price, she could tell them their future. She soon discovered that the gullible Perrigos had a lot of money, and she charged them even more, especially when her guesswork about the Perrigos' immediate futures, through sheer luck, turned out to be pretty accurate. The Perrigos began to ask too many questions, however, and Bateman, fearing exposure, fed them arsenic. Mrs. Perrigo soon died, but her husband survived and, never thinking that his wife had been murdered, continued to consult the surprised fortune-teller.

She demanded a large amount of money to ensure that Perrigo would not go blind. The widower did not go blind, but he did go to the police. They burst into Bateman's home and found a bottle of mercury chloride and a jar of honey laced with arsenic.

The hanging of the fortune-teller in 1809 drew a huge crowd of spectators. Someone decided to raise money for local charities by laying out Mary's corpse on a table and charging the public a fee to view it; hundreds did. Then her body was skinned, and pieces of the skin were sold to townspeople as souvenirs. The hefty profits went to charity.[53]

Murders by poison in America were just as shocking as those in England and Europe at the time of Wythe's death. By the end of the eighteenth century, newspapers frequently carried accounts of them. Murder stories, then and now, sell papers, and articles about poisonings from one city's newspaper were often carried on the pages of another city's. Newspapers often printed lengthy stories of grisly murders by poison, usually with spouses killing each other.

America had poisonings not only among family members, but of masters by their slaves, who often used arsenic. This was something that slave owners in the colonies had feared since the beginning of bondage in the early seventeenth century. The poisoning of whites by black slaves was a serious problem in Virginia and in Richmond during Wythe's last years. Slave "conjurers," or mystics, were renowned for concocting poisons out of the roots of plants or mixing together easily found medicines into toxic substances. Their poisons worked, too. Several hundred murders of whites were committed by blacks using poisons during the eighteenth century and in the first few years of the nineteenth. From 1740 to 1785, slaves were prosecuted in 179 murder trials for poisoning whites and other blacks. Most of the murderers were hanged. From 1800 to 1816, another forty-one slaves were hanged for poisoning their masters. The three doctors all knew of slave poisons and were aware of the elements of the poison mixtures from treating their victims.[54]

Long-term illness was a convenient cover for murder by arsenic. Someone who wanted to get rid of a wife by using arsenic could successfully argue to a doctor and a jury that the deceased had complained of stomach troubles all winter and finally succumbed to them.

Sometimes high levels of arsenic found their way into everyday life and had catastrophic results. In London around 1800, arsenic once turned up in the green coloring used by pastry chefs in icing; dozens of children were poisoned by it. Seven horses in Paris around that same time were accidentally given food with arsenic in it; they all died. One of the most frightening events was the mass arsenic poisoning of more than two hundred people in West Yorkshire, England, in 1858. A candy manufacturer wanted to use a cheaper compound, calcium sulfate, to replace sugar in a batch of peppermint candies. A pharmacist's assistant accidentally sold him twelve pounds of arsenic trioxide instead. Twenty-two people died in the poisoning.

For centuries, arsenic was alluded to in the deaths of several members of the Stuart family, which ruled Scotland in the sixteenth century.

Charles Darwin scholars often claimed that he died of arsenic poisoning over an extended period of time. In one of history's maddening arsenic mysteries, it was at first charged that Napoleon Bonaparte was killed in his exile on St. Helena island by chronic arsenic poisoning, topped off with a dose of mercury cyanide—toxins that were administered by his enemies. Later, others said that he died accidentally by continually breathing in high levels of arsenic that was contained in the coloring of the wallpaper in his home. (In 1960, at the Harwell Nuclear Research Lab of Scotland's University of Glasgow, and in 1965, at the Toxicology Crime Lab of the U.S. Federal Bureau of Investigation, tests conducted on the wallpaper and on hairs from Napoleon confirmed very high levels of arsenic.)[55]

So much was known about body organs through dissection by the end of the eighteenth century that in 1794 the Scottish doctor John Bell was able to write a comprehensive book on organs. His *Engravings Explaining the Anatomy of Bones, Muscles and Joints* was filled with information and sketches. The book was popular in Great Britain and Europe, and copies were sold in the United States. By 1806, Bell's work with organs had been well known in the medical profession around the globe for twelve years but was apparently unknown to the doctors assigned to examine the bones, muscles, joints, and other body parts of Judge Wythe.[56]

A Spanish doctor, Mathieu Bonaventure Orfila, who also dabbled in chemistry, was involved in new studies of body organs and poisons at the time of George Wythe's death. His book on the subject, *Treatise on Poison*, would be published in 1814.[57]

So when the team of Richmond physicians conducted the autopsy on Wythe in the spring of 1806, they knew that arsenic poisoning was a well-known means of murder. Everybody in Richmond was convinced that arsenic had been used to murder the popular old man, and people were certain that the doctors would find it in his body and in young Michael Brown's.

When Dr. McClurg took the stand during the George Wythe Sweeney trial, the courtroom was packed with men in stylish suits and women in their finest dresses. The doctor proceeded to report on the autopsy. He testified that the lower part of the teenager Michael Brown's stomach was severely inflamed and appeared to be filled with black bile, but he did not know what had caused the bile. McClurg, a world-renowned expert on stomach bile, told the jury that he had visited Brown just before he died and said that the boy was running a high fever and had experienced no passage in his bowels for more than twelve hours. His tongue was discolored and "foul." The teenager was very ill, McClurg told the court, and his symptoms *indicated* the *possible* use of arsenic, and that was what the doctor tried to discover in his forensic examination. He could not say with certainty, however, that arsenic had killed Brown.

Shock filled the courtroom. Everyone had been certain that Dr. McClurg's expert opinion would pin down a definitive cause of death. Now the doctor's autopsy report created doubt in the minds of the spectators.

15

The Forensics Nightmare, Part II: The Autopsy

THE EMINENT DR. McCLURG, who was well known as a U.S. political figure and one of the nation's most respected physicians, sat on the witness stand with his notes in front of him and testified about the autopsy of the judge. He told the jury that Wythe's stomach and intestines had a very bloody appearance, far bloodier than expected, which *could* have been produced by arsenic. But, McClurg said with conviction, arsenic should have killed Wythe much sooner than fourteen days. It should have taken his life within a few days, not two weeks. Then, with great authority as a physician who had treated the aging Wythe on a regular basis for a long period of time, the doctor told the jury that other factors, rather than arsenic, might have contributed to Wythe's death. For example, McClurg said that the old man had suffered from very irregular bowels for more than three years and that perhaps his bowel troubles had something to do with his vomiting, diarrhea, and death. His medical history of bowel problems might explain the obvious inflammation and redness of the bowels that the doctors discovered in the autopsy.

McClurg told the jury, as did the other doctors, that when he arrived at Wythe's home on May 25, he had not attributed the judge's violent illness to arsenic poisoning. All three doctors were certain that he was suffering from cholera. The doctors did not oblige the judge in his request for a search of Sweeney's room until two days later. They did find a mixture of arsenic and sulfur there but still did not believe that Sweeney had given him a dose of this.[1]

What had killed the judge, then? McClurg shrugged. It was probably the buildup of black bile, with no connection to arsenic. The defense lawyer must have reminded the jury that few doctors in the world knew as much about black bile as Richmond's Dr. McClurg. He had, after all, written a book on bile. He was one of the world's leading experts on bile.

McClurg continued. He looked at the jurors and, as if lecturing a class of students, carefully explained that the judge had all the symptoms of death by bile. Bile was caused by the dehydration of the body, and Wythe's diarrhea and vomiting had drained his body of its fluids. Bile was a direct product of a high fever; Wythe ran a fever for two weeks. Bile usually affected older people, and Wythe was eighty. It could be fatal in hot weather, and, in the first week of June, summer had already arrived. Black bile could be found in the stomachs of emaciated people, and Wythe was thin, frail, and wan-looking. Bile caused diarrhea and puking, the judge's primary symptoms. Bile affected those who drank wine, and the judge was known for his love of good wine. And, most important, older people who exhibited bowel and stomach disorders for a period of time tended to have a severe buildup of bile. McClurg himself had treated Wythe for bowel problems for three long years. It was bile that had probably killed the judge, McClurg said.[2]

Dr. McCaw took the stand after McClurg and told the jury that he first saw Wythe at 4 P.M. on Monday, May 26, the day after the judge fell ill, in the bedroom of his home. That afternoon Wythe suffered "violent puking and purging," as he had the entire previous day. Dr. McCaw gave him an opiate to serve as a sedative and told the jury that Wythe's health improved after swallowing the medicine. Then, the next day, May 27, after Wythe was told of the check forgeries, he became very ill once more, puking and purging badly. Dr. McCaw tried to treat Wythe, who by then was weak and trembling from pain, but the medicine did no good. According to McCaw, Wythe's condition worsened all week, and he remained very ill until he died. McCaw also said that the examination showed that Wythe's stomach had an enormous amount of black bile, but that it was not necessarily caused by arsenic.

When asked about the teenager, McCaw agreed with McClurg. He said that he thought the boy had died from an extraordinary buildup of bile in his stomach that his body had not been able to pump out. He was not so certain that Michael Brown had been poisoned, either.

Dr. Foushee, too, was tentative in his testimony. He told the jury that when he examined Wythe's stomach with the other medical experts, he was convinced that it was greatly inflamed. He noticed that there was much bile in the stomach but very little in the liver. He offered no further testimony about the liver. It was his expert opinion, Foushee said, that the judge's death *could* have been caused by arsenic or by any other acrid matter that was harsh in taste or smell, but he was *not sure*.

And what about ratsbane? The white powder arsenic compound found in Sweeney's room, and in the paper tossed over the jail yard wall was ratsbane, and everybody knew it. Wythe's friends had been certain that the doctors would attribute his death to ratsbane. Surely, the doctors would have directly connected it to the old man's demise because, probably without much thought, Sweeney had chosen the single most common arsenic poison in the world: the popular ratsbane. Wythe's friends knew that to obtain a conviction for Sweeney, the prosecutors needed the doctors to state conclusively that ratsbane had killed the judge. Yet even if McClurg had sworn that ratsbane was the probable cause of death, the defense attorneys could charge that the common rat poison was found throughout Richmond and the United States and had often been employed to kill rats and other vermin for years. Sweeny had ratsbane in his room? So what? Most people did.

Ratsbane had been the toxin of choice to exterminate rats since the middle of the seventeenth century. Its use was chronicled in medical texts in England as early as 1669, as "rattesbane," and in British oral histories and letters as far back as 1590. It was a quick and effective poison that the British needed to combat the hordes of rats that descended on London and other cities following their arrival on merchant ships. Thousands of the dreaded black rats came ashore each week in busy ports. Rats were often infected with diseases. In the fourteenth century, rats that were brought from port to port on ships carried bubonic plague, which killed one-third of the population of Europe. People were terrified of them.

Ratsbane with its arsenic compound was a welcome weapon when it was developed in the 1650s.[3] Ratsbane became a very popular poison in murders in England but was such a common and widely sold poison that until the latter half of the nineteenth century, the authorities never held any merchants who sold it accountable for homicides committed with it. A bill passed in 1851 required some guidelines for its sale, but they were usually ignored.[4]

When pressed, none of the three Richmond doctors could state categorically that they believed Wythe had been poisoned with ratsbane. They were also inconclusive in their determination regarding the autopsy of Michael Brown. Their combined opinion was simply that both men *might* have been poisoned. Then again, all three doctors agreed, Brown might have died from the bile buildup. They were simply *not sure*.

What defense counsel William Wirt knew and kept silent about was that the three highly regarded physicians had conducted only a single, rather cursory, examination for arsenic and instead had concentrated on the bile in Wythe's stomach, McClurg's specialty, so naturally the exam was inconclusive. Stomach inflammation and the buildup of bile could have accompanied several other stomach or intestinal diseases, the doctors told the jury. Yet the doctors should have known that these symptoms *always* occur with arsenic poisoning; however, they halted their examination. They did not continue the autopsy by conducting numerous other routine tests on the stomach and the intestines to determine whether Sweeney had poisoned his granduncle. They also did not examine other organs of the body, such as the liver, the windpipe, the esophagus, and the eyes, which would have proved whether the judge had been poisoned.

The doctors obviously had to know how to complete an autopsy. They had studied anatomy and witnessed autopsies at the University of Edinburgh, where a course in that subject had been required for students since the 1720s. The head of the university while McClurg studied there had insisted that in all of medicine, "There is nothing that has been of more service than the dissection of morbid bodies." The three doctors

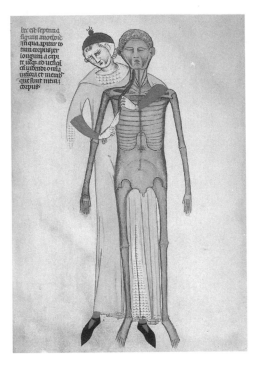

The Chinese were performing dissections and autopsies long before the English and the British were, as illustrated in this 1300s painting of the body and the organs of a Chinese man.

In the eighteenth century, autopsies and dissections were conducted in medical colleges in front of large groups of students and townspeople.

also worked with cadavers at nearby hospitals that the university used as training centers.[5] They should have read all of the most important medical textbooks and journals, as evidenced by their knowledge of cholera. Yet they halted the autopsy, eliminating numerous steps that would have enabled them to determine whether arsenic was in the various bodily systems and organs of the boy and the judge.

Several well-known textbooks on autopsies had been published during the three doctors' careers, which they should have read or at least consulted. These works detailed numerous autopsy case studies for every possible cause of death. The most prominent was Théophile Bonet's *Sepulchretum:sive anatomia practica ex cadaveribus morbo denalis*, published in Lyons, France, in 1693, which featured a compilation of more than three thousand autopsies. Two other noted medical texts on autopsies were published while McClurg was a student at Edinburgh and had easy access to them. Joseph Lieutaud wrote *Historia anatomica medica*, a two-volume study published in Paris in 1767, which included the case studies of several hundred autopsies. (McClurg worked as a resident in Paris from 1771 to 1773.) In 1769, Giovanni Battista

The German physician Johann Kulmus is shown here preparing to begin an autopsy, one of many that were performed in Great Britain and Europe in the late eighteenth century.

Morgagni published *De sedibus et causis morborum* (Seats and Causes of Disease, Investigated by Anatomy), a massive three-volume set of hundreds of his autopsies and analyses. The autopsies enabled him to discover the causes of infantile cerebral palsy and to determine that lesions on the brain cause paralysis. The individual analyses were the most complex ever published, and in case after case, Morgagni explained how doctors examined all of the major organs of the body to detect poisons, abrasions, heart damage, and clogged arteries. In addition to those texts, McClurg and the others should have read about Dr. John Pringle's exhaustive studies of diseases contracted by British soldiers in America's French and Indian War, 1756–1763, and other conflicts. His analyses of autopsies were collected and published in *Observations on the Diseases of the Army* in 1774.[6]

The three surgeons were veteran physicians and should have been reading all of the medical books and journals of the day to keep abreast of advances in medicine. They had easy access to these books. The bookstores in America sold British medical books and translations of European medical texts. Nearly every doctor in the United States belonged to Britain's Royal Society of London and as a member was mailed its medical journal. Most U.S. doctors were also members of the American Philosophical Society, a medical group, and could obtain its literature. Many American newspapers reprinted articles from British newspapers on English and European diseases and their treatments. There were even self-help medical books for the average reader that the three doctors could have consulted, such as John Tennent's *Every Man His Own Doctor; or the Poor Planter's Physician.*

They all knew doctors who had performed autopsies and surely had performed some themselves. They all had had opportunities to hear one of the many lectures delivered by leading autopsy specialists, such as Rhode Island's Dr. William Hunter, who gave numerous public talks on anatomy. These three Richmond doctors should have known how to perform a complete autopsy.[7]

The trio should also have been aware of the many tests that would have conclusively proved whether George Wythe and Michael Brown had been murdered with a dose of arsenic in their coffee.[8]

The standard test was to submerge in a solution pieces of flesh cut from an autopsied human body and then to bubble hydrogen sulfide gas through the solution. If the flesh contained arsenic, there would be a yellow precipitate (leftover sediment) of arsenic sulfide present. This test had been used for years, yet the doctors not only neglected to perform it, but did not take any biopsies of Wythe's organ tissue.[9] In another chemical procedure used at the time, a suspected arsenic fluid was tested in three ways. First, it was mixed with hydrochloric acid and then hydrosulfuric acid. The two acids washed the solution. If a yellow precipitate appeared, the solution contained arsenic. In a second test, a solution of silver nitrate and ammonia was applied to a fluid that was suspected of containing arsenic. Again, a yellow precipitate indicated arsenic. The third test required doctors to mix ammonia with copper sulfate and to use that mixture to wash the suspected arsenic solution; the result would be an apple-green precipitate. None of these three tests by itself was considered conclusive, but if all three indicated arsenic, chemists of the day were certain that it definitely was arsenic.[10] The trio of Richmond doctors did not conduct any of these tests. They demonstrated no awareness of the work published only months earlier by the German chemist Valentin Ross, whose tests detected different types of poison in the walls of the stomach. And Ross's work was merely an expansion of similar experiments conducted thirty years before that by the Swedish chemist Carl Wilhelm Scheele.

Primitive, but effective, tests had been used in autopsies to discover poison for hundreds of years. The simplest was for the doctor to dip his finger into the deceased's stomach fluid and taste it. Stomach fluid turns acrid when exposed to arsenic. If the solution has a foul taste, it is poison. In the 1570s, it was charged that the Scottish regent Morton had poisoned the Earl of Atholl, Scotland's treasurer, at a banquet. The accusation was so serious and was believed by so many that the king ordered an autopsy to be performed by five surgeons. Three of them said the earl had been poisoned, but two could not make up their minds. Several Edinburgh public officials were asked to witness the autopsy, and most of them ruled the death to be murder by poison. A randomly chosen citizen was brought in, who took one look at the Earl of Atholl's inflamed insides, jerked his head back in revulsion, and told the inquest that it was "cold poyson." Then one of the doctors at the autopsy performed the taste test. He gagged, collapsed, and nearly died.[11]

In 1611, an autopsy was performed on the Scottish nobleman George Home, the Earl of Dunbar. In an unusual twist on the common poison test, the doctor conducting the autopsy put stomach fluid on his finger, rubbed the fluid on the earl's heart, and then licked it. The doctor slumped to the ground and died several days later.

Another common and easy-to-perform test was to carefully examine the stomach. Sometimes the bodies of people who had been killed with arsenic still contained visible traces of it as tiny grains stuck to the stomach lining. By this easy test, nineteenth-century physicians were occasionally able to determine exactly how many grams of arsenic had been ingested. In one case, doctors found 154 grams of arsenic in the stomach of a suitor poisoned by a Glasgow, Scotland, woman who had fallen in love with another man.[12]

More efficient tests were developed later, after Wythe's demise. In 1836, the English scientist John Marsh developed a procedure in which body tissue was heated with acids that dissolved organic matter and any arsenic in the tissue. The poisoned liquid was then converted into the gas arsine (AsH_3). Metallic zinc was next added to the acidified solution to ascertain whether the deceased had been poisoned. In 1842, Edgar Reinsch devised another test in which a piece of copper foil was dipped into a fluid made from the dissolved body tissue. The copper strip was then heated to show whether any arsenic residue had been deposited on it.[13]

When doctors in Europe and America, circa 1806, suspected that arsenic had caused a death but found it difficult to determine this conclusively, they ignored the autopsy and ran tests on any powder that looked like arsenic that had been confiscated from the alleged killer's residence. Guilt would seem obvious if that powder proved to be arsenic. A common two-step test, which by 1806 had been used for more than sixty years, was simply to burn the confiscated powder on an iron fireplace poker and smell it to see whether an acrid arsenic smell was produced by the flame. The second step was to rub bona fide arsenic onto the poker and burn it, to see whether the smells matched each other.

Another method was to wash the suspicious confiscated powder in a bowl of warm water and then slowly decant it to see whether the substance tended to stick to the sides of the bowl. Doctors would then use a knife to scrape the powder that stuck to the bowl. Arsenic that was washed with water would oxidize and turn into a black powder. If the knife turned black, the substance was arsenic.[14] Or the Richmond doctors could have performed the following water test: dissolve white arsenic powder in a bowl of water for an extended period of time. The arsenic powder would produce large crystal grains, like sugar, that would expand in the water to a size that was easy enough to spot with the naked eye.[15] The doctors could have tried this with the arsenic found in the paper tossed into the garden from the jail, as well as on the mixture of arsenic and sulfur found in Sweeney's room. One more reliable test was simply to put pieces of charcoal into a test tube with the confiscated arsenic powder and heat it. The arsenic would then stick to the outside and inside edges of the remaining charcoal flakes as a white crust, which would be obvious to the eye. In his landmark 1845 book on toxicology, A Treatise on Poisons, in Relation to Medical Jurisprudence, Physiology, and the Practice of Physic, Professor Robert Christison of Edinburgh University wrote that the popular charcoal test was foolproof, and that the arsenic grains that turn to a crust "are imitated by no substances in nature."[16] It would have been the perfect way to prove that the white powder confiscated from Sweeney was arsenic, but the Richmond doctors never conducted this test.

If the arsenic found in Sweeney's room and outside the jail wall had been unwrapped and exposed to air for a prolonged period of time, it would have turned into a fine, gray powder called "fly powder." A common arsenic used to kill flies (sold commercially as "King's Yellow" in just about any apothecary or general store), the gray powdered arsenic could have been placed in a metal test tube and heated. If the powder was arsenic, it would have turned into a white crystalline powder with a metallic crust. In another heat test of the era, the doctors could have heated the powder with a type of carbonaceous matter. If the combination, heated at 425 degrees Fahrenheit, turned into a crystalline powder, this would have proved it was arsenic. Since it was suspected that Sweeney used ratsbane to kill his uncle, ratsbane procured from a druggist could have been tested and matched against the powder found in Sweeney's room.

These were only a few tests available at the time. There were so many others that could have been conducted, and that had been undertaken in numerous other autopsies, that when Christison wrote his medical text, he devoted a hundred pages to descriptions of arsenic; forty of those pages detailed the various tests to detect the poisonous substance. In fact, Christison wrote "that there are few substances in nature, and perhaps hardly any other poison, whose presence can be detected in such minute quantities and with so great certainty." Yet the Richmond doctors did not conduct *any* of those tests.[17]

The men on the jury, who could not know anything about forensics testing, believed that the highly praised doctors were among the best in the nation. Surely, the jurors assumed, the trio had done everything medically possible to determine whether Wythe had been poisoned. In addition to their expertise, the three men were political associates and close personal friends of Wythe's and, more than anyone, would have wanted to solve his murder.

But, in fact, the very best doctors in Virginia had completely botched the autopsies of both the justice and the teenage boy. They were given as much time as they needed, yet they did nothing more than open the body and look at a few different organs, note the areas of inflammation and discoloration, and agree that the stomach had a bile buildup. They did not perform any of the standard tests to discover arsenic and even ignored the simple 240-year-old taste test that would have at least alerted them to a poison of some kind. The autopsies that should have conclusively proved that arsenic was responsible for the deaths of Michael Brown and George Wythe were, in short, colossal forensics failures.

Even worse, the doctors ignored the well-known signs of arsenic poisoning that they should have noticed in Wythe while he was alive, on the very first day that they were summoned to his bedside, as well as when he was dead. The justice first complained of hot skin, then later of cold, clammy skin. He told those who visited him that he felt drained and weak, which, along with low blood pressure, was a symptom of arsenic poisoning. He exhibited all of the classic signs of arsenic poisoning, so much so that the doctors should have realized that no other cause of death was possible.

In the autopsy, the doctors did not carefully check Wythe's liver and kidneys.[18] According to Joseph Plenck's *Elementa medicinae et chirurgiae forensis*, which had been published twenty-five years earlier, general autopsy procedure at the time was to check all of the body's vital organs for signs of poisoning, not only the stomach, which was always red and inflamed in arsenic deaths. Arsenic was sometimes not apparent in one organ but might be detectable in another.[19] None of the doctors examined Wythe's liver for anything but bile; it would have shown signs of deterioration caused by arsenic. No one thought to look at the victims' eyes to see whether they had been damaged by arsenic; the eyes would usually display conjunctivitis, which was another tell-tale sign of poisoning.[20]

The investigation should have led the doctors to suspect a type of ratsbane or another vermin arsenic, in white crystalline powder form. Those poisons result in a pattern of damage to the body that is similar to Wythe's symptoms before and after death. The types of arsenic in that family produce purging within eight hours, headaches, and a period of delirium and convulsions, and they bring on kidney failure and jaundice. Postmortem, vermin poisons cause the rupture of gastrointestinal blood vesicles, which results in extensive bleeding and severe inflammation in the stomach and gives the stomach lining a very red hue.[21]

McClurg, McCaw, and Foushee contended that a buildup of black bile in young Michael Brown's stomach might have killed him. They were seemingly unaware that a buildup of black bile was perhaps the most common sign of arsenic poisoning. In fact, European doctors had removed as much as three pounds of black bile from the stomachs of arsenic victims.[22]

McClurg seemed to suggest that much of the inflammation he found in Wythe's stomach and intestines was connected to bowel irregularities that the deceased had experienced for some time; the physician therefore dismissed the inflammation as unimportant. Yet doctors in England had previously detected arsenic poisoning in other men who had also exhibited bowel disorders for extended periods of time. In fact, the reddened inflammation that the doctors found in Wythe's bowels was proof that arsenic had poisoned the judge. European doctors had also found that the longer a victim lingered from arsenic poisoning, the redder the inner coat of the stomach became. But the Richmond doctors did not check that coloring, either.[23]

Foushee was next to testify. He said that he had examined Wythe's stomach, intestines, and liver. He, too, said that the stomach and the intestines were inflamed and the stomach was bloated with black bile. He did examine the liver but only for bile. He did not offer any opinion on the amount of damage, if any, that might have been done to the liver. Arsenic always damages the liver; bile has nothing to do with arsenic in the liver.

The doctors did not examine the lungs to see whether they had a redness that would have indicated arsenic poisoning or the inner surface of the heart, which would have had a pinkish hue if arsenic had been present in the bloodstream. The doctors did not check the windpipe or the esophagus, which would have been inflamed and red, especially in victims who had lingered for some time. There was no scrutiny of the justice's penis, which, after two weeks of arsenic in the body, would have started to turn black.

The biggest mistake they made was in assuming that arsenic had not been used because Wythe died two long weeks after becoming ill. The teenager had lingered for a full week. McClurg testified that if Wythe had been poisoned, he should have died much sooner. The doctor had accepted the common belief that arsenic kills all victims within twelve to thirty-six hours, and that in really slow arsenic deaths, the patient lingers up to four days. Wythe had lived for fourteen days, far too long for arsenic poisoning, McClurg contended. His view of arsenic as an immediate killer was shared by many. Just nine years later, in 1815, most of the population of London was outraged at the conviction of Eliza Fenning, a servant, on charges that she had poisoned a family of five by lacing their apple dumplings with arsenic. Although they all became ill and exhibited all of the symptoms of arsenic poisoning, none had died. Many residents tried to get her conviction overturned because they could not believe that people who had been poisoned with arsenic could live.

The Richmond doctors should have known that while patients usually died within thirty-six hours, there had been a considerable number of cases in which victims had lingered much longer. One Frenchman who had been poisoned with arsenic lived for six days. In a famous European case, Mrs. Mary Blandy slipped arsenic into her husband's dinner; he lived for nine days. Another French victim lived for three weeks. Doctors in Europe reported dozens of cases of arsenic victims living more than two weeks, and one person miraculously survived for ten weeks. Many more people who had been poisoned with very small amounts of arsenic by amateur killers remained ill for weeks, even months, but then lived. Later investigations showed that depending on the dosage, many victims of fatal arsenic poisoning lived for four weeks or more before expiring.

The doctors should have been aware that the amount of time it takes for someone to die from arsenic is due to several critical factors. One is the amount of the dose. Large doses, nine or ten grains of arsenic powder, or 200 mg or so, can kill someone in only a few hours. Fewer grains of the dose take longer to achieve their effect, and men and women who are poisoned with 125 mg or less, or only three grains or less, take much longer, usually days, to die.

Another factor to consider is whether the victim has eaten anything prior to the poisoning. People who have not consumed any type of food, even fruit or crackers, die much more quickly than those who have because there is nothing in the stomach to absorb the arsenic and prevent it from going directly into the bloodstream. A person who has just eaten a meal and is then poisoned tends to vomit up the food in his stomach within minutes, thus purging out part of the arsenic dose. All three residents of the Wythe household had finished a full breakfast with their coffee that morning and experienced violent bouts of purging directly afterward. The coffee itself was also a factor. Warm solutions cause arsenic to dissolve very quickly and to act rapidly. Tests done around the time of Wythe's murder showed that people who were poisoned with arsenic in their coffee reacted to it very quickly and began purging within ten minutes.[24] Finally, there is age and metabolism. Older people tend to live longer when poisoned; children usually die much sooner. Some people have a slower body metabolism that causes arsenic to work less rapidly. Just as there were dozens of cases in which victims lived for many weeks, there were also many instances of death within only a few hours. One fourteen-year-old girl in England who was intent on killing herself took 90 grams of arsenic and died in five hours. A man who ingested an ounce of arsenic died in four hours. In another suicide case, a man consumed a quarter pound of arsenic; he died in two hours. Back in that era, the basic arsenic ore bases, realgar and orpiment, were still sold in stores, and they worked quickly. In a case reported at the time, a German woman who was poisoned with realgar had died within a few hours after her stepdaughter mixed it into her red cabbage soup. A dog that swallowed orpiment died in nine hours.[25] In addition, because George Wythe's friends suspected arsenic poisoning, they might have given him daily doses of magnesium, which was thought to be an antidote at the time and which might have slowed the arsenic from acting in his system. The medicine might have prolonged his life.

What the doctors should have concluded was that eighteen-year-old Sweeney, despite all of his planning, knew very little about poisoning. He simply poured too small a dose of arsenic into the coffeepot, a dose so tiny that it took days to work. That misjudgment on Sweeney's part was compounded by his administering arsenic with a large meal. These were the primary reasons why the poison took so long to kill.

Another mistake the doctors made was in assuming that any type of gastrointestinal illness could have caused Wythe's death, as they contended at the trial and for years afterward. In fact, their examination of Wythe, Broadnax, and Brown before two of the victims died, along with the cursory exams that were conducted during Brown's and Wythe's autopsies, should have proved to the doctors that the deterioration of the bodies and the victims' very specific symptoms could *only* have been caused by arsenic poisoning.[26]

What happened? Didn't the three best doctors in Virginia, perhaps even in America, know about the tests for arsenic that most of the medical profession seemed to be aware of? Didn't they remember what they had been taught about arsenic and poisons at their alma mater, the University of Edinburgh, the preeminent school in the world for the study of arsenic poisoning? Hadn't they read the dozens of books about arsenic and its detection that were written in the centuries prior to the judge's death? Or the thick encyclopedia that defined dozens of poisons, including arsenic, in English, which was published in London in 1661? Or a manual about arsenic symptoms, A *Treatise of Poisons Vegetable, Animal and Mineral, with Their Cure*, by J. Cooke, that had been in print since 1770?[27]

Hadn't they read the medical journals, as doctors were supposed to do? In 1806, there were more than thirty regularly published medical journals in Great Britain, Europe, and the United States, and articles about arsenic poisoning and its detection were printed in most of them.[28]

McClurg had studied medicine in Edinburgh and had then done postgraduate work in London and Paris. British medical journals had been published in London since the 1770s; they all contained articles not only about arsenic and toxicology, but about homicide trials for arsenic poisoning. Among these were *The Transactions of a Society for the Improvement of Medical and Chirurgical Knowledge*, the *London Medical Journal*, the *London Medical Review and Magazine*, *Medical Communications of the Society for Promoting Medical Knowledge*, *Medical Facts and Observations*, the *Medical Museum*, *Medical Observations and Inquiries by a Society of Physicians in London*, the *Medical and Physical Journal*, the *Medical Spectator*, and the *Medical Transactions of the Royal College of Physicians*. Of course, they could also have subscribed to their alma mater's *Edinburgh Medical and Surgical Journal*, which probably published more accounts of arsenic poisoning and its detection than any medical book or journal in the world during that era.

All of the medical journals featured articles on arsenic and tests for detecting it and provided accounts of arsenic murder trials. The English-language publications, especially those from London and Edinburgh, carried numerous articles on arsenic detection, as did dozens of French and German medical journals. These were all published during the last decades of the eighteenth century and in the early years of the nineteenth century. In fact, the very year that Wythe died, a German medical journal published yet another article on arsenic poisoning and its effects.[29]

In the United States, by even easier delivery access, the physicians could have subscribed to the *Transactions of the College of Physicians of Philadelphia* (available since 1793), the *New York Medical Repository* (since 1797), *Transactions of the Medical Society for the State of New Jersey* (since 1766), *Medical Communications of the Medical Society of the Massachusetts Medical Society* (since 1790), and the *Philadelphia Journal of Medical and Physical Sciences*. The latter was a publication that McClurg himself wrote for, and, by 1806, it had been in print for nearly twenty years.

A few years after the judge's death, the world's medical journals routinely began to publish articles about arsenic murders and their detection. The journals used crimes from around the turn of the century as case studies and usually got their information from old newspaper articles. Some of these specifically described detection tests, such as "Some Remarks on the Use of Nitrate of Silver for the Detection of Minute

Portions of Arsenic," "Observations on the Best Methods of Detecting Poisonous Substances Taken into the Stomach, Particularly Arsenic," and "Case of Recovery from Arsenic, with Remarks on a New Mode of Detecting the Presence of This Metal." In 1812, one author even wrote an article for the *Medical and Physicians Journal* in London, in which he discussed numerous specific cases of arsenic homicide during recent years.[30]

The doctors should have read the many published articles that dealt with the signs of arsenic poisoning—signs that they ignored in their autopsies of Wythe and Brown. For example, in 1799 the *London Medical Review and Magazine* carried an article specifically on the condition of the penis and the scrotum caused by arsenic ingestion. Articles were written about ways to discover traces of arsenic in autopsies, too.[31]

Articles about arsenic murders filled the *Newgate Calendar*, which was the English publication that chronicled the most important trials at Old Bailey, the premier London courthouse. Newspaper accounts of those trials were read by thousands of Londoners, who seemed to have developed a thirst for news about gruesome slayings. The three doctors had to have been familiar with those articles and trials.

In fact, during Dr. McClurg's final year of study at the University of Edinburgh, 1770, the *Newgate Calendar* and British newspapers accorded heavy press coverage to Robert Evans and William Evans, who were tried for murdering an elderly spinster by sprinkling white arsenic powder in her cup of gin. Doctors who autopsied the woman found the arsenic while performing a routine examination of her stomach, something that the doctors in Richmond did not do.

There were murder and attempted-murder cases very similar to Wythe's, too, as would have been apparent in any reading of the *Newgate Calendar* or British newspapers, which were available in America. Just six weeks prior to Wythe's poisoning, there was a strikingly similar case in London. Henry Wyatt, fifteen, was accused of stealing arsenic powder from the workshop of James Goldsmith, which Goldsmith had used to kill rats. Wyatt then sprinkled the powder into a pot of coffee on a Sunday morning before Goldsmith and his wife and daughter went to church. The three fell ill instantly. The teenage Wyatt then carefully took what appeared to be a sip of coffee from the pot, making certain that Mrs. Goldsmith saw him do so. He did not become sick.

The Richmond doctors also would have learned from these stories and hundreds of others that many victims of rat poisoning, such as the judge, lived for two weeks or more before dying or, as in the case of Lydia Broadnax and others, survived.

In almost all arsenic cases in London and America, druggists testified that people were sold ratsbane, wrapped in a paper package, to poison rats that had overrun their homes. It was a common procedure and one that Sweeney himself followed.[32]

The trio of Richmond doctors did not seem to be aware of all the possible tests for arsenic that were rather commonplace. In fact, tests to discover arsenic were so well-known that following Wythe's death, his neighbor William Claiborne applied fire to the white powder residue on the wheelbarrow where Sweeney had pounded the white substance. The fire mixed with the residue to create a particular smell that Claiborne, a layman with no medical training at all, immediately knew was arsenic just from his own general knowledge of arsenic tests. If an untrained layman such as Claiborne could detect arsenic with a simple test of fire, why couldn't three of the best doctors in the United States?[33]

Did the Richmond physicians care about finding truth and justice in this case? What can account for their negligence? For one thing, they were general practitioners, not experts on chemistry or toxins. McClurg disdained doctors who were chemical authorities and saw them as nuisances at best or, at worst, quacks. He wrote condescendingly of them, "While the knowledge of chemists was confined to the operations within the laboratory, their art, though destined to throw a light on so many parts of nature, was full of mystery and confusion. The variety of phenomena, multiplied by every day's experience, inspired an admiration that arose to enthusiasm, and gave probability to their absurdest fancies. . . . They behold everywhere the operation of acid, alkalis, nitre and sulphur; and corrupted the theory of medicine."[34]

Or did McClurg merely ignore all signs of arsenic poisoning? Did he simply open up his friend's stomach, see the huge buildup of black bile, and, being one of the world's foremost experts on bile, immediately assume that black bile killed Wythe? Why go any further? Did the egomaniacal McClurg turn to his colleagues, point to the bile, announce his decision, and tell them there was no need for further tests? Did the

other two, who knew that McClurg was the expert on bile, stare down
at the bile in Wythe's stomach, shrug their shoulders, and decide that
he had to be right? McClurg had literally written the book on bile, and
it was such a well-respected book that it had been published in numerous languages. Who was Foushee to question his close friend, the great
doctor, the signer of the Constitution, the man who had followed him
as mayor, his friend on the city council, the man who was twice almost
the secretary of state? Who was the much-younger McCaw to challenge McClurg, whose textbook on bile he had studied as a student at
Edinburgh and whom he looked up to as one of the finest physicians in
America? McClurg, who had paid for McCaw's medical education and
let the youth live in his Richmond mansion? And how could young
McCaw doubt his own uncle?

Or had all three of the physicians who performed the autopsy and
who held so many public offices among them spent so much time and
effort becoming good politicians that they had forgotten how to be
good doctors?

The Virginia court was just as responsible as the doctors were for
the bungled investigation and autopsy. If there were lingering doubts
about the cause of death, and there were among thousands of people,
the courts always could have ordered Wythe's body disinterred and
autopsied again for signs of arsenic. In Europe at that time, it was
common practice for bodies that had been buried, even those lying in
graves for several months, to be exhumed and autopsied. One man's
body was dug up after fourteen months so that doctors could examine
the corpse; they found arsenic poisoning. In one notable case, arsenic
was found in the corpse of a man who had been buried in a cemetery for
three years.[35] Digging up Wythe's slowly decaying body several months
later would have enabled doctors to prove conclusively whether he
was poisoned with arsenic because the decomposition of the body after
several weeks releases hydrogen gases in the corpse. These mix with
any arsenic in the body to create numerous large bright-yellow streaks
and patches on the coating of the stomach and sometimes the large
intestine. These vivid yellow patches, undeniable evidence of arsenic
poisoning, would have been noticed immediately in a second autopsy.
They would have created a bizarre yellow finger pointing up from the
grave at young George Sweeney. The doctors should have known about

this from the numerous articles about the odd postmortem coloring of the stomach that frequently appeared in medical journals.[36]

The doctors' inability to find a cause of death and to state categorically that while it *might* have been arsenic, it might have been something else, or was, as McClurg insisted, stomach bile, shocked everyone. It did not shock William Wirt, however. The defense attorney had known the conclusion of the trio's autopsy ever since he took the case because the most informed man in the state, the governor, had told him what the doctors had found.

Dr. McClurg, always eager to ingratiate himself with important political figures, had let it slip in a conversation with Virginia governor Thomas Cabell soon after the autopsy that the results were inconclusive. A surprised Cabell, who should have known better, immediately informed Wirt of the autopsy findings. It was highly improper for the governor to do so because he represented the state of Virginia, and it was the state that was prosecuting George Sweeney. The governor was secretly informing the defense counsel of privileged information.

Why? Because Wirt was his brother-in-law.

So Wirt knew all along that according to the doctors, the autopsy showed no cause of death. He was thus able to frame an entire line of questioning to pound away at the doctors' inability to conclude what killed the old man and to showcase their reluctance to attribute his death to arsenic.

There was much confusion in the courtroom and the jury box when the three doctors finished their testimony. Jurors and courthouse attendants had been convinced by the rumors that swept through the city that the two decedents had been poisoned; now they were perplexed. The weak and inconclusive autopsy reports had turned the case upside-down. If the judge's teenage nephew had not poisoned him, how did he die? Did Wythe, in fact, die of natural causes? Few people lived to be eighty in 1806. Maybe Wythe had died of a common malady connected to old age and the inability of the elderly to fight off diseases and physical trauma. Maybe McClurg, who had treated Wythe for years, was right. Perhaps his lengthy bowel disorders had brought about his death. Maybe it was the black bile in his stomach that had killed him. Perhaps he had merely died of old age.

But if Wythe had died from old age, what had happened to Michael Brown? He was only sixteen and a very healthy young man. He hadn't died of old age. What had killed him?

Most of the townspeople believed that both men had died from arsenic poisoning. Through gossip and rumors, they had heard that Sweeney did have ratsbane arsenic in his room, had used an axe to cut it into fine grains, and had thrown papers full of it over the jailhouse wall. Now, however, the doctors could not prove that he had used arsenic to kill his uncle. Jurors could not hang someone for having rat poison in his possession, even the illegal, very powerful ratsbane that could be procured by anyone. Different types of rat poison were readily available in downtown stores to whoever asked for it. Many people in Richmond used it to rid their homes and warehouses of rodents in the vermin-infested city where new buildings were being constructed every day and the streets were strewn with garbage. The construction and the refuse attracted large armies of rats that swarmed throughout the city, to the dismay of the residents, who used all of the poison they could procure to kill the ugly rodents. If the jury hanged Sweeney for keeping rat poison in his room, they would have to hang half the population of Richmond.

The doctors' bungled autopsy had cast a huge shadow of doubt over Sweeney's guilt.

Ah, but there was an eyewitness to the poisoning, and a very reliable one: the chancellor's cook of more than twenty years, Lydia Broadnax. Chemical tests were one thing, but an eyewitness description of a murder was another. Lydia had seen the teenager pour the poison into the coffee pot with her own eyes. Her testimony would surely send Sweeney to the gallows.

16

Lydia Broadnax: The Eyewitness

I N ADDITION TO THE AUTOPSY REPORT, which everyone had been certain would reveal that Wythe had been poisoned by Sweeney, the prosecution had Wythe's black freedwoman cook Lydia Broadnax. She was an unimpeachable eyewitness to the murders of Wythe and Michael Brown and, in fact, to her own attempted murder. Broadnax had been a faithful slave and later a freed servant of George Wythe's for more than twenty years. She admired the judge so much that she asked her sister to name her two sons after him (Philip and Benjamin Wythe Judah).[1] The personable Lydia possessed a sterling reputation among both black and white Richmonders. She was trusted by all. No one could be counted on more than Lydia to tell the truth about the events of the morning that the entire household had fallen so ill.

She was the perfect eyewitness for several reasons: (1) she said that she saw Sweeney pour what she assumed was arsenic out of a piece of white paper into the coffee; (2) she saw Sweeney reading Wythe's will, in which Wythe left half of his estate to Brown; (3) she knew Sweeney well; (4) she must have known that Sweeney had stolen books and other things from the judge and that Wythe was angry about the thefts; (5) she undoubtedly had known about the forged checks; and (6) she had no motive to lie about the incident. Disparaging or protecting Sweeney did not help or hurt her at all. And in addition to those reasons for her

credibility, all of the judges and the attorneys involved in the case had
known Lydia for years through the judge. Most people were certain that
her testimony would bring about a guilty verdict and a hanging.

Lydia's damning testimony did not worry defense attorneys William
Wirt or Edmund Randolph at all. They knew that Lydia Broadnax would
never be permitted to take the stand. Lydia Broadnax was black.

RICHMOND HAD BEEN a mixed-race city since it became the state capital
in 1780. The city was like no other in the South. Its busy shipyards and
new manufacturing mills required thousands of slaves to assist immigrants from around the world and local laborers in work that made the
city so prosperous. Richmond was surrounded by tobacco plantations
whose owners sent millions of pounds of tobacco to Richmond for rolling, packing, and shipping to U.S. and foreign ports each year. Over the
last two decades of the eighteenth century, the rapids of the James River
above Richmond had become a source of waterpower for mills in town.
The city was soon home to a string of large grain and flour mills that used
waterpower to operate their machines and slaves to do the work. The
combination of industrial and shipping needs meant that Richmond
required a huge labor force. There were far too few whites to fill the
ever-growing number of jobs; slaves were essential, and lots of them.

City slavery, though, was quite different from plantation bondage.
On the plantation, slaves were housed on the farm, were fed on the
farm, and worked on the farm. In the city, slaves had to be housed in
town and fed wherever it was possible, and they worked in numerous
places. To profit from slave labor, the city industries had to reinvent
slave life. Slaves had to live wherever housing could be found, eat
on their own, and work in places where they had the proper skills
and experience. Most important, slaves had to be hired from their
owners. The shippers and the mill operators did not want to own
slaves but merely wanted to profit from their work. These employers
hired the slaves from their plantation or city owners and brought
them to the shipyards or the mills. Under the terms of these contracts,
the slaves were given money for rent and food, and they found housing wherever they could. Since they lived on their own, slaves had
enormous freedom. At the end of the workday, they could dine out at

restaurants, go shopping, visit taverns, gamble, attend races, romance women, and do just about everything that white citizens did. No one cared as long as they were back at work the next day.

Slaves were usually hired out for a year but could be hired for shorter periods of time, even a single day. Employers liked this flexibility because it saved them money. They had to pay yearly wages to free white workers and keep them employed, but they could hire slaves to work when business was good and release them when it was bad. When poor harvests hit the tobacco industry, companies could simply release their slave workers and save enormous amounts of money. Even overall hiring on yearlong contracts was a cost-saver for industries. The average male slave could be hired out at $70 per year. To buy that same slave cost $900. Another benefit to hiring slaves to work in the city was that the abundance of labor for factories and the docks made it difficult for slaves to stage work slowdowns, as they often did on plantations.[2]

Many Richmonders warned the leaders of industry that hiring slaves was a bad idea. They said that slaves did not have the motivation to work that free white workers had, they could not learn the skills of particular trades, and they were lazy. Richmonders also argued that whites would not work alongside black slaves. Finally, they stated that slaves given money and so much freedom would continually demand more of each and in time would rebel against the system and seek the same freedom that the white men beside them had.

Slaves with special skills who could work in various industries had been living in Richmond for years. During the Revolution, the government had selected hundreds of slaves and put them to work in lead and iron mines in the area to make ammunition for the Continental Army. After the war, they had continued to work in these industries or in related jobs in the city. Hundreds of others worked on the small ships that made up part of the American Navy, serving as repairmen, crewmen, and even captains. The skills from these jobs were transferable and were used later in Richmond's shipping industry.

The shippers and the millers negotiated with slave owners to hire slaves for specific jobs, and they often bargained with the slaves themselves, agreeing to pay a certain amount of money to cover the slaves' living costs. Slaves were allowed to travel through Richmond on their own and required only written passes from employers.

Richmond's city slaves learned skills to become blacksmiths, iron-makers, tailors, workers in the ropewalks who made riggings for ships, mill machinery operators and spinners, woodcutters, sail repairers, shipping maintenance workers, and, most important, tobacco processors and bailers.[3]

The biggest single employer of city slaves was the tobacco industry. Wagons full of raw tobacco leaves packed into 1,400-pound barrels arrived daily and needed to be processed in warehouses. The tobacco leaves were moistened in wet cloth, and the cloth was later cut from the leaves by men working at long wooden benches in one room. The tobacco leaves were then twisted into plugs. In some warehouses, workers rolled tobacco into cigars and cigarettes for sale. Warehouses with numerous large, high-ceilinged rooms and at least two floors were required for these operations. In the late 1790s, there were three processing houses in Richmond, employing twenty-two slave workers, but by 1840 that number had grown to more than thirty houses employing more than nine hundred workers, most of them slaves. The workforce was gender- and age-mixed, too, with hundreds of women and children, usually teenagers, working alongside the men. At first, women, in bulky dresses and bright white aprons, made up nearly 25 percent of the workforce and children close to 40 percent, although the percentage of women and children declined to almost zero by the 1820s. They worked side by side with paid white laborers and black freedmen.[4]

The Virginia legislature forbade the manumission of any slaves after 1723, but hundreds had been freed by their owners prior to that. Those freed blacks had families, and the freed black population grew. It swelled even more after 1782, when an antislavery faction in the State Legislature managed to pass a bill to once again permit manumission (the act included only slaves over the age of forty-five or under eighteen, and their owners had to provide them with money to live and had to pay taxes if they did not give them financial support).[5] Hundreds of slaves were freed under that bill. The law stated that any children of freed blacks were born free, so even though the bill was rescinded a few years later, all of the offspring of the freed slaves were free. By 1806, there were thousands of freed blacks in Virginia and more than two thousand in Richmond alone.[6]

Black and white laborers worked together in the large mills that began to flourish in Richmond at the turn of the century. The mixed-race workforce also thrived in just about every industry in Richmond. From 1798 and for decades thereafter, blacks and whites worked side by side constructing the Kanawah Canal, roads, bridges, docks, and Jefferson's capitol building, along with other government structures. Mixed-race workforces could be found in the Richmond Towing Company, whose sailors towed large merchant ships up and down the James River, and in companies that hauled tons of coal from mountain mines to Richmond. Later, large mixed-race workforces appeared in the weaving and cotton industries. In 1806, slaves constituted anywhere from one-third to two-thirds of the mixed-race working population in town.[7]

Another reason that the city's companies hired so many slaves was because free whites, especially immigrant workers, did not want to do the hard work or the menial tasks that slaves would do. Some companies that began with half of their workforces as slaves soon eliminated all of their white workers and became 100 percent slave workforces.

Thomas Jefferson designed the Virginia capitol building to resemble the most beautiful buildings of ancient Rome and Greece. It overlooked the city as one of America's architectural wonders. Wythe's courtroom was on the first floor.

During that era, aggressive white workers demanded higher wages than slaves did. Plus, they engaged in strikes and work slowdowns when they did not get the salaries they desired. Whites were all cognizant of the generally higher wages that were paid to shipyard and mill workers in Northern cities because sailors brought the news to town. One company executive complained, "I am plagued by the worthless white men who pretend to labor around here."[8]

The city slaves were young, with a high percentage of them between the ages of eighteen and forty-five, which were prime years for workers. Two-thirds of the city slaves who worked in the shipping, tobacco, or milling industries were men.[9]

Finding slaves was easy. Prospective employers talked to plantation owners or ran ads in the Richmond newspapers, specifying the jobs, the skills needed, and the number of slaves sought. Employers would also seek workers in the taverns and on the streets of Richmond, where slave workers spent their time and could be found quickly. A slave who had finished working six months for one employer for $30 could easily be talked into working for another person for three or six more months for the same pay or higher. Many slave owners permitted their slaves to travel to Richmond, some of them dressed in suits, to seek employment. Many slaves even carried letters of recommendation from previous employers.

Slaves who were hired for city jobs often protested that their working conditions were miserable. Eager to keep the skilled labor they needed, employers would often permit slaves to change their assignments in order to have more acceptable conditions. Slaves complained that they were not provided with enough food or sufficient money to purchase it. They also said that the two suits of clothing allowable, one for summer and one for winter, were not enough. Some employers did not even furnish the two suits, and plantation owners who hired their slaves out took these employers to court for not doing so.[10] Many owners gave their slaves hand-me-down clothes from their own families to supplement the slaves' clothing. Owners also permitted slaves to run their own small businesses in town, such as selling crafts or fruits and vegetables, to make more money to buy food and clothing.

Employers in town provided medical care, too. Slaves were sent to city doctors for treatment, or factories paid physicians to visit several times a week to examine any slaves who claimed they were sick.

Hardworking slaves were appreciated and were often rehired for additional contracts. Sometimes they were given incentive bonuses for their work. The bonuses were substantial, ranging from $3 to $10 a week, which, if earned weekly, would nearly double their annual salary.[11]

The industries that employed the unique mixed-race workforce became quite successful. The tobacco and mill industries, as well as others, with blacks and whites working side by side, grew rapidly throughout the early years of the nineteenth century and really thrived in the following decades. One visitor to Richmond, noting all of the African Americans in the industrial workforce, wrote, "All the work in Richmond is done by slaves."[12]

By the 1850s, Richmond was the nation's largest manufacturer of tobacco, it ranked second in flour milling, and it was among the top five cities in iron production. The three big industries in the city employed more than five thousand workers, half of them slaves. The workers in these top three industries made up nearly 70 percent of the city's adult male population. Collectively, they had gross revenues of nearly $9 million.[13]

Richmond's slaves had near-complete autonomy. They were, as Frederick Douglass wrote of ship workers in Baltimore who lived in similar circumstances, "almost free citizens." Compared to plantation slaves, the city slave was "much better fed and clothed, less dejected in his appearance, and enjoys privileges altogether unknown to the whip-driven slave on the plantation."[14]

The freedoms of a city slave were extensive. The "for hire" slaves in the city formed their own churches and social organizations and developed secret societies. They congregated at mixed-race taverns and grocery stores and regularly visited one another. It was common for twenty or more slaves to spend evenings as the guests of the house slaves of a rich merchant in town. They enjoyed all of the freedom that freed blacks enjoyed and many of the liberties that whites had.[15]

And they helped to form a racially mixed social community in Richmond, particularly in the working-class neighborhoods around Main Street at Rockett's Landing, the shipping district. Blacks, both freed and slave, and whites congregated together at the racetrack, in taverns, and in gambling houses. They lived next door to one another in large boardinghouses in the crowded warehouse district on the James River's northern shore. The boardinghouses had been built for the thousands of newly arrived workers in the city, black and white. They socialized together, along with the French and the Portuguese, and freed blacks were often seen dancing with white women, which was a social taboo just about everywhere else in the South. The foreigners, white men and black men, freedmen and slaves, played cards, drank together, and fought with one another. The odd mix of residents, especially the single men—black and white, native and foreign—who made up nearly two-thirds of the city's population, created an unusual melting pot of people in Richmond in the early 1800s. It was probably the most socially and racially mixed city in the United States prior to the Civil War, and this terrified white residents throughout all of Virginia. The slaves of planters who lived in other parts of the state complained that they had no freedom at all. They all seemed to know a slave in Richmond who had plenty of freedom. The country slaves resented this and wanted those liberties, too.[16]

The problem for whites was not the predominance of nonwhites in the population, the sight of blacks and whites together in bars and at dances or at the track, or even black men socializing with white women. The problem was that the whites were losing control over the blacks, and the blacks were getting a very healthy taste of freedom. They would want more; they would want it all. The white South needed slaves for its plantations, shipyards, and tobacco warehouses. Therefore, whites had to preserve slavery and regain control over the black population, both freed and slave, which seemed on the verge of complete assimilation into white society. And whites needed to take control quickly.

In 1798, harsh new laws were passed to curtail the freedom of blacks in Richmond. Blacks could no longer hire themselves out to employers; their owners had to do this. Regardless of where they worked in town, slaves had to carry passes twenty-four hours a day or face a public whipping. Slaves were barred from visiting the racetrack, gaming houses, or cockfight pits. They could not gamble privately, either. Slaves were banned from participating in any of the numerous fistfights that broke out in the streets of the town. They could not gather in large groups or make political speeches that criticized the government of the city, the state, or the nation. Any black who was caught criticizing the government was burned in the palm of his or her left hand with a hot poker.[17]

The new restrictions did not dissuade slaves from seeking more freedom but instead emboldened them. The added restraints made many slaves feel that the future did not hold more freedom but far less. In the summer of 1800, Gabriel, the bright, educated blacksmith-carpenter slave of planter Thomas Prosser, who lived six miles from Richmond and often hired out to work on other plantations, organized a revolt. The goal was the murder of Prosser, dozens of other planters, and Richmond city officials, as well as the kidnapping of Virginia governor James Monroe. At a signal, some slaves were to set fire to all of the wood-frame buildings in the city, and during the conflagration, another group of slaves would seize Main Street and its businesses and residential homes and occupy them. Another battalion of rebel slaves was to take control of the capitol and other key city buildings, along with the munitions arsenal at the state penitentiary. Orders were also given to murder hundreds of whites throughout Richmond and in the surrounding villages. Quakers, Methodists, Frenchmen, and poor white women were to be spared because Gabriel had always been grateful for their kindness toward slaves. Gabriel and his lieutenants were certain that their rebellion, which had been planned to take place within twenty-four hours, would spur a general slave uprising throughout the South.

Informers and a sudden rainstorm prevented the well-planned revolt from taking place. Two slaves who heard of the plot told their owner, who alerted other planters. They went looking for Gabriel and his men on the evening the insurrection was to start. That same night an unexpected rainstorm hit Richmond, forcing most slaves to arrive late at the meeting spot because of muddy roads and washed-out bridges. The planters had formed their own posse and captured many slaves who gathered at the meeting place. The posse rounded up more black rebels throughout the county. Gabriel managed to escape and hid out for nearly two weeks before he was apprehended on a schooner in Norfolk.

Gabriel and those who had planned the revolt with him were hanged shortly afterward.[18]

Just two years later, Richmond was again stunned when yet another slave insurrection was uncovered and put down. This one, led by a slave named Sancho, involved hundreds of blacks who worked as pilots or crewmen on boats that sailed in and out of Richmond and other waterways in Virginia. It was a far-flung conspiracy that stretched to cities throughout the state and into North Carolina. Thirty-seven slaves were hanged. Five other, much smaller, planned insurrections were quashed between 1800 and 1806.[19]

Fear of a slave revolt in Virginia was not new. Planters had worried about it for years. In 1782, Thomas Jefferson bluntly predicted that a slave revolt would result in the murder of thousands of whites. Following Gabriel's revolt and the hanging of the blacks, a very scared white Richmond dramatically reined in its freed blacks and slaves again. New laws were passed to substantially curb blacks' liberties and restrict their freedom of movement. Whites were worried not only because of the scope of the plots, but because newspapers throughout the South and even in New York City had published stories about them. The press coverage might inspire other slaves to revolt.

Now, all slaves needed their passes twenty-four hours a day, but any slave traveling at night also had to carry a special second pass from his or her master or employer. Freed blacks had to carry their "register," or proof of freedom, at all times. Blacks could not walk near the state capitol building or city hall without written permission from a white official. Blacks could not smoke tobacco; carry weapons of any kind, even a fruit-paring knife; or congregate near a church, on a sidewalk, at a street corner, or in a public alley in groups larger than five. Slaves could not make their own arrangements for lodgings if they were hired out by their owners; their masters or employers had to do that. Blacks had to step aside to let whites pass on city streets and sidewalks.[20]

Interactions between blacks and whites were curbed, too. New laws that were passed after the revolt, some prior to Judge Wythe's murder and some shortly afterward, made it illegal for slaves working on barges or boats to step off the boats to visit a town where the ship docked. No black slave could be hired as the pilot of any boat. Freed black men could not marry slave women. Whites could not teach adult slaves how to read, write, or do mathematical problems. Slaves who came into Richmond on business had to leave the city as soon as their work was finished. Whites could not sell to or purchase goods from slaves. Whites could not forge traveling passes for slaves, sell them liquor, provide them religious instruction, help them cross a bridge, or permit them to board a ship illegally. A law that was passed in 1802 forbade any white owner of a restaurant, a tavern, or a bakery to sell food to slaves on Sunday without written permission from city authorities; this restriction was later extended to seven days a week. Any white person who urged a slave to flee his owner or rebel against the owner would be hanged.[21]

Some planters had "hired out" slave children to work as domestics in the city. In 1805, a law was passed that forbade their city owners to teach these children how to read or write. In 1811, a school run by independent black freedmen was burned down, and a year later the legislature prohibited black tutors from teaching in the state. White working-class women were forbidden to live with or socialize with black freedmen or slaves. Any slave who wanted to attend church on Sunday needed a special pass to do so.[22]

Despite all of the laws passed by the State Legislature and the city council, Richmonders remained terrified of further slave revolts. They were so frightened that a special city paramilitary unit was established, called the Public Guard, with its two-story headquarters near Capitol Square. Its sole responsibility was to monitor the activities of blacks, day and night, throughout the city. Members of the guard imprisoned and routinely beat any slaves they caught without papers roaming the city streets after 9 P.M.

The fear of all blacks was so great that in January 1800, several months after the insurrection, the state legislature passed its "transportation law." This law permitted judges to order slaves who were convicted of certain crimes to be deported out of Virginia to other states or nations in the Caribbean, South America, or Africa. Judges routinely lumped "troublemakers" who had not been convicted of major crimes into that group to ensure local tranquility. The white population was panicked in 1804 when a bloody slave revolt succeeded in overthrowing the government of Haiti. Many Frenchmen fled from Haiti to Richmond, frightening residents with stories of the conflict. Two years later, in the year that Wythe died, Virginia passed a law that ordered all freed slaves, such as Lydia Broadnax, to leave the state within six months. This law, however, was never successfully executed.[23]

The people of Richmond, although shaken by Gabriel's revolt, soon began to disregard the new laws, ignore the paramilitary army, and once again do business with slaves and freedmen and freedwomen. After a few months, the gaming houses let them back in and gladly accepted their bets, the taverns once again served them as much beer and liquor as they could drink, merchants sold them goods, and whenever more than five slaves congregated in an alley or on a street corner, the constables paid no attention to them. Small "grogshops," storefront taverns, welcomed them back right away, and the sight of white bartenders serving black and white customers through the windows was common. The women in the houses of prostitution were still happy to entertain blacks as well as whites, as long as they had money.

The businessmen of white Richmond disregarded the laws because they realized that the sizable black freedman and slave population of the city had accounted for a very large percentage of their income. Their revenue plunged under the new restrictions, and they did not like it. Collectively, they decided to ignore the laws, being certain that the courts would not imprison the entire business population of the city. They were right. From time to time, a tavern owner or a clothing store merchant was arrested, convicted, and fined a small amount of money for breaking the new slave laws, but not often. A tavern owner's income from hundreds of slaves drinking his beer each week far exceeded a few small fines.[24]

The townspeople's reluctance to obey the new laws angered city and state officials. This laxity on the part of the people could only encourage slaves to push for more freedom. At some point, slaves would want to be completely free, and that could not be permitted. The only weapons the city fathers had left were those of the legal system, with which the people could not interfere. These were the weapons that would silence Lydia Broadnax.

17

The Black and White Legal Codes

T HE MOST POTENT of the restrictive laws against blacks, which
had been on the books for years, was the statute that prohibited
any black person from testifying against whites in a criminal
trial. Whites believed that blacks, freed or slave, could not be trusted
and would surely perjure themselves in any criminal proceeding to help
themselves, a relative, or a friend escape punishment. All of the blacks
would supposedly stick together, lie, and subvert justice. Therefore, no
black was allowed to testify against whites in any court of law: federal,
state, county, or local.

That law had been on the books in Virginia since 1732. The statute was revised slightly in 1748. It remained the law in 1785, when
the new criminal and civil statutes of Virginia were approved by the
State Legislature. The law was amended slightly in 1801, following
Gabriel's Revolt, to read, "Any Negro or mulatto, bond or free, shall be
a good witness in pleas of the commonwealth for or against Negroes or
mulattos, bond or free, or in civil pleas where free Negroes or mulattos
shall alone be parties."[1]

That state law, always revered by the city council and the State
Legislature, was invoked at the trial of George Wythe Sweeney to pre-
vent Lydia Broadnax, the eyewitness to the poisoning, from testifying.
Not only was the cook prohibited from taking the witness stand, but the

228

information that she provided on Sweeney's pouring of the apparent arsenic powder into the coffee was forbidden to be divulged by any of the white witnesses to whom she had told her story firsthand.

In addition, judges ruled that none of the testimony of the blacks who saw Sweeney cut the arsenic on an axe could be admitted, nor could that of the black girl who found a piece of paper containing arsenic that Sweeney allegedly threw from the jail yard. None of this information from blacks could be believed, the arbiters of the legal system in Virginia had decided. Therefore, none of the blacks had been permitted to testify in the earlier hearings of the Sweeney trial, but whites had apparently been permitted to repeat the blacks' testimony, secondhand. In the actual District Court trial, the whites were not allowed to repeat anything said to them by the black witnesses.

Those laws against black testimony had been inviolate in Virginia as a colony since 1732 and in Virginia as a state for nearly thirty years. And in a final bit of irony, who had been responsible for the continuance of those state laws? George Wythe.

When the judge, Jefferson, and Pendleton revised all of the laws for the state of Virginia from 1777 through 1779, they had decided not to change the old colony slave statutes because they believed the time was not right to liberalize them. Those slave laws, which forbade any blacks to testify in a trial, remained intact when the legislature voted on the 126 laws proposed by the trio. The slave laws were never considered again.

Thus, Lydia Broadnax, the eyewitness to the poisoning whose testimony would have sent George Wythe Sweeney to the gallows, and the other black witnesses never told their stories to the jury.

THE MEN ON THE JURY were justifiably confused. The three best doctors in the state, among the most renowned in the country—educated at Edinburgh, no less—had said that after performing their expert autopsy, they were *not sure* the cause of death was arsenic.

The prosecuting attorneys were stymied from every angle in presenting their case. Did Sweeney put the ratsbane arsenic in the coffee? They had no eyewitness to put on the stand. Wythe did not see it happen because he was upstairs in the main house. Michael Brown might have, but he was dead. Lydia Broadnax had told everyone she met that Sweeney had put arsenic in the coffee pot, but she was not allowed to testify.

And the defense had a logical rebuttal for every piece of circumstantial evidence. The ratsbane that was found in Sweeney's room? All of the jurors probably had ratsbane in a drawer or a closet somewhere in their own homes. Having ratsbane did not prove anything.

The will? Prosecutors said that a possible motive for murder was that Sweeney feared being cut out of the will. But members of families everywhere cut their relatives out of their wills for numerous reasons, some of them valid and others petty. The prosecutors also told the jury that Sweeney would obtain all of Wythe's estate if Michael Brown died first. If the bodies of all of the men and the women who had been cut out of angry relatives' wills were lined up head to foot, they would reach from one end of America to the other. If Sweeney feared being eliminated from the old man's will, this did not mean that Sweeney killed Wythe, just as being cut out of a will did not lead the thousands of Americans who had suffered the same fate to murder their relatives.

It must have been Sweeney because he was the only one not stricken after drinking the coffee? So what? Maybe he had a single sip. Maybe he wanted to drink some, put the coffee cup to his lips, and then, because he was in a hurry, as many had said, merely put it down without tasting the coffee. Broadnax could not take the stand to tell the jury whether he drank any or how much he consumed.

The court had listened to Wirt deliver an eloquent defense of Sweeney. The handsome young attorney was legendary in arguing murder defenses. His first case had been a murder trial, and he had won it. He had also won the seemingly unshakable case against Shannon, the Williamsburg shotgun slayer. Defense attorney Wirt had made a strong case for the jurors in the Wythe case. They needed evidence, but none was presented. They needed eyewitnesses, but none took the stand. They needed an official cause of death, but the doctors could not give them one. The evidence that Sweeney had been seen pounding arsenic powder with an axe could not be presented because the eyewitnesses to that incident were black. The story of the arsenic found near the wall of the jail was not presented, either, because the girl who found it was black. Her master's testimony was only hearsay. The jury at least needed a decent motive, and the only one that had been presented, fear of being cut out of Wythe's will, seemed flimsy. The one thing the jurors did know for sure was that George Wythe at eighty was a very old man, and, as the defense attorneys suggested, citing the eminent physicians, he might have died from complications of any of the ailments that had afflicted him for years—as had so many of the jurors' own elderly relatives.

All that the jurors had was a very circumstantial case. Could they send a teenager to the gallows without witnesses, evidence, a cause of death, or a strong motive—a boy with no prior arrest record?

Did they think that Sweeney had murdered his granduncle? Probably. Could they prove it beyond a shadow of a doubt? No.

The jurors wanted to be fair and, like all juries in Virginia, they were influenced by recent anti–capital punishment crusades that had begun in America and England. (Wythe's friend Benjamin Rush, who had worked with him in the Continental Congress, led one of the most highly publicized ones in the United States.)[2] The jurors were also swayed by the decades-old code of leniency that had begun in the late 1770s, which led many Virginia juries to avoid sending anyone to the gallows without substantial proof of guilt. And to whom did the jury look for guidance in leniency when determining whether there was enough evidence to execute Sweeney?

None other than George Wythe.

He, Jefferson, and Pendleton had substantially reduced the number of capital offenses and the punishments for them when, as the Revisors, they had rewritten the state's criminal codes in the late 1770s. Everyone remembered that Wythe, Jefferson, and Pendleton had begged for clemency, even in murder cases, and that clemency had become part of the judicial life in the state. In 1777, everyone had felt stirred by Jefferson's note on behalf of Wythe and Pendleton, stating, "An eye for an eye, and a hand for a hand, will exhibit spectacles in execution whose moral effect would be questionable." Now, in 1806, people still took this sentiment to heart. The ghost of George Wythe helped prevent the jury from hanging the murderer of George Wythe.

The jury returned in less than an hour, and the foreman announced that young George Wythe Sweeney was not guilty of murdering his granduncle, the high chancellor of Virginia.

The press and the public were shocked. The evidence against Sweeney was overwhelming, and now he had been acquitted in what many saw as a gross miscarriage of justice. The city's newspapers were outraged at the acquittal, but journalistic anger was not directed at the jury or the prosecutor but at the racist laws of Virginia. Editor Thomas Ritchie, in his story in the *Enquirer*, seethed, "Some of the strongest testimony exhibited before the called court and before the grand jury was kept back from the petit jury. The reason is that it was gleaned from the evidence of Negroes, which is not permitted by our laws to go against a white man."[3]

For years, the residents of Richmond and of the entire South had lived in fear that they would be murdered by foreigners or slaves. In this case, one of their most beloved neighbors had been murdered, not by angry slaves or devious foreigners, but by his own nephew. They all knew that Sweeney was guilty, too, but the racist laws they had embraced for so long let the killer get away and escape the murder charges.

All was not lost, though. People were certain that Sweeney would at least spend several years in prison for forgery. The case against him was indisputable. He had forged checks, signing his uncle's name, one of them only two days after he poisoned the judge. Then, as further evidence, there were the six previously forged checks, which turned up in the files of the Bank of Virginia. The jurors might not have been certain that Sweeney had poisoned everyone in the Wythe home on May 25, but they were positive that he had forged the checks. They had seen the checks, the forged signatures, and the copies of the judge's signature. There was no doubt of Sweeney's guilt on that charge. Like many juries who are uncertain about a major charge, they felt that justice would still be served if they convicted him on the minor charge of forgery, a charge they would hear on the following day. Sweeney would go to prison and at least serve several years for forgery and, in an indirect way, for killing George Wythe.

Sweeney was clearly guilty of breaking the latest forgery law, passed in 1789, which decreed guilt "if any person or persons, shall falsely and deceitfully obtain or get into his or their hands or possession, any money, goods or chattels of any other person or persons, by colour and means of any such false token or counterfeit letter, made in any other man's name."[4]

What Sweeney's lawyer, Wirt, knew that no one else seemed to realize was that, in fact, the revised laws of Virginia, which had been completed from 1777 to 1779 and amended from time to time since, contained language regarding only personal forgery and not forgery against a public institution, such as a bank. There was no language in those laws to provide for forgery against a bank because there were no banks in the U.S. in the 1770s. The first Virginia financial institution, the Bank of Alexandria, was chartered in 1792. The state's second bank was the Bank of Richmond, which opened its doors on January 30, 1804, and remained in business until the end of the Civil War. This bank, one of the largest and most successful in the South, eventually had branches in Norfolk, Petersburg, Fredericksburg, Danville, Portsmouth, Lynchburg, Buchanan, Charleston, and Union. It was soon joined by the Bank of Virginia.[5]

The State Legislature had approved the personal forgery laws as part of the overall crime package that the Revisors sent to it by 1786. Over the next twenty years, the State Legislature never rewrote the forgery laws to include forgeries against banks. The old laws were so accepted that no one in the Bank of Virginia even thought to have them amended to protect the bank or any other financial institution.

Wirt quietly told the judge and the jury that Sweeney could not be convicted of breaking a law that did not exist. An uproar ensued. Wirt quieted everyone by giving the court a background description of the forgery laws and the history of banking in the city and the state. The men who had written the forgery laws, he reminded everyone, incredibly forgot to envision public banks, which were already important institutions in England and Europe. Over the next twenty years, those same men had apparently assumed that their law covered the banks that had since opened their doors and thus had never amended it. Neither had the State Legislature. Sweeney had not broken any law. The forgery charges against him were dismissed.

The men who had written those forgery laws had left a huge loophole that, nearly thirty years later, enabled Sweeney to avoid prosecution for forgery, even though he had clearly forged seven different checks.

And who had written those forgery laws in such a way that, thirty years later, Sweeney was off the hook? None other than George Wythe.

Sweeney had the best lawyers in America, but in the end, his escape from prosecution for what appeared to everyone to be blatant premeditated murder and the forging of numerous checks was thanks mainly to the man he had killed, his granduncle. Judge Wythe, in his eagerness to bring some mercy to the legal codes of Virginia during the 1770s, had helped to seat a jury three decades later that would not hang his own killer because he himself had advocated judicial leniency. The key witness in the case, Lydia Broadnax, who had seen Sweeney put poison into the coffeepot, could not testify because she was black, and the legal restrictions on blacks testifying against whites, upheld by Wythe, meant that she could not take the stand and point a finger of guilt at Sweeney. Due to some inexplicable reason, the judge, Jefferson, and Pendleton had forgotten to include forgery against a bank as a crime when they revised the state's laws; this omission meant that young Sweeney could not be charged with that crime, either, and that all of those forged checks could not be held against him. It could be said that the judge had freed his own killer. It could also be argued that the racism of Virginia freed the murderer of one of its heroes.

A fury overtook Richmond when Sweeney walked out of the city jail a free man. Sensing the anger of the people, Wirt and Randolph advised Sweeney to get out of the city and the state as fast as he could. The teenager left right away, probably aided by receiving a horse and money from his family, and he traveled west, never to see Virginia again.

18

Washington, October 1806

PRESIDENT JEFFERSON missed his dear friend George Wythe. The president always told people that throughout his life, he had treasured most those whom he had come to admire as a young man, and the judge was one of them. He once wrote, "As I grow older, I set a higher value on the intimacies of my youth, and am more afflicted by whatever loses one of them to me."[1]

The president's personality seemed to sour after the murder, and he complained more and more about the emptiness he often felt in his life. He should have been ebullient in the fall of 1806, the time of the trial. He had been reelected president in a landslide in 1804. The Lewis and Clark expedition had successfully navigated the Louisiana Territory, which Jefferson had purchased from France in August 1805, and in September 1806 the explorers had returned to St. Louis.[2] Yet the president was melancholy. On most days, Jefferson went horseback riding in the countryside around Washington, D.C., for recreation and to take a break from his presidential responsibilities. He spent much time thinking on those excursions, as his mounts carried him through miles of thick forests, across narrow streams, and along the shores of the Potomac River. One afternoon a few weeks after Sweeney's acquittal, President Jefferson returned to the Executive Mansion extremely depressed and penned a melancholy letter to his daughter. Perhaps he was thinking about all the years he had spent with George Wythe as a student, a law clerk, a political colleague, and a friend. He wrote, "Having been so long in the midst of a family, the lonesomeness of this place is more intolerable than I ever found it. My daily rides, too, are sickening for want of some interest in the scenes I pass over: and indeed I look over the two ensuing years as the most tedious of my life."[3]

GEORGE WYTHE was appropriately buried in St. John's Cemetery, in the hilly southeastern section of Richmond, near the church where he listened to Patrick Henry give his immortal "Give me liberty or give me death" speech. The cemetery overlooks the James River and the city Wythe loved, which has grown into one of America's thriving and most historic metropolises. His tombstone boasts his legacy to the United States. It reads:

THIS TABLET IS DEDICATED

TO MARK THE SITE WHERE LIE

THE MORTAL REMAINS OF

GEORGE WYTHE

BORN 1726–DIED 1806

JURIST AND STATESMAN

TEACHER OF RANDOLPH

JEFFERSON AND MARSHALL

FIRST PROFESSOR OF LAW

IN THE UNITED STATES

FIRST VIRGINIA SIGNER OF THE

DECLARATION OF INDEPENDENCE

Epilogue

T HE WYTHE MURDER remained a heated topic of conversation in Virginia and throughout the nation for generations. Everyone was certain that Sweeney had murdered the judge, regardless of the unpopular verdict. In letters written throughout their lifetimes, people referred to Wythe's death as a murder and called Sweeney his killer. One of Wythe's friends, Littleton Tazewell, told people twenty years later that the chancellor had been murdered. His demise "was produced by poison, administered in his coffee, by a reprobate boy, a relation of his who he had undertaken to educate, and who was afterwards convicted of having committed many forgeries of checks in his name."[1] Perhaps Henry Clay, writing forty-five years after the passing of his mentor, summed up everyone's feelings. He wrote heatedly that Sweeney "poisoned him, and others—the black members of his household—by putting arsenic into a pot in which coffee was prepared for breakfast. . . . The coffee having been drank by the Chancellor and his servants, the poison developed its usual effects."[2]

None of the people involved in the investigation or the trial suffered from the legal and medical fiasco. The trio of doctors who had bungled the autopsy flourished. They left the courtroom and went right back to their successful medical practices. McClurg continued to be considered one of the most skilled doctors in the country. He was so highly regarded that when the prestigious Medical Society of Virginia was formed in 1820, its members elected McClurg as its first president. Dr. Foushee's reputation did not suffer, either. He followed McClurg as a president of the Medical Society of Virginia. His medical practice grew, and he became one of the wealthiest doctors in the country. His house was so large that when a bank sought out the biggest building in the city for its offices, they bought it because it dwarfed all of the businesses and the warehouses in Richmond. His gardens were left to the city when he died, and they became a tourist attraction. Dr. McCaw's fame as a physician also grew. Over the next several decades, he became renowned as one of the South's most distinguished doctors. His son followed in his footsteps and even surpassed him in stature as a physician. His grandsons and nephews became physicians, too, and founded one of the largest family medical dynasties in the nation.

Wirt had wanted to get attention by winning an acquittal, and he did. Wythe's friends, understanding how the legal profession worked, never held it against him that he had represented Sweeney. In fact, Wythe's best friend, the president, named Wirt as the chief prosecutor of Aaron Burr a year later, when Burr went on trial for treason in Richmond. And who defended Burr, obviously looking for attention, too? It was Edmund Randolph. Burr was found not guilty, despite a magnificent attack by Wirt. Burr was exonerated not by Randolph's work, however, but by a ruling from Chief Justice Marshall, who heard the case. The ruling forbade the government to file particular charges against Burr.

Wirt, who was as popular for prosecuting Burr in 1807 as he was unpopular for defending Sweeney in 1806, was named attorney general of the United States by President James Madison. His successor, President James Monroe, asked Wirt to stay on as attorney general for the duration of his two administrations, another eight years, which made Wirt the longest-serving attorney general in American history.

Randolph went back to his legal business after the Sweeney trial. He defended Burr and then pursued dozens of complex civil suits filed by his clients in Virginia. He recovered his legal reputation and died ten years later, still owing that vast sum of money to the U.S. government.

And Sweeney? The seventeen-year-old left Virginia and vanished. Years later, it was learned that he had drifted into Tennessee. There, the impulsive and mischievous Sweeney was arrested and convicted for horse theft, a serious crime everywhere during that era. He served several years in prison and was then released. Once again, he disappeared. Several investigations by historians and the author of this book could not turn up any additional biographical information on Sweeney. Tennessee did not inaugurate a state-wide prison system until the 1820s, so all records of Sweeney's life and local incarceration in Tennessee were lost.

The news that Sweeney had spent several years in a Tennessee prison satisfied the friends and admirers of George Wythe. Sweeney might have eluded justice in Virginia, but he had been unable to do so in Tennessee. Virginians, a religious people, had hoped that after Sweeney was acquitted, at least God would punish him. They never knew what the Lord did to him, but at least Tennessee had imprisoned him for a period of time.

Today in Virginia there is a county named after George Wythe, as well as a town, several schools, and numerous streets in various cities. There are also monuments. His Williamsburg home serves as a museum for the millions of Americans who visit the restored colonial capital each year. But nowhere does his memory live on more than at the bottom of the Declaration of Independence, where in 1776 he signed "George Wythe" with enormous pride.

Acknowledgments

From the beginning, I traveled a fascinating path in my study of the murder of George Wythe and found myself knee-deep in the history of both homicide and forensics. I had much assistance along the way.

I owe a great deal of gratitude to Rachel Merkley, a historian at Colonial Williamsburg, who helped me with the story of Wythe's life there. I did work at the Rockefeller Library at Williamsburg, and I thank the staffers there who aided me. Many thanks to the staffs of several libraries, among them those at New Jersey City University (and Fred Smith), the Rutgers Library of Science and Medicine, John Jay College Library, the Morris County library, the Randolph (N.J.) library, the New York Historical Society, the Virginia Historical Society, the Massachusetts Historical Society, and the State Library of Virginia.

I appreciate the help of several photo experts. They include Andrea Ashby-Lareras, Independence Hall, in Philadelphia; Jeff Ruggles, at the Virginia Historical Society; and Marianne Martin, at Colonial Williamsburg.

I am grateful for all the help extended to me by my editor at John Wiley & Sons, Stephen S. Power. Also at Wiley, Rachel Meyers skillfully shepherded the book through production. Patricia Waldygo thoughtfully copyedited the manuscript. Thanks, as always, to my loving wife, Marjorie, for reading the book, several times, and offering suggestions. I would also like to acknowledge my agents Elizabeth Winick and Rebecca Strauss at the MacIntosh and Otis Literary Agency for their work.

Thanks, too, to all the good people of Virginia, who are directly and indirectly connected to my investigation of the murder of George Wythe and who offered their encouragement and assistance to me.

Notes

CHAPTER 1. "I AM MURDERED"

1. Lewis Mattison, "Life of the Town" in *Richmond, Capital of Virginia: Approaches to Its History* (Richmond, Va.: Whittet & Shepperson, 1938), pp. 47–55.
2. William Munford to John Coalter, September 30, 1791, Brown-Coalter Papers, William and Mary College Library.
3. Joseph Gutmann and Stanley Chyet, eds., *Moses Jacob Ezekiel: Memoirs from the Baths of Diocletian* (Detroit: Wayne State University Press, 1975), p. 82.
4. *Richmond Enquirer*, October 11, 1859.
5. Wythe delighted the delegates to the Continental Congress with his classical references, as mentioned by John Adams in his diary notes of October 12 and October 21, 1775. See L. H. Butterfield, *The Adams Papers: The Diary and Autobiography of John Adams* (Cambridge, Mass.: Belknap Press, 1962), vol. 2, pp. 214–215, p. 208. Many of Wythe's letters from Philadelphia are in Paul Smith, *Letters of Delegates to Congress, 1774–1789*, 26 vols. (Washington, D.C.: Library of Congress, 1976).
6. *Virginia Gazette*, August 17, 1775.
7. Imogene Brown, *American Aristides: A Biography of George Wythe* (Teaneck, N.J.: Fairleigh Dickinson University Press, 1981), pp. 144–147.
8. *Virginia Gazette*, January 23, 1778.
9. John Adams to James Warren, October 23, 1775, in L. H. Butterfield, *The Adams Papers: The Diary and Autobiography of John Adams*, vol. 2 (Cambridge, Mass.: Belknap Press, 1962), pp. 231–232.
10. Mattison, "Life of the Town," p. 44.
11. Hugh Grigsby, *The History of the Virginia Federal Convention of 1788: With Some Account of the Eminent Virginians of That Era Who Were Members of the Body*, vol. 1 (Richmond: Virginia Historical Society, 1855), p. 75.
12. Colonial Williamsburg Online, *George Wythe Biography*, available at http://www.colonial williamsburg.com/Almanack/people/bios/biowythe.cfm, last accessed June 30, 2008.
13. Joyce Blackburn, *George Wythe in Williamsburg* (New York: Harper and Row, 1975), p. 60.
14. Herbert Ezekiel, "The Newspaper," in *Richmond, Capital of Virginia*, pp. 163–176. Richmond was one of many cities that had at least two newspapers by 1806. The first U.S. daily paper, the *National Intelligencer*, debuted in 1814.
15. *Richmond Enquirer*, Friday, May 23, 1806.
16. Warren Billings, John Selby, and Thad Tate, *Colonial Virginia: A History* (White Plains, N.Y.: KTO Press, 1986), pp. 354–355.
17. Mattison, "Life of the Town," p. 44.
18. Billings, Selby, and Tate, p. 360.
19. Mordecai, p. 227, U.S. Census for 1800, 1810, and 1820.

20. *Virginia Gazette*, December 14, 1739.
21. Rhys Isaacs, *The Transformation of Virginia, 1740–1790* (New York: W. W. Norton, 1982), p. 100.
22. Harry Ward and Harold Greer Jr., *Richmond during the Revolution, 1775–1783* (Charlottesville: University of Virginia Press, 1977), pp. 112–113.
23. Ibid., pp. 109–111.
24. Mayor William Foushee's petition to the governor for more jail guards, Virginia State Library.
25. Julian Boyd and W. Edwin Hemphill, *The Murder of George Wythe, Two Essays* (Williamsburg, Va.: The Institute of Early American History and Culture, 1955), pp. 12–13.
26. Another account of his poisoning is from Alonzo Dill, *George Wythe, Teacher of Liberty* (Williamsburg, Va.: Colonial Williamsburg Foundation, 1979), pp. 66–69.

CHAPTER 2. THE FUNERAL

1. Lydia Broadnax to Thomas Jefferson, April 9, 1807, in Jack McLaughlin, ed., *To His Excellency Thomas Jefferson, Letters to a President* (New York: W. W. Norton, 1991), pp. 128–129. Through a cousin, the president sent her $50.
2. Thomas Jefferson to William DuVal, June 14, 1806, in Julian Boyd, ed., *The Papers of Thomas Jefferson*, 33 vols. (Princeton, N.J.: Princeton University Press, 1950); microfilm, papers of 1806, Dice Robins Anderson, "The Teacher of Jefferson and Marshall," *South Atlantic Quarterly* 16 (1916): 343.
3. William Munford's oration, *Richmond Enquirer*, June 13, 1806, and in the *Virginia Argus*, June 13, 1806.
4. Foushee was one of three men who handled the sale, *Virginia Gazette and General Advertiser*, July 8, 1795.
5. *Richmond Enquirer*, June 10, 1806.
6. Ibid.
7. Ibid.
8. Henry Clay to Benjamin Minor, May 3, 1851, in Edward Maxwell, ed., *Virginia Register* (Richmond, Va.: McFarland and Co., 1852), chap. 5, p. 166.
9. William Brown to Joseph Prentis, September 24, 1804, Prentis Papers, University of Virginia Library, Brown, p. 283.

CHAPTER 3. HOMICIDE: THE INVESTIGATION, PART I

1. Calvin Jarrett, "Was George Wythe Murdered?" *Virginia Cavalcade* (Winter 1963–1964): 33–39.
2. John Little, *History of Richmond* (Richmond, Va.: Dietz, 1933), pp. 80–85.
3. Joyce Blackburn, *George Wythe in Williamsburg* (New York: Harper and Row, 1975), p. 137; George Munford, *Two Parsons, Cupid's Sports, the Dream and the Jewels of Virginia* (Richmond, Va.: J.D.K. Sleight, 1884), pp. 422–424.
4. Roderick McGraw, *Russia and the Cholera, 1823–1832* (Madison: University of Wisconsin Press, 1965), pp. 20–21; W. E. van Heyningen and John Seal, *Cholera: The American Scientific Experiment, 1947–1980* (Boulder, Colo.: Westview, 1983), pp. 12–13.
5. McGraw, *Russia and the Cholera, 1823–1832*, p. 22.
6. Joann Krieg, *Epidemics in the Modern World* (New York: Twayne, 1992), p. 73.
7. *Edinburgh Medical and Surgical Journal* 16 (1820): 458; 15 (1826): 180.
8. Herbert Thoms, *The Doctors Jared of Connecticut* (Hamden, Conn.: Shoe String Press, 1958), p. 2.
9. Krieg, *Epidemics in the Modern World*, pp. 72–75.
10. Charles Rosenberg, *The Cholera Years: The United States in 1832, 1849 and 1866* (Chicago: University of Chicago Press, 1962), p. 42.

11. Christopher Wills, *Yellow Fever, Black Goddess: The Co-Evolution of People and Plagues* (New York: Addison-Wesley, 1996), pp. 112–113, 116; Abraham Lilienfeld, MD, ed., *Times, Places and Persons: Aspects of the History of Epidemiology* (Baltimore, Md.: Johns Hopkins University Press, 1980), p. 4.

12. Robert Hewitt, "The Influence of Somatic and Psychiatric Medical Theory on the Design of Nineteenth Century American Cities," http://www.priory.com/homol/19c.htm, p. 9, last accessed October 1, 2007.

13. J. MacPherson, *The Annals of Cholera from the Earliest Periods to the Year 1817* (London, 1872).

14. Heyningen and Seal, *Cholera: The American Scientific Experiment, 1947–1980*, pp. 4–5; Geoffrey Marks and William Beatty, *Epidemics* (New York: Charles Scribner's Sons, 1976), pp. 192–193.

15. William McNeill, *Plagues and People* (Garden City, N.Y.: Doubleday, 1976), pp. 266–267.

16. Richard Evans, *Death in Hamburg: Society and Politics in the Cholera Years, 1830–1910* (Oxford: Clarendon Press, 1987), p. 229.

17. Little, *A History of Richmond*, p. 98.

18. Frederick Cartwright and Michael Biddiss, *Disease and History* (New York: Thomas Crowell, 1972), pp. 119–121.

19. J. N. Hays, *The Burdens of Disease: Epidemics and Human Response in Western History* (New Brunswick, N.J.: Rutgers University Press, 1998), pp. 135–154.

20. John Duffy, *Epidemics in Colonial America* (Baton Rouge: Louisiana State University Press, 1953), pp. 41–43, 69–109; Donald Hopkins, *Princes and Peasants: Smallpox in History* (Chicago: University of Chicago Press, 1983), p. 261; Horace Ogden, *CDC and the Smallpox Crusade* (Washington, D.C.: U.S. Department of Health, Center for Disease Control, 1972), pp. 3–4; Herve Bazin, *The Eradication of Smallpox* (New York: Academic Press, 1984), p. 6; Patrice Boudelais, *Epidemics Laid Low: A History of What Happened in Rich Countries*, translated by Bart K. Holland (Baltimore: Johns Hopkins University Press, 2003), pp. 40–41; William McNeill, *Plagues and People*, pp. 249–250; Carl Binger, MD, *Revolutionary Doctor, Benjamin Rush* (New York: W. W. Norton, 1966), p. 122; *Smallpox in Colonial America* (New York: New York Times/Arno Press, 1971), all of section 4; Oscar Reiss, MD, *Medicine and the American Revolution: How Diseases and Their Treatments Affected the Colonial Army* (Jefferson, N.C.: McFarland, 1998), p. 68.

21. John Ellis, *Yellow Fever and Public Health in the New South* (Lexington: University of Kentucky Press, 1992), p. 31; Krieg, *Epidemics in the Modern World*, pp. 59–60.

22. Arno Karlen, *Man and Microbes: Disease and Plagues in History and Modern Times* (New York: Touchstone Books, 1995), p. 106.

23. Gerald Grob, *The Deadly Truth: A History of Disease in America* (Cambridge, Mass.: Harvard University Press, 2002), p. 102.

24. Ellis, *Yellow Fever and Public Health in the New South*, p. 4.

25. Duffy, *Epidemics in Colonial America*, pp. 138–139; George Kahn, ed., *Encyclopedia of Plague and Pestilence* (New York: Facts on File, 1995), p. 100; Marks and Beatty, *Epidemics*, pp. 150–151; Alan Bewell, *Romanticism and Colonial Disease* (Baltimore, Md.: Johns Hopkins University Press, 1999), pp. 72–75.

26. Wynham Blanton, MD, *Medicine in Virginia in the Nineteenth Century* (Richmond, Va.: Garrett & Massie, 1933), pp. 224–225, 277.

27. Virginia Dabney, *Richmond: The Story of a City* (Garden City, N.Y.: Doubleday, 1976), pp. 45–46; Blanton, *Medicine in Virginia in the Nineteenth Century*, p. 228.

28. Rolla Thomas, MD, *Eclectic Practice of Medicine*, Colonial Williamsburg research study, 1993; M. E. Bradford, *Founding Fathers: Brief Lives of the Framers of the United States Constitution* (Topeka: University Press of Kansas, 1981), p. 162.

29. Norfolk Herald, in William Forrest, *The Great Pestilence in Virginia, Being an Account of the Origin, General Character and Ravages of the Yellow Fever on Norfolk and Portsmouth in 1855, Together with Sketches of Some of the Victims* (Philadelphia: J. B. Lippincott, 1856), p. 87.
30. Blanton, *Medicine in Virginia in the Nineteenth Century*, p. 260.
31. Jarrett, "Was George Wythe Murdered?" pp. 33–39; Julian Boyd and W. Edwin Hemphill, *The Murder of George Wythe, Two Essays* (Williamsburg, Va.: The Institute of Early American History and Culture, 1955), p. 35.
32. Ibid., p. 48.

Chapter 4. Williamsburg: George Wythe and Thomas Jefferson

1. Thomas Jefferson to Alexander Donald, September 17, 1787, in Julian Boyd, ed., *The Papers of Thomas Jefferson*, 33 vols. (Princeton, N.J.: Princeton University Press, 1950), vol. 12, p. 133.
2. Thomas Jefferson to John Saunderson, August 31, 1820, in Thomas Jefferson, *Autobiography, The Writings of Thomas Jefferson*, 3 vols., edited by H. A. Washington (Washington, D.C.: Baylor & Maury, 1858), vol. 1, p. 111; Thomas Jefferson to William DuVal, June 18, 1806, *Papers of Thomas Jefferson*, Princeton University.
3. Fawn Brodie, *Thomas Jefferson: An Intimate History* (New York: W. W. Norton, 1974), p. 62.
4. Thomas Jefferson to John Page, February 21, 1770, in Joseph Gardner, ed., *The Founding Fathers: Thomas Jefferson: a Biography in His Own Words* (New York: Newsweek Publishing, 1974), pp. 37–38.
5. George Wythe to Thomas Jefferson, March 9, 1770, in Joyce Blackburn, *George Wythe in Williamsburg* (New York: Harper and Row, 1975), p. 63.
6. Andrew Burstein, *Jefferson's Secrets: Death and Desire at Monticello* (New York: Basic Books, 2005), p. 161.
7. Brodie, *Thomas Jefferson: An Intimate History*, p. 60; Thomas Jefferson to L. H. Girardin, January 15, 1815, in Boyd, *Papers of Thomas Jefferson*, vol. 4, p. 231.
8. Thomas Jefferson to John Saunderson, August 31, 1820, in Washington, ed., *Writings of Thomas Jefferson*, vol. 1, pp. 111–113.
9. Marquis de Chastellux, *Travels in North America in the Years 1780, 1781 and 1782*, translated by Howard Rice (Chapel Hill: University of North Carolina Press, 1963), pp. 443–444.
10. Gardner, *The Founding Fathers*, p. 23; Robert Rutland, ed., *James Madison and the American Nation, 1751–1836* (New York: Simon & Schuster, 1994), p. 331.
11. Thomas Jefferson to Dr. Vine Utley, March 21, 1819, in Gardner, *The Founding Fathers*, p. 23–24.
12. Gardner, *The Founding Fathers*, pp. 28–29; Lewis Powell, 1990 lecture to the Supreme Court Historical Society, printed in the organization's *Society Publications* archives, Washington, D.C., 1990, p. 2.
13. *Virginia Gazette and General Advertiser*, July 8, 1795.
14. Alonzo Dill, *George Wythe: Teacher of Liberty* (Williamsburg, Va.: Colonial Williamsburg Foundation, 1979), pp. 3, 5; Robert Kirtland, *George Wythe: Lawyer, Revolutionary, Judge* (New York: Garland, 1986), pp. 20–40; Dice Anderson, "The Teacher of Jefferson and Marshall," *South Atlantic Quarterly* 15 (1916): 329.
15. "Will of Richard Taliaferro," *William and Mary Quarterly* 12, no. 2 (October 1903): 124–125.
16. Blackburn, George Wythe in Williamsburg, p. 56; Wythe's orders were recorded in Francis Mason, ed., John Norton and Sons, *Merchants of London and Virginia, Being the Papers from Their Counting House for the Years 1750–1795* (Richmond, Va.: Dietz Press, 1937); Imogene Brown, *American Aristides: A Biography of George Wythe* (Teaneck, N.J.: Fairleigh Dickinson University Press, 1981), pp. 87–89.
17. Blackburn, *George Wythe in Williamsburg*, pp. 20–28.

18. Elizabeth Merkley, Colonial Williamsburg Research Files.

19. Leola Walker, "Officials in the City Government of Colonial Williamsburg," *Virginia Magazine* 75 (1967): 42–43.

20. E. M. Halliday, *Understanding Thomas Jefferson* (New York: HarperCollins, 2001), p. 21.

21. George Munford, *The Two Parsons, Cupid's Sports, the Dream and the Jewels of Virginia* (Richmond, Va.: J.D.K. Sleight, 1884), pp. 549–550.

22. Ironically, this information was from a sketch of Henry that Jefferson wrote in 1810 for a biography of Henry written by William Wirt, who had just defended the murderer of Jefferson's close friend George Wythe.

23. Thomas Jefferson to Peter Carr, August 10, 1787, in Gardner, *The Founding Fathers*, p. 22.

24. Dill, *George Wythe: Teacher of Liberty*, p. 13.

25. Blackburn, *George Wythe in Williamsburg*, pp. 40–45; Anderson, "The Teacher of Jefferson and Marshall," p. 334.

26. William Wirt, *Sketches of the Life and Character of Patrick Henry* (Philadelphia: Claxton, Remsen, Haffelfinger, 25th ed., 1878), p. 48; Littleton Tazewell, *Sketches of His Own Family Written by Littleton Tazewell, for the Use of His Children* (Norfolk, Virginia, 1823), p. 116; Grigsby, *The Virginia Convention of 1776* (Richmond, 1855), p. 121.

27. Blackburn, *George Wythe in Williamsburg*, p. 45.

28. Brown, *American Aristides*, pp. 96–97.

29. Andrew Burnaby, *Travels through the Middle Settlements in North America in the Years 1759 and 1760, With Observations on the State of the Colonies*, (London: T. Payne, 1798), p. 58.

30. Brown, *American Aristides*, pp. 98–104; Blackburn, *George Wythe in Williamsburg*, pp. 80–81.

31. L. H. Butterfield, *The Adams Papers: The Diary and Autobiography of John Adams* (Cambridge, Mass.: Belknap Press, 1962), vol. 2, pp. 214–216.

32. Brown on the two men, *American Aristides*, pp. 115–116; John Adams to Abigail Adams, October 19, 1775, in Butterfield, *Adams Papers*, vol. 2, pp. 201–202; Charles Tansill, ed., *The Making of the American Republic: The Great Documents, 1774–1789* (New Rochelle, N.Y.: Arlington House Press, 1972), p. 98.

33. Blackburn, *George Wythe in Williamsburg*, pp. 86–87; Charles Francis Adams, ed., *The Works of John Adams, Second President of the United States, with a Life of the Author* (Boston: Little, Brown, 1854)10: 94–96.

34. Blackburn, *George Wythe in Williamsburg*, pp. 97–99; *Journals of the Continental Congress, 1774–1789*, 34 vols. (Washington, D.C.: U.S. Government Printing Office, 1904–1937), vol. 4, pp. 401–402.

35. L. H. Butterfield, *The Autobiography of John Adams*, 4 vols. (Cambridge, Mass.: Harvard University Press, 1961), vol. 2, p. 172.

36. Dill, *George Wythe: Teacher of Liberty*, p. 25.

37. George Corner, ed., *The Autobiography of Benjamin Rush* (Princeton, N.J.: Princeton University Press, 1948), p. 151.

38. Hugh Grigsby, quoted in Oscar Shewmake, *The Honorable George Wythe* (Williamsburg, Va.: Colonial Williamsburg Foundation, 1954), p. 33.

39. Dill, *George Wythe: Teacher of Liberty*, p. 28.

40. Adams's notes on Wythe's speeches, Butterfield, *The Autobiography of John Adams*, vol. 2, p. 248; vol. 3, p. 335.

41. Benjamin Minor, ed., introduction, in George Wythe, *Decisions of Cases in Virginia by the High Court of Chancery with Remarks upon Decrees by the Court of Appeals Reversing Some of Those Decisions* (Richmond, Va.: J. W. Randolph, 1852), p. xviii; Adams's notes on Wythe's Hessian letter, Butterfield, *The Adams Papers*, vol. 4, pp. 110–112.

42. George Washington to Patrick Henry, December 19, 1777, in John Fitzpatrick, *The Writings of George Washington*, 38 vols. (Washington, D.C.: U.S. Government Printing Office, 1932), vol. 10, pp. 172–173.

43. Minor, *Decisions of Cases in Virginia*, p. xvi; Blackburn, *George Wythe in Williamsburg*, pp. 108–109.

44. Alexander Macauley, "Alexander Macauley's Journal," *William and Mary Quarterly*, Series 1, vol. 11 (1902–1903): 186–188; Warren Billings, Warren Selby, and Thad Tate, *Colonial Virginia: A History* (White Plains, N.Y.: KTO Press, 1996); Johann Doehla, "The Doehla Journal," translated by Robert Tilden, *William and Mary Quarterly*, Series 2, vol. 22, no. 7, (1942): pp. 229–274.

45. Journal of Lord Adam Gordon, in Newton Mereness, *Travels in the American Colonies* (New York: Antiquarian Press, 1961), pp. 403–404.

46. Albert Beveridge, *The Life of John Marshall*, 8 vols. (Boston: Houghton Mifflin, 1916), vol. 1, p. 157.

47. Tutor Philip Fithian, in Edmund Morgan, *Virginians at Home* (Charlottesville, N.C.: Dominion Books, 1968), pp. 78–80; June Sprigg, *Domestick Beings* (New York: Alfred Knopf, 1984), p. 84; Arthur Styron, *The Last of the Cocked Hats: James Monroe and the Virginia Dynasty* (Norman: University of Oklahoma Press, 1945), pp. 20–22.

48. Elizabeth Ambler to Mildred Smith, from Richmond, 1780, in Elizabeth Carrington, "An Old Virginia Correspondence," *Atlantic Monthly*, October, 1899, pp. 535–549; Jean Edward Smith, *John Marshall, Definer of a Nation* (New York: Henry Holt, 1996), p. 81.

49. Clifford Dowdy, *The Golden Age: A Climate for Greatness: Virginia, 1732–1775* (Boston: Little, Brown, 1970), p. 62; William Ewing, *The Sports of Williamsburg* (Richmond, Va.: Dietz Press, 1937), pp. 31–33. Washington gambled extensively in Williamsburg and at parties elsewhere, and he attended horse races in several colonies; see John Fitzpatrick, ed., *Diaries of George Washington*, 6 vols. (New York: Houghton Mifflin, 1925), vol. 2, pp. 168–169; his card-playing marathons and lottery ticket fanaticism were recorded in vol. 2, p. 57, and vol. 1, p. 238.

50. George Munford Diary, July 22, 1791, April 23, 1791, "Glimpses of Old College Life," *William and Mary Quarterly* 8, no. 3 (January 1900): 154.

51. Robert Hughes, "William and Mary, the First American Law School," *William and Mary Quarterly*, Series 2, vol. 2 (January 1922): 43.

52. Littleton Tazewell Papers, Virginia State Library; Brown, *American Aristides*, pp. 220–221.

53. George Munford, "Glimpses of College Life," pp. 153–160.

54. Burstein, *Jefferson's Secrets*, p. 130.

CHAPTER 5. JEFFERSON AND WYTHE REMAKE VIRGINIA

1. Jefferson letter to John Saunderson, August 31, 1820, in H. A. Washington, ed., *Writings of Thomas Jefferson*, 3 vols. (Washington, D.C.: Baylor & Maury, 1858), vol. 1, pp. 111–113; Joseph Gardner, ed., *The Founding Fathers: Thomas Jefferson: A Biography in His Own Words* (New York: Newsweek Publishing, 1974), p. 20.

2. James Bear Jr. and Lucia Stanton, eds., *Jefferson's Memorandum Books: Accounts, with Legal Records and Miscellany, 1767–1826*, 2 vols. (Princeton, N.J.: Princeton University Press, 1997), vol. 1, pp. 153, 206, 263, 426, 428, 455, 456, 466, and 476.

3. E. M. Halliday, *Understanding Thomas Jefferson* (New York: HarperCollins, 2001), p. 43.

4. Adrienne Koch and William Peden, "Autobiography," in *The Life and Selected Writings of Thomas Jefferson* (New York: Modern Library, 1949), p. 43.

5. Julian Boyd, *The Papers of Thomas Jefferson*, 33 vols. (Princeton, N.J.: Princeton University Press, 1950), vol. 2, pp. 572–572; George Wythe, *Decisions of Cases in Virginia by the High Court of Chancery with Remarks upon Decrees by the Court of Appeals Reversing Some of Those Decisions*, edited by Benjamin Minor (Richmond, Va.: J. W. Randolph, 1852), pp. xvii–xviii.

6. Gardner, *The Founding Fathers*, pp. 80–81.

7. Jefferson's notes on the revised criminal code, in Washington, *Writings of Thomas Jefferson*, vol. 1, pp. 148–159.

8. "Glimpses of College Life," *William and Mary Quarterly* 8, no. 3 (January 1900): 153–160.
9. Koch and Peden, *The Life and Selected Writings of Thomas Jefferson*, pp. 45–47.
10. Thomas Jefferson to Jean Demeunier, June 1786, in Boyd, *The Papers of Thomas Jefferson*, vol. 10, pp. 62–63.
11. Koch and Peden, *The Life and Selected Writings of Thomas Jefferson*, p. 51.
12. Ibid.
13. Merrill Peterson, *Thomas Jefferson and the New Nation* (New York: Oxford University Press, 1970), pp. 111–112.
14. Merrill D. Peterson, ed., *James Madison: A Biography in His Own Words* (New York: Newsweek Publications, 1974), pp. 89–90.
15. Koch and Peden, *The Life and Selected Writings of Thomas Jefferson*, p. 51; Peterson, *Thomas Jefferson and the New Nation*, pp. 111–112; Charles Cullen, "Completing the Revisal of the Laws in Post-Revolutionary Virginia," *Virginia Magazine* 82 (1974): 85–86.
16. Thomas Jefferson to Richard Price, in Boyd, *The Papers of Thomas Jefferson*, vol. 8, p. 357.
17. Charles Francis Adams, ed., *The Works of John Adams, Second President of the United States, with a Life of the Author* (Boston: Little, Brown, 1854), vol. 3, p. 50.
18. *William and Mary Quarterly*, Series 1, vol. 5 (July 1896): 182–183.
19. David Hume, *Treatise on Human Nature* (London: J. Noon, 1739); Charles Montesquieu, *Spirit of Law*, 2 vols., translated by Thomas Nugent (London: J. Nourser and Peter Vaillant, 1750), sect. 6, chap. 10, p. 153.
20. Jean Smith, *John Marshall: Definer of a Nation* (New York: Henry Holt, 1996), pp. 77–80; W. Edwin Hemphill, *George Wythe: America's First Law Professor and the Teacher of Jefferson, Marshall and Clay*, dissertation, Emory University, 1933, p. 44.
21. John Tyler to Thomas Jefferson, in a series of 1810 letters, in Boyd, *The Papers of Thomas Jefferson*, Series 2, vol. 81, p. 110.
22. Smith, *John Marshall*, p. 80.
23. George Wythe to John Adams, December 5, 1785, in Oscar Shewmake, *The Honorable George Wythe*, oration (Williamsburg, Va.: Colonial Williamsburg Foundation, 1954), p. 16.
24. Thomas Shippen to Dr. William Shippen, February 5, 1784, in Shippen Papers, Library of Congress.
25. Dice Robins, "The Teacher of Jefferson and Marshall," *South Atlantic Quarterly* 15 (1916): 341.
26. Albert Beveridge, *The Life of John Marshall*, 8 vols. (Boston: Houghton-Mifflin, 1916), p. 158; Robert Rutland, ed., *James Madison and the American Nation, 1751–1836* (New York: Simon & Schuster, 1994), p. 294.
27. Anderson, D. R. "Chancellor Wythe and Parson Weems," *William and Mary Quarterly* 25, no. 1 (July 1916).
28. Fawn Brodie, *Thomas Jefferson: An Intimate History* (New York: W. W. Norton, 1974), p. 110.
29. Jefferson referred to Wythe as his "second father" in a series of letters to John Tyler several years after Wythe's murder, in Boyd, *The Papers of Thomas Jefferson*, Series 2, no. 81, p. 110; *William and Mary Quarterly*, Series 1, vol. 6 (July 1897): 182–183.
30. Robert Hughes, "William and Mary, the First American Law School," *William and Mary Quarterly*, Series 2, vol. 2, no. 1 (January 1922): 41.
31. Arthur Styron, *The Last of the Cocked Hats: James Monroe and the Virginia Dynasty* (Norman: University of Oklahoma Press, 1945), pp. 62–63, 67, 76–77.
32. Styron, *The Last of the Cocked Hats*, p. 87; Harry Ward and Harold Greer Jr., *Richmond during the Revolution, 1775–1783* (Charlottesville: University Press of Virginia, 1977), pp. 8–9, 16; Stuart Brown, ed., *The Autobiography of James Monroe* (Syracuse, N.Y.: Syracuse University Press, 1959), pp. 224–225; Imogene Brown, *American Aristides: A Biography of George Wythe* (Teaneck, N.J.: Fairleigh Dickinson University Press, 1981), p. 207.
33. Brown, *American Aristides*, p. 217.
34. Boyd, *The Papers of Thomas Jefferson*, vol. 13, p. 372.

35. Letters between Wythe, Carr, and Jefferson, in Boyd, vol. 10, pp. 592–593; vol. 11, p. 299; and vol. 12, pp. 15, 677.
36. Thomas Jefferson to George Wythe, September 16, 1781, in Boyd, vol. 33, p. 563.
37. Lyon Taylor, "George Wythe," in William Draper Lewis, ed., *Great American Lawyers*, 8 vols. (Philadelphia: John Winston, 1907–1909), vol. 1, p. 87.
38. Jane Carson, *We Were There: Descriptions of Williamsburg, 1699–1859, Compiled from Contemporary Sources and Arranged Chronologically* (Williamsburg, Va.: Colonial Williamsburg Foundation, 1965), p. 94.
39. *Virginia Gazette*, June 28, 1786; William Wirt, writing in *The Letters of a British Spy*, 10th ed. (New York: Harper and Bros., 1832), pp. 132–133.
40. Samuel Mordecai to Ellen Mordecai, September 10, 1828, in Jacob Mordecai Papers, Duke University.
41. Boyd, *The Papers of Thomas Jefferson*, vol. 16, p. 150.
42. George Wythe to Beverley Randolph, June 16 and July 16, 1787, in Randolph Papers, Historical Society of Pennsylvania.
43. *Virginia Gazette*, August 23, 1787.
44. Colonial Williamsburg Research Archives.
45. Brown, *American Aristides*, pp. 271–273.

CHAPTER 6. RICHMOND: BOOMTOWN AND THE DECADENT NIGHTLIFE OF GEORGE WYTHE SWEENEY

1. Historical Statistics, *Colonial Times to 1970*, Series A, pp. 57–72, 11–12.
2. Myron Berman, *Richmond's Jewry, 1769–1976, Shabbat in Shockoe* (Charlottesville: University of Virginia Press, 1979), p. 30; William Lewis, ed., *The Great American Lawyers*, 8 vols. (Philadelphia, 1907–1909), p. 72.
3. Elna Green, *This Business of Relief: Confronting Poverty in a Southern City, 1740–1940* (Athens: University of Georgia Press, 1993), p. 24.
4. H. R. McIlwaine and John Pendleton Kennedy, eds., *Journals of the House of Burgesses of Virginia*, Richmond, Virginia, (1905–1915, 1752–1755, 1756–1758), p. 100; Rhys Isaacs, *The Transformation of Virginia, 1740–1790* (New York: W.W. Norton, 1982), p. 100; Jackson Lears, *Something for Nothing: Luck in America* (New York: Penguin, 2003), p. 87; James Sidbury, *Ploughshares into Swords: Race, Rebellion, and Identity in Gabriel's Virginia, 1730–1810* (New York: Cambridge University Press, 1997), pp. 172–173; Richmond Hustings Court Order Books #3 (1797), #4 (1797), others.
5. H. J. Eckenrode, ed., *Richmond, Capital of Virginia: Approaches to Its History* (Richmond: Whittet & Shepperson, 1938), p. 34; Henrico County Records, 1687, in Eckenrode, p. 34n, p. 35n, p. 39; "Journal of a French Traveler in the Colonies, 1765, I," *American Historical Review* 26 (1920–1921): 743; Isaacs, pp. 94–95.
6. Harold Gill, Jr., "Williamsburg and the Demimonde: Disorderly Houses, the Blue Bell and Certain Hints of Harlotry," *Journal of the Colonial Williamsburg Foundation* (Autumn 2001): 27–31.
7. F. F. Ferguson to Dr. William Sanger, September 15, 1856, in William Sanger, *The History of Prostitution: Its Extent, Causes and Effects throughout the World* (New York: Eugenics Publishing), pp. 810–811, 523; Richmond Hustings Court Order Books, #4–9, 1810.
8. Robert Bailey, *The Life and Adventures of Robert Bailey, from His Infancy up to December, 1821* (Richmond, Va.: J & G. Cochran, 1822), p. 49; *Richmond Daily Dispatch*, August 27, 1853; Sanger, *The History of Prostitution*, pp. 524, 580.
9. Sanger, *The History of Prostitution*, pp. 452, 624, 529.
10. David Schwarz, *Roll the Bones: The History of Gambling* (New York: Gotham Books, 2006), pp. 138, 147.

11. T. H. Breen, "Horses and Gentlemen: The Cultural Significance of Gambling among the Gentry in Virginia," *William and Mary Quarterly* (April 1977): 339–357; *Virginia Gazette*, April 4, 1768.

12. Schwarz, *Roll the Bones*, p. 148.

13. Linda Sturtz, "The Ladies and the Lottery: Elite Women's Gambling in Eighteenth Century Virginia," *Virginia Magazine of History and Biography* 104, no. 2 (Spring 1996): 177–184; *Virginia Gazette*, May 26, 1768.

14. Sturtz, "The Ladies and the Lottery," p. 178.

15. *Pennsylvania Evening Post*, May 13, 1777; *Journal of the Continental Congress 1904–1937*: 192.

16. "Diary of a Little Colonial Girl," *Virginia Magazine of History and Biography* 11 (1903–1904): 213.

17. Lears, *Something for Nothing*, p. 69.

18. Breen, "Horses and Gentlemen," pp. 339–357; John Fitzpatrick, ed., *Diaries of George Washington*, 4 vols., Mount Vernon Ladies Association of the Union (Boston: Houghton-Mifflin, 1925), vol. 2, p. 57, and vol. 1, p. 238; *Washington in Williamsburg*, monograph, Morristown National Historical Park collections, Morristown, N.J., 1956, pp. 22–25; Schwarz, *Roll the Bones*, pp. 152–153.

19. Ann Fabian, *Card Sharps, Dream Books and Bucket Shops: Gambling in Nineteenth Century America* (Ithaca, N.Y.: Cornell University Press, 1990), pp. 23–25, 48–49.

20. Richmond Hustings Court Order Books, #4–9, 1810.

21. Recollection of Richmond by Bernard Henley, "Of Main Street, the Eagle Hotel and Gambling, c. 1830," *Richmond Quarterly* 4 (Fall 1981): 37–39.

22. Fithian entry, October 3, 1774, in Hunter Farish, ed., *Phillip Fithian, Journal and Letters of Phillip Fithian, 1773–74: A Plantation Tutor of the Old Dominion* (Williamsburg, Va.: Colonial Williamsburg Foundation, 1943), also see p. 282.

23. Ibid., pp. 37–39.

24. Bailey, *The Life and Adventures of Robert Bailey*, p. 44.

25. Ibid., p. 53.

26. Ibid., p. 44.

27. Fabian, *Card Sharps, Dream Books & Bucket Shops: Gambling in Nineteenth Century America*, p. 23; Isaacs, *The Transformation of Virginia, 1740–1790*, p. 247.

28. Bailey, *The Life and Adventures of Robert Bailey*, pp. 48–49.

29. Virginius Dabney, *Richmond: The Story of a City* (Charlottesville: University Press of Virginia, 1976), p. 36.

30. George Munford, *Two Parsons, Cupid's Sports, the Dream and the Jewels of Virginia* (Richmond: J.D.K. Sleight, 1884), p. 349.

31. Sidbury, *Ploughshares into Swords*, pp. 248–249.

32. Samuel Mordecai, Papers, Duke University, pp. 248–250; Dabney, *Richmond: The Story of a City*, p. 36.

33. Bailey, *The Life and Adventures of Robert Bailey*, pp. 43–44.

34. Mordecai, p. 247.

35. Breen, "Horses and Gentlemen," pp. 249–254; November 25, 1773, in Farish, ed., *Phillip Fithian, Journal and Letters of Phillip Fithian, 1773–1774: A Plantation Tutor of the Old Dominion*, p. 32; Dabney, *Richmond: The Story of a City*, p. 36.

36. T. J. Macon, *Life Gleanings* (Richmond, Va.: W. H. Adams, 1913), p. 35.

37. Ibid., p. 37.

38. Dabney, *Richmond: The Story of a City*, p. 36.

39. David Johnson, *Policing the Urban Underworld: The Impact of Crime on the Development of the American Police, 1800–1887* (Philadelphia: Temple University Press, 1942), p. 49; *Aurora* (N.Y.) *General Advertiser*, July 17, 1800; *Philadelphia Public Ledger*, June 17, 1840.

40. Dr. William Foushee to the governor of Virginia, August 29, 1782; William Palmer, ed., *Calendar of Virginia State Papers and Other Manuscripts, 1652–1869*, 11 vols. (Richmond, Va.: State of Virginia, 1875–1893), vol. 3, p. 274.

41. *Report of the Minority of the Committee of Twenty Four on the Subject of Gambling in the City of Richmond* (Richmond, Va.: T. W. White Publishers, 1833 [its office, coincidentally, was next door to one of the infamous gaming dens, Bell's Tavern, and it advertised that location in its books and pamphlets to attract business]), pp. 14–17.

42. 1833 Virginia legislative report on gambling in Richmond, p. 15.

43. Jefferson Wallace to Charles Wallace, April 1, 1855, Clopton Family Papers, Duke University.

44. Bailey, *The Life and Adventures of Robert Bailey*, p. 44.

45. Gregg Kimball, *American City, Southern Place: A Cultural History of Antebellum Richmond* (Athens: University of Georgia Press, 2000), p. 48.

46. *Report of the Minority of the Committee of Twenty Four on the Subject of Gambling in the City of Richmond*, p. 4.

47. Dabney, *Richmond: The Story of a City*, p. 39; Lears, *Something for Nothing*, p. 114.

48. Robert Saunders, "Crime and Punishment in Early National America: Richmond, Virginia, 1784–1820," *Virginia Magazine of History and Biography* 86 (1978): 35, 37; Records of the Richmond Hustings Court for 1784–1820, *Uniform Crime Statistics, Federal Bureau of Investigation*, 2007.

49. *Pittsburgh Gazette*, November 28, 1833.

50. Hustings Court records, 1784–1820; Saunders, "Crime and Punishment in Early National America: Richmond, Virginia, 1784–1820," p. 38.

51. Hustings Court records, 1784–1820; Saunders, "Crime and Punishment in Early National America: Richmond, Virginia, 1784–1820," p. 41.

52. U.S. Census of 1810.

53. Dabney, *Richmond: The Story of a City*, p. 49; Saunders, "Crime and Punishment in Early National America: Richmond, Virginia, 1784–1820," p. 42; *U.S. Bureau of the Census Reports for Virginia and Richmond*, 1790, 1800, 1810; Virginia: Personal Property and Real Estate, 1788, 1789, 1791, 1795, 1800, 1805; black criminal codes were mandated by a number of legislative acts going back to 1705.

54. Saunders, "Crime and Punishment," pp. 41, 43; Philip Schwarz, *Slave Laws in Virginia* (Athens: University of Georgia Press, 1996), p. 85 (Schwarz used Virginia county court records for his statistics); murder quote from Eckenrode, *Richmond, Capital of Virginia*, 35n.

55. *Richmond Enquirer*, February 6, 1806; William Crawford, *Report on the Penitentiaries of the United States* (Montclair, N.J.: Patterson Smith, 1969), p. 111.

56. Dabney, *Richmond: The Story of a City*, pp. 48–49.

57. Jay Worrall, *Friendly Virginians: History of America's First Quakers*, unpublished manuscript, 1992, Virginia Historical Society.

Chapter 7. The Dying George Wythe Changes His Will

1. George Munford, *Two Parsons, Cupid's Sports, the Dream and the Jewels of Virginia* (Richmond, Va.: J.D.K. Sleight, 1884), pp. 427–429.

2. Thomas Jefferson to George Wythe, August 13, 1786, in Julian Boyd, *The Papers of Thomas Jefferson*, 33 vols. (Princeton, N.J.: Princeton University Press, 1950), vol. 10, p. 244.

3. Thomas Jefferson to George Wythe, October, 1794, in Jack McLaughlin, *To His Excellency Thomas Jefferson: Letters to a President* (New York: W. W. Norton, 1991), p. 258.

4. Joseph Gardner, ed., *The Founding Fathers: Thomas Jefferson: A Biography in His Own Words* (New York: Newsweek Publishing, 1974), pp. 273–274.

5. Thomas Jefferson to George Wythe, August 13, 1786, in Boyd, *The Papers of Thomas Jefferson*, vol. 10, p. 244.

6. Jacob Marcus, *Early American Jewry, the Jews of Pennsylvania and the South, 1655–1790* (Philadelphia: Jewish Publication Societies of America, 1953), vol. 2, p. 180.

CHAPTER 8. MOVING DAY: A SECOND LIFE IN RICHMOND AND THE RETURN OF GEORGE WYTHE

1. Clement Eaton, *Henry Clay and the Art of American Politics* (Boston: Little, Brown, 1957), p. 7.
2. Joyce Blackburn, *George Wythe in Williamsburg* (New York: Harper and Row, 1975), p. 275.
3. James City County Court deed poll, October 8, 1787; slave manumissions recorded September 15, 1788, York County Deed Book 6 (1777–1791, pp. 351, 371, 390–391); George Wythe to Richard Taliaferro on the return of slaves, August 20, 1787, *William and Mary Quarterly*, Series 1, vol. 12: 125–126.
4. Thomas Jefferson to Richard Price, August 7, 1785, in Julian Boyd, *The Papers of Thomas Jefferson*, 33 vols. (Princeton, N.J.: Princeton University Press, 1950), vol. 8, pp. 356–357.
5. Thomas Jefferson, *Notes on the State of Virginia* (London: John Stockdale, 1782, reprinted, by Chapel Hill: University of North Carolina Press, 1955), p. 87; Imogene Brown, *American Aristides: A Biography of George Wythe* (Teaneck, N.J.: Fairleigh Dickinson University Press, 1981), p. 269 note.
6. Jefferson, *Notes on the State of Virginia*, pp. 139–143.
7. Thomas Jefferson to Edward Coles, August 25, 1614, in *Notes on the State of Virginia*, p. 287 note.
8. Jean Smith, *John Marshall: Definer of a Nation* (New York: Henry Holt, 1996), pp. 251–252; William Henning and William Munford, *Reports of Cases Argued and Determined in the Supreme Court of Appeals of Virginia: With Select Cases, Relating Chiefly to Points of Practice Decided by the Superior Court of Chancery for the Richmond District*, 2d ed., 4 vols. (Charlottesville: University Press of Virginia, 1903, reprint), pp. 71–74.
9. Blackburn, *George Wythe in Williamsburg*, Colonial Williamsburg Research Files, p. 123.
10. Virginius Dabney, *Richmond: The Story of a City* (Charlottesville: University Press of Virginia, 1976), p. 38.
11. Hugh Grigsby, *Collections of the Virginia Historical Society: The History of the Virginia Federal Convention of 1788*, 2 vols. (Richmond, Va.: Virginia Historical Society, 1858), vol. 1, p. 65.
12. Dabney, *Richmond: The Story of a City*, p. 39.
13. Henry Clay to Benjamin Minor in *Decisions*, quoted in the address of Oscar Shewmake, a College of William and Mary professor, on December 18, 1921, in *The Honorable George Wythe: Teacher, Lawyer, Jurist, Statesman* (Williamsburg, Va.: William and Mary Publications, 1921, 2nd printing in 1922), p. 34.
14. George Wythe, *Decisions of Cases in Virginia by the High Court of Chancery with Remarks upon Decrees by the High Court of Appeals Reversing Some of Those Decisions*, edited by George Minor (Richmond: J.W. Randolph, 1852), p. 94.
15. James Paulding, *Letters from the South*, 2 vols. (New York: James Eastburn, 1817), vol. 1, p. 50.
16. Address by Oscar Shewmake, p. 20.
17. Fiske Kimball, *The Capitol of Virginia: A Landmark in American Architecture*, edited by Jon Kukla (Richmond: Virginia State Library and Archives, 1989), p. 13; Gregg Kimball, *American City, Southern Place: A Cultural History of Antebellum Richmond* (Athens: University of Georgia Press, 2000), p. 3; William Draper Lewis, ed., *Great American Lawyers*, 8 vols. (Philadelphia: John Winston, 1907), vol. 1, p. 86.
18. Blackburn, *George Wythe in Williamsburg*, p. 129.
19. Dabney, *Richmond: The Story of a City*, p. 34; H. J. Eckenrode, ed., *Richmond, Capital of Virginia: Approaches to Its History* (Richmond: Whittet & Shepperson, 1938), p. 41.

20. Dabney, *Richmond: The Story of a City*, pp. 34–35.

21. Ibid., p. 34.

22. Ibid., p. 40.

23. Harry Ward and Harold Greer Jr., *Richmond during the Revolution: 1775–1783* (Charlottesville: University Press of Virginia, 1977), pp. 8–9, 16.

24. J.D.B. DeBow, *Statistical View of the United States . . . Being a Compendium of the Seventh Census* (Washington, D.C.: Beverly Tucker, 1854), pp. 398–399; *Population of the United States for 1860, Compiled from the Original Returns of the Eighth Census* (Washington, D.C.: U.S. Government Printing Office, 1864), xiii, xxxii.

25. Allan Nevins, *The Diary of Phillip Hones, 1828–1851*, 2 vols. (New York: Dodd, Mead, 1927), vol. 1, p. 209.

26. Ward and Greer, *Richmond during the Revolution*, p. 109.

27. Jefferson, *Notes on the State of Virginia*, pp. 84–85.

28. Eaton, *Henry Clay and the Art of American Politics*, pp. 118–119; Daniel Mallory, ed., *The Life and Speeches of Henry Clay*, 2 vols. (New York: Van Amringe and Bixby, 1844), vol. 1, pp. 10–11.

29. Eaton, *Henry Clay and the Art of American Politics*, pp. 6–7, 118–119.

30. Thomas Jefferson to George Wythe, May 29, 1799, in Boyd, *The Papers of Thomas Jefferson*, Library of Congress.

31. Smith, *John Marshall*, p. 95; Dice Anderson, "The Teacher of Jefferson and Marshall," *South Atlantic Quarterly* 16 (1916): 336–337.

32. R. J. Hoffman, "Classics in the Courts of the United States, 1790–1800," *American Journal of Legal History* 22 (1978): 55–84.

Chapter 9. The Arrest

1. Julian Boyd, "The Murder of George Wythe," *William and Mary Quarterly* (October 1955): 33.

2. Joyce Blackburn, *George Wythe in Williamsburg* (New York: Harper & Row, 1975), p. 136.

3. There was speculation that the teenage Brown was Wythe's illegitimate son, whom he had with Lydia Broadnax. Lengthy investigations by one of his biographers, Imogene Brown, and two researchers at Williamsburg's Rockefeller Library, Louis Powers and Linda Rowe, have disproved that contention. They pointed out that Michael was born about 1790, just after the death of Wythe's wife. Wythe might have been sterile. But if he was not, it would have been very unlikely that Broadnax, nearly fifty then, could have borne a child. Slave sons had their mother's last names, and he was called Brown. In copious population records that were kept at the time, Lydia was never listed as a mother, and no Michael Brown or Michael Broadnax was mentioned in Wythe's household, or in tax records. The teenager would have been born free, since Lydia had been freed in 1787, yet Wythe referred to him as his "freed boy," meaning that he had at one time been a slave. Childless owners often provided for slaves in their wills. Wythe had a long history of tutoring both black and white teenagers, and Michael was just one more. Wythe was also a rather pious man, and it seems out of character for him to enter into a relationship with his cook, or anyone, after his wife's death.

Chapter 10. The Investigation, Part II

1. Julian Boyd and Edward Hemphill, *The Murder of George Wythe, Two Essays* (Williamsburg, Va.: Institute of Early American History and Culture, 1955), pp. 49–50.

2. *Richmond Enquirer* and *Argus* coverage in the first week of May 1806.

3. Imogene Brown, *American Aristides: A Biography of George Wythe* (Teaneck, N.J.: Fairleigh Dickinson University Press, 1981), p. 83.

4. John Page to St. George Tucker, June 29, 1806, Tucker-Coleman Papers, Colonial Williamsburg Collection, Rockefeller Library; see also vol. 1, p. 152; *Petersburg Republican*, reprinted in the Philadelphia's *Paulson's American Daily Advertiser*, June 17, 1806; M. L. Weems, *Charleston (S.C.) Times*, July 1, 1806.

CHAPTER 11. FOR THE DEFENSE: WILLIAM WIRT

1. John P. Kennedy, *Memoirs of the Life of William Wirt, the Attorney General of the United States*, 2 vols. (Philadelphia: Lea and Blanchard, 1849), vol. 1, pp. 16, 66, and vol. 2, p. 433.

2. Kennedy, *Memoirs of the Life of William Wirt*, vol. 1, p. 66.

3. John Little, *History of Richmond* (Richmond, Va.: Dietz, 1933), pp. 110–111; F. W. Thomas, *John Randolph of Roanoke and Other Sketches of Character, including William Wirt, Together with Tales of Real Life* (Philadelphia: A. Hart, 1853), pp. 38–39.

4. William Wirt to his wife, July 18, 1806, in Kennedy, *Memoirs of the Life of William Wirt*, vol. 1, pp. 52–53.

5. Description of Norfolk by Lord Adam Gordon on his 1765 tour of America, in Newton Mereness, ed., *Travels in the American Colonies* (New York: Antiquarian Press, 1961), pp. 406–407.

6. William Wirt to Dabney Carr, February 13, 1803, in Kennedy, *Memoirs of the Life of William Wirt*, vol. 1, pp. 94–95.

7. William Wirt to Dabney Carr, March 20, 1803, in Kennedy, *Memoirs of the Life of William Wirt*, vol. 1, pp. 96–97.

8. Gregory Glassner, *Adopted Son: The Life, Wit and Wisdom of William Wirt, 1772–1834* (Madison County, Va.: Kurt-Ketner, 1997), p. 34.

9. Francois La Rochefoucauld-Liancourt, *Voyages dans les Etats-Unis d'amerique, fait en 1795, de 1797*, 4 vols. (Paris: DuPont de la Republique, 1799), vol. 4, pp. 256–257; *Norfolk Gazette and Public Ledger*, September 12, 1806, in Glassner, *Adopted Son: The Life, Wit and Wisdom of William Wirt, 1772–1834*, pp. 33–34.

10. William Wirt to Benjamin Edwards, March 17, 1805, in Kennedy, *Memoirs of the Life of William Wirt*, vol. 1, pp. 133.

11. Kennedy, *Memoirs of the Life of William Wirt*, vol. 1, pp. 118–123.

12. Anya Jabour, *Marriage in the Early Republic: Elizabeth and William Wirt and the Companionate Ideal* (Baltimore, Md.: Johns Hopkins University Press, 1998), p. 29.

13. Ibid., pp. 30–32.

14. William Wirt to Elizabeth Wirt, July 26 and August 9, 1805, and Elizabeth Wirt to William Wirt, August 5, 1805, Wirt Papers, Maryland Historical Society.

15. Ibid.

16. James Callender to Thomas Jefferson, August 10, 1788, in Washington Chauncey Ford, ed., "Thomas Jefferson and James Thomson Callender," *New England Historical and Genealogical Register* 50 (1896): 446.

17. James Callender, *The Prospect before Us* (Richmond, Va.: M. Jones, S. Pleasants and J. Lyon, 1800), preface, part 1, p. 179; part 3, p. 58.

18. "Sedition in the Old Dominion," in James Smith, *Freedom's Fetters: The Alien and Sedition Cases and American Civil Liberties* (Ithaca, N.Y.: Cornell University Press, 1956), pp. 344–345.

19. Smith, *Freedom's Fetters*, pp. 354–355.

20. E. M. Halliday, *Understanding Thomas Jefferson* (New York: HarperCollins, 2001), pp. 172–174; Fawn Brodie, *Thomas Jefferson: An Intimate History* (New York: W. W. Norton, 1974), pp. 322–323.

21. William Wirt to Elizabeth Wirt, October 16, 1802, Wirt Papers.

22. Letters of William Wirt to his wife, in Kennedy, *Memoirs of the Life of William Wirt*, vol. 1, pp. 140–142.

23. William Taylor, "William Wirt and the Legend of the Old South," in *Cavalier and Yankee: The Old South and American National Character* (New York: G. Braziller, 1961), pp. 67–94; William Wirt to Benjamin Edwards, March 17, 1805, in Kennedy, *Memoirs of the Life of William Wirt*, vol. 1, pp. 133–139.

24. William Wirt to James Monroe, June 10, 1806, Monroe Papers.

25. Littleton Tazewell, "Sketches of His Own Family," Norfolk, 1823, Virginia State Library.
26. Julian Boyd, "The Murder of George Wythe," *William and Mary Quarterly* (October 1955): 55.
27. Kennedy, *Memoirs of the Life of William Wirt*, vol. 1, pp. 106–108.
28. William Wirt to Elizabeth Wirt, July 13, 1806, in Kennedy, *Memoirs of the Life of William Wirt*, vol. 1, pp. 152–155.
29. D. L. Southard, *Discourse on the Professional Character and Virtues of the Late William Wirt* (Washington, D.C.: Gales and Seaton, 1834), p. 12.
30. Kennedy, *Memoirs of the Life of William Wirt*, vol. 1, pp. 86.
31. Southard, *Discourse on the Professional Character and Virtues of the Late William Wirt*, pp. 12, 15.
32. Kennedy, *Memoirs of the Life of William Wirt*, vol. 1, p. 86.
33. Ibid., p. 66; Southard, *Discourse on the Professional Character and Virtues of the Late William Wirt*, p. 16.
34. Kennedy, *Memoirs of the Life of William Wirt*, vol. 2, pp. 436–437.
35. Ibid., vol. 2, pp. 443–444.

CHAPTER 12. FOR THE DEFENSE: EDMUND RANDOLPH

1. John Reardon, *Edmund Randolph: A Biography* (New York: Macmillan, 1974), pp. 20–22.
2. Mary K. Tachau, "George Washington and the Reputation of Edmund Randolph," *Journal of American History*, 73, no. 1 (June 1986): 15–38.
3. Moncure Conway, *Omitted Chapters in History Disclosed in the Life and Papers of Edmund Randolph* (New York: G. P. Putnam's Sons, 1888), p. 359.
4. Conway, *Omitted Chapters in History*, p. 359.
5. Reardon, *Edmund Randolph*, pp. 316–319.
6. Jonathan Daniels, *The Randolphs of Virginia* (Garden City, N.Y.: Doubleday, 1972), pp. 162–163.
7. Ibid., pp. 325–329.
8. Conway, *Omitted Chapters in History*, p. 371.
9. Reardon, *Edmund Randolph*, pp. 349–357.
10. Harry Ammon, *James Monroe: The Quest for National Identity* (New York: McGraw-Hill, 1971), p. 70.
11. Ibid., pp. 66–67.
12. Reverend M. L. Weems letter to the *Charleston* (S.C.) *Times*, July 1, 1806.
13. George Wythe to Robert Alexander, in M. L. Weems letter to the editor, *Charleston Times*, July 1, 1806.
14. D. R. Anderson, "Chancellor Wythe and Parson Weems," *William and Mary Quarterly* 25, no. 1 (July 1916): 15.
15. Gregory Glassner, *Adopted Son: The Life, Wit and Wisdom of William Wirt, 1772–1834* (Madison County, Va.: Kurt-Ketner, 1997), pp. 36–37; William Wirt, *The Letters of a British Spy*, 10th ed. (New York: Harper and Bros., 1832), pp. 207–208.
16. William Wirt to Dabney Carr, January 16, 1804, in John P. Kennedy, *Memoirs of the Life of William Wirt, the Attorney General of the United States*, 2 vols. (Philadelphia: Lea and Blanchard, 1849), vol. 1, pp. 111–123.

CHAPTER 13. MOURNING AT THE EXECUTIVE MANSION

1. Dumas Malone, *Jefferson and His Time*, 5 vols. (Boston: Little, Brown, 1974), vol. 5, p. 135.
2. William DuVal to Thomas Jefferson, June 29, 1806, and November 21, 1806, Jefferson Papers, Library of Congress, Princeton University.
3. Dumas Malone, *Jefferson and His Time*, vol. 5, p. 139.
4. Ibid., vol. 5, p. 139.

5. Thomas Jefferson to John Saunderson, August 31, 1820, *Writings of Thomas Jefferson*, vol. 1, pp. 111–113.

6. Andrew Burstein, *Jefferson's Secrets: Death and Desire at Monticello* (New York: Basic Books, 2005), p. 13; Julian Boyd, "The Murder of George Wythe," *William and Mary Quarterly*, Series 3, vol. 12 (1955): 512–541.

7. Eliphalet Adams, *A Sermon Preached on the Occasion of the Execution of Katherine Garret* (New London, Conn.: T. Green, 1738), p. 42.

CHAPTER 14. THE FORENSICS NIGHTMARE, PART I: ARSENIC, THE POISON OF CHOICE

1. Mary Roach, *Stiff: The Curious Lives of Human Cadavers* (New York: W. W. Norton, 2003), pp. 39–40.

2. Dudley Weber, Eugene Fazzani, and Thomas Reagan, *Autopsy Pathology Procedure and Protocol* (Springfield, Ill.: Charles Thomas, 1973), p. ix.

3. Rolla Hill and Robert Anderson, *The Autopsy: Medical Practice and Public Policy* (London: Butterworth, 1988), pp. 112–113.

4. *Beitrage Zur Gerichtllichen Medizin* 49 (1991): 297–305.

5. E. J. Wagner, *The Science of Sherlock Holmes: From Baskerville Hall to the Valley of Fear, the Real Forensics behind the Great Detective's Greatest Cases* (New York: John Wiley & Sons, 2006), p. 6.

6. Martin Kaufman, *American Medical Education: The Formative Years, 1765–1910* (Westport, Conn.: Greenwood), p. 10.

7. Christopher Lawrence, "Ornate Physicians and Learned Artisans: Edinburgh Medical Men, 1726–1776"; W. F. Bynum and Roy Porter, *William Hunter and the Eighteenth Century Medical World* (Cambridge: Cambridge University Press, 1985), pp. 57, 160–161.

8. *New York Gazette*, July 18 and 20, 1799.

9. Kelley autopsy from *Pediatrics* 61 (1978): 572; Mary Roach, *Stiff: The Curious Lives of Human Cadavers*, pp. 40–46.

10. Jean Folkets and Dwight Teeters, *Vision of a Nation: A History of Media in the United States* (New York: MacMillan, 1989), pp. 92, 130–149; *Massachusetts Spy*, July 7, 1778.

11. Kaufman, *American Medical Education*, pp. 28–29.

12. Albert Lyons and R. Joseph Petrucelli, *Medicine: An Illustrated History* (New York: Harry Abrams, 1978), p. 534.

13. Clarence Meyer, *American Folk Medicine* (New York: Thomas Crowell, 1973), pp. 2–9; Kaufman, *American Medical Education*, pp. 10–14.

14. Ronald Numbers, ed., *Medicine in the New World: New France, New Spain, New England* (Knoxville: University of Tennessee Press, 1987), p. 141.

15. Ibid., p. 11; General James Varnum to George Washington, January 3, 1778, George Washington Papers, Library of Congress; General Jedidiah Huntington to George Washington, January 1, 1778, George Washington Papers, Library of Congress; Benjamin Rush to Nathanael Greene, in Richard Showman and Dennis Conrad, *Papers of Nathanael Greene*, 12 vols. (Chapel Hill: University of North Carolina Press, 1976–2002), vol. 2, pp. 257; Dr. John Beck, *Medicine in the American Colonies, an Historical Sketch of the State of Medicine in the American Colonies, from Their First Settlement to the Period of the Revolution* (Albany, N.Y.: C. Van Benthuysen, 1850), pp. 34, 36.

16. Whitfield Bell, *The Colonial Physician and Other Essays* (New York: Science History Publications, 1975), p. 6.

17. *Virginia Gazette*, May 1745; David Copeland, *Colonial American Newspapers: Character and Content* (Newark: University of Delaware Press, 1997), pp. 183–187.

18. Maurice Gordon, MD, *Aesculapius Comes to the Colonies: The Story of the Early Days of Medicine in the Thirteen Original Colonies* (Ventnor, N.J.: Ventnor Publishers, 1949), p. 33.

19. Gerald Grob, *The Deadly Truth: A History of Disease in America* (Cambridge, Mass.: Harvard University Press, 2002), pp. 50–52; Maurice Gordon, *Aesculapius Comes to the Colonies*, pp. 19–21; Thomas Hughes, *Medicine in Virginia, 1607–1699* (Williamsburg: Virginia's 350th Celebration Corporation, 1957), p. 72.

20. Kaufman, *American Medical Education*, pp. 23–24.

21. James McClurg to a friend, *William and Mary Quarterly*, Series 2, vol. 4 (October 1922).

22. John Reardon, *Edmund Randolph: A Biography* (New York: Macmillan, 1974), p. 248.

23. H. J. Eckenrode, ed., *Richmond, Capital of Virginia: Approaches to Its History* (Richmond, Va.: Whittet & Shepperson, 1938), p. 229; Wynham Blanton, *Medicine in Virginia in the Nineteenth Century* (Richmond, Va.: Garrett & Massie, 1933), vol. 13, pp. 75–76; W. Asbury Christian, *Richmond: Her Past and Present* (Richmond, Va.: L. H. Jenkins, 1912), p. 545.

24. James McClurg, *Experiments upon the Human Bile and Reflections on the Biliary Secretions* (London: T. Cadell, 1772); M. E. Bradford, *Founding Fathers: Brief Lives of the Framers of the United States Constitution* (Topeka: University of Kansas Press, 1981), p. 162; Gordon, *Aesculapius Comes to the Colonies*, pp. 46–47.

25. Blanton, *Medicine in Virginia in the Nineteenth Century*, pp. 116–117, 261, 367.

26. Ibid., pp. 75–76; Christian, *Richmond: Her Past and Present*, pp. 57–58; *Richmond Enquirer*, August 24, 1824.

27. Midori Takagi, *Rearing Wolves to Our Own Destruction: Slavery in Virginia, 1782–1865* (Charlottesville: University Press of Virginia, 1999), p. 44.

28. *Richmond Enquirer*, July 15, 1824.

29. James McClurg, "On Reasoning in Medicine," *Philadelphia Journal of Medical and Physical Sciences* (Philadelphia: M. Carey and Son, 1820), pp. 34–35; McClurg, *Experiments upon the Human Bile and Reflections on the Biliary Secretions*, pp. 118, 196, 208, 210–214.

30. Dr. Jonathan Miller, "An Account of an Epidemic Fever which Has Prevailed in Certain Parts of Virginia for the Last Eight Years," in *Philadelphia Journal of Medical and Physical Science*, vol. 5 (Philadelphia: Carey & Lea, 1822); *Virginia Argus*, March 1 and 29, 1815.

31. *Tyler's Quarterly*, vol. 5, p. 21, cited in Blanton, *Medicine in Virginia in the Nineteenth Century*, p. 134.

32. Colonial Williamsburg research query, 1994.

33. McClurg, "On Reasoning in Medicine," pp. 220–223.

34. McClurg, "On Reasoning in Medicine," p. 234.

35. McClurg, *Experiments upon the Human Bile and Reflections on the Biliary Secretions*, introduction.

36. Boyd, "The Murder of George Wythe," *William and Mary Quarterly*, Series 3, vol. 12 (October 1955): 28.

37. M. Alice Ottoboni, PhD, *The Dose Makes the Poison* (Berkeley, Calif.: Vincente Books, 1984), p. 33.

38. Curtis Klaasen, Mary Amdur, and John Doull, *Casarett and Doull's Toxicology: The Basic Science of Poison*, 3rd ed. (New York: Macmillan, 1986), pp. 843–844.

39. A. Wallace Hayes, ed., *Principles and Methods of Toxicology* (New York: Raven Press, 1994), pp. 2–8.

40. B. Gorman and D. L. Kaplan, "The Affliction of Job: Poisoned!" *Journal of the American Academy of Dermatology* 40, no. 1 (January 1999): 126–128.

41. C.J.S. Thompson, *Poisons and Poisoners, with Historical Accounts of Some Famous Mysteries in Ancient and Modern Times* (New York: Barnes & Noble, 1993), pp. 26–27.

42. Richard Glyn Jones, *Poison! The World's Greatest True Murder Stories* (Secaucus, N.J.: Lyle Stuart, 1987), p. 8.

43. Thompson, *Poisons and Poisoners*, pp. 41–42.

44. Ibid., p. 90.

45. Serita Deborah Stevens and Anne Klarner, *Deadly Doses: A Writer's Guide to Poisons* (Cincinnati, Ohio: Writer's Digest Books, 1990), p. 6.

46. Klaasen, Amdur, and Doull, *Casarett and Doull's Toxicology*, pp. 843–844.

47. Michael Gorby, "Clinical Conference: Arsenic Poisoning," *Western Journal of Medicine* 149 (September 1988): 308–315.

48. John Emsley, *Elements of Murder* (Oxford: Oxford University Press, 2005), pp. 74–87.

49. Charles Spear, *Essays on the Punishment of Death* (Boston: C. Gilipin, 1851), p. 13.

50. Pamphlet by William Smith, *A Just Account of the Horrid Contrivance of John Cupper and Judith Brown, His Servant, in the Poysoning of His Wife*, Shrewsbury, England, 1684.

51. Reverend John Quick, *Hell Open'd, or the Infernal Sin of Murther Punished*, Plymouth, England, 1676; *Horrid News from St. Martins, or, Unheard-of Murder and Poyson*, St. Martin's, England, 1677.

52. Thompson, *Poisons and Poisoners*, p. 97; Robert Christison, *A Treatise on Poisons, in Relation to Medical Jurisprudence, Physiology and the Practice of Physic*, 2nd ed. (Edinburgh: Edinburgh University Press, 1832), p. 196; Journal de chimie Medicale, Paris (1842): 656.

53. Emsley, *Elements of Murder*, pp. 71–72.

54. Stuart Banner, *The Death Penalty in American History* (Cambridge, Mass.: Harvard University Press, 2002), p. 12; Philip Schwarz, *Twice Condemned: Slaves and the Criminal Cases of Virginia, 1705–1865* (Baton Rouge: Louisiana State University Press, 1988), pp. 103–113.

55. Anthony Campbell, "Darwin's Illness Revealed," *Postgraduate Medical Journal* 81 (2005): 248; Ben Weider and John Fornier, "Activation Analysis of Authenticated Hairs of Napoleon Bonaparte Confirm Arsenic Poisoning," *American Journal of Forensic Medicine and Pathology* 20, no. 4 (December 1999): 1; X. Lin, D. Alber, and R. Henkelman, "Elemental Contents in Napoleon's Hair Cut before and after His Death: Did Napoleon Die of Arsenic Poisoning?" *Analytical and Bioanalytical Chemistry Journal* 379, no. 2 (May 2004): 218–219; F. Mari, E. Bertol, V. Fineschi, and S. B. Karch, "Channeling the Emperor: What Really Killed Napoleon?" *Journal of the Royal Society of Medicine* 97, no. 8 (August 2004): 397–399.

56. Wagner, *The Science of Sherlock Holmes* (New York: John Wiley & Sons, 2006), p. 4.

57. Ibid., p. 48.

Chapter 15. The Forensics Nightmare, Part II: The Autopsy

1. Julian Boyd, "The Murder of George Wythe," *William and Mary Quarterly*, Series 3, vol. 12 (October 1955): 50.

2. James McClurg, *Experiments upon the Human Bile and Reflections on the Biliary Secretions* (London: T. Cadell, 1772), pp. 92–94, 105, 182, 196, 199–200.

3. "London Coroner's Inquests for 1590," *Journal of the History of Medicine and Allied Sciences* 28, no. 4 (1973): 376–386; Dennis Chitty, ed., *Control of Rats and Mice*, 3 vols. (Oxford, England: Clarendon Press, 1954), vol. 1, pp. 26–27, vol. 2, pp. 490; Arien Mack, ed., *In Time of Plague: The History and Social Consequences of Lethal Epidemic Diseases* (New York: New York University Press, 1991), p. 103.

4. P. Bartrip, "A Pennurth of Arsenic for Rat Poison: The Arsenic Act of 1851, and the Prevention of Secret Poisoning," *Medical History* 36, no. 1 (January 1992): 53–69.

5. A. Doig, J.P.S. Ferguson, I. A. Milne, and R. Passmore, eds., *William Cullen and the Eighteenth Century Medical World* (Edinburgh: Edinburgh University Press, 1993), pp. 192–193; Elisha Bartlett, *An Introductory Lecture on the Objects and Nature of Medical Science* (Lexington, Ky.: N. L. and J. W. Fineall, 1841), p. 4.

6. Théophile Bonet, *Sepulchretum: sive anatomia practica ex cadaveribus morbo denalis* (Lyons: Sumptibus Cramer and Perachon, 1693); Joseph Lieutaud, *Historia anatomica-medica*, 2 vols. (Paris: I.S. Zolling, 1767); Giovanni Battista, *De sedibus et causis morborum*, 3 vols.

(London: A Millar and T. Cadell, 1769); Lester King, MD, *Transformations in American Medicine, from Benjamin Rush to William Osler* (Baltimore, Md.: Johns Hopkins University Press, 1991), pp. 32–33; Matthew Baillie, *Morbid Anatomy of Some of the Most Important Parts of the Human Body* (London: Barber and Southwick, 1795); John Pringle, *Observations on the Diseases of the Army* (London, 1774); Lester King, *The Medical World of the Eighteenth Century* (Chicago: University of Chicago Press, 1958), pp. 260–270.

7. John Cassedy, *Medicine in America: A Short History* (Baltimore, Md.: Johns Hopkins University Press, 1991), pp. 14–20; Maurice Gordon, *Aesculapius Comes to the Colonies: The Story of the Early Days of Medicine in the Thirteen Original Colonies* (Ventnor, N.J.: Ventnor Publishers, 1949), pp. 256–266, photo plates 305.

8. Wynham Blanton, *Medicine in Virginia in the Nineteenth Century* (Richmond, Va.: Garrett & Massie, 1933), p. 246.

9. John Emsley, *Elements of Murder* (Oxford: Oxford University Press, 2005), p. 149.

10. Robert Christison, *A Treatise on Poisons, in Relation to the Medical Jurisprudence, Physiology and the Practice of Physic*, 2nd ed. (Edinburgh: Edinburgh University Press, 1832), p. 207.

11. C.J.S. Thompson, *Poisons and Poisoners, with Historical Accounts of Some Famous Mysteries in Ancient and Modern Times* (New York: Barnes & Noble, 1993), p. 140. The jurors, fearful of the politically charged investigation, however, agreed to swear that the results of the autopsy were uncertain and Morton was freed. Everyone in Scotland believed he was guilty, though, and enjoyed some satisfaction when he was executed for other crimes in 1581.

12. Thompson, *Poisons and Poisoners*, p. 261.

13. J. Thorwald, "The Winding Road of Forensic Toxicology," in *The Century of the Detective* (New York: Harcourt, Brace & World, 1964), pp. 267–292.

14. Thompson, *Poisons and Poisoners*, p. 253.

15. Christison, *A Treatise on Poisons*, p. 202.

16. Ibid., p. 205.

17. Ibid., pp. 223–324.

18. Robert Dreisbach, *Handbook of Poisoning and Diagnostic Treatment*, 9th ed. (Los Altos, Calif.: Lange Medical Publications, 1998), pp. 210–214.

19. Joseph Plenck, *Elementa medicinae et chirurgiae forensis* (Vienna: Rudolphum Graeffer, 1781), p. 11.

20. C. P. Stewart, ed., *Toxicology: Mechanism and Analytical Methods*, 2 vols. (New York: Academic Press, 1961), vol. 2, pp. 830–831.

21. Curtis Klaassen, Mary Amdur, and John Doull, *Casarett and Doull's Toxicology: The Basic Science of Poison*, 3rd ed. (New York: Macmillan, 1986), pp. 1012–1015.

22. Christison, *A Treatise on Poisons*, p. 268.

23. Ibid., p. 201 note.

24. Tests by J. H. Stallard of Leicester, England, and Robert Christison of Edinburgh, Scotland, in Christison, *A Treatise on Poisons*, p. 235.

25. Christison, *A Treatise on Poisons*, p. 231.

26. Ibid., p. 261. Great Britain's foremost arsenic expert of the Wythe era argued that the total number of symptoms in several trials suggested arsenic as the only possible cause of physical disorders, even when the victims lived, given that they were not suffering from food poisoning or a lengthy illness; a 2004 study in M. J. Kosnett, "Arsenic, the Old Poison Rediscovered," *Clinical Toxicology Journal* 42, no. 4 (2004): 423–424, showed that while many people died within twenty-four hours or a week, many more lived for a month.

27. J. S. Billings, ed., *The Index of the Library of the Surgeon-General: Office, U.S. Army*, 15 vols. (Washington, D.C.: Government Printing Office, 1879–1899), vol. 14, pp. 681–682; W. Ramesey, *Treatise of Poysons, Their Sundry Sorts, Names, Natures and Virtues, with Their Several Symptoms, Signs[,] Diagnosticks and Antidotes. Wherein Are Divers Necessary Questions Discussed, the Truth by the Most Learned, Confirmed, by Many Instances, Examples*

and Stories Illustrated and Both Philosophically and Medicinally Handled (London, 1661); J. Cooke, A Treatise on Poisons, Vegetable, Animal and Mineral, with Their Cure (London: Edward and Charles Dilly, 1770).

28. Billings, ed., The Index of the Library of the Surgeon-General: Office, U.S. Army, vol. 14, pp. 666–681, vol. 1, pp. 569–578.

29. W. Remer, "Uutersuchung einer sonderbaren Vergiftungsgeschichte nebst angehangtem Gutachten, Arzene," Geburtsh Surgical Journal, Arznk, Jena 4 (1906): 647–673.

30. "Some Remarks on the Use of Nitrate of Silver for the Detecting of a Minute Portion of Arsenic," Transactions of the Medical-Chirurgical Society 3 (London, 1812): 312–347; V. Mott, "Observations on the Best Methods of Detecting Poisonous Substances Taken into the Stomach, Particularly Arsenic," Medical Repository of New York 2 (1811): 113–116; P. M. Roget, "Case of Recovery from Arsenic, with Remarks on a New Mode of Detecting the Presence of this Metal," Transactions of the Medical Chirurgical Society, London, 2 (1817): 157–161; J. Hume, "On Poisoning with Arsenic," Medical and Physicians Journal, London, 39 (1818): 27–33; W. J. Crowfoot, "On the Effects of Poisoning with Arsenic," Medical and Physicians Journal, London, 34 (1815): 441–443; D. H. Davies, "Cases," Medical and Physicians Journal, London, 28 (1812): 345–350.

31. N. Washbourn, "A case of swelling, accompanied with sphacelation of the scrotum, etc. from the imprudent external use of arsenic, successfully treated," London Medical Review and Magazine 2 (1799–1800): 197–199; J. A. Smith, "History of a case in which a large quantity of arsenic was taken, with the appearances on dissection," New York Medical and Philosophical Journal and Review 3 (1811): 6.

32. Proceedings of the Old Bailey, OldBaileyOnline.org, trials of Robert and William Evans, June 30, 1770; Henry William Wyatt, April 16, 1806; and others. Last accessed July 15, 2007.

33. Edward Hemphill, George Wythe: America's First Law Professor and the Teacher of Jefferson, Marshall and Clay, dissertation. Emory University, 1933, p. 48.

34. McClurg, "On Reasoning in Medicine," Philadelphia Journal of the Medical and Physical Sciences (Philadelphia: M. Carey and Son, 1820), p. 228.

35. Christison, A Treatise on Poisons, p. 270.

36. J. J. Bigsby, "On the effects of Arsenic as they Appear in the Human Body after Death," London Medical Repository 5 (1816): 97–105; J. A. Symonds, "An account of the examination and appearances of a corpse fourteen months after death, and of the detection of poisoning by arsenic," Transactions of the Provincial Medical and Scientific Association, London, 3 (1835): 432–472; J. Rayner, "Alleged Murder by Poisoning of the Body with arsenic: exhumation of the body after six weeks," Lancet, London, 1 (1838): 103.

Chapter 16. Lydia Broadnax: The Eyewitness

1. The Last Will and Testament of Lydia Broadnax, City of Richmond Will Book, February 26, 1827.

2. Midori Takagi, Rearing Wolves to Our Own Destruction: Slavery in Virginia, 1782–1865 (Charlottesville: University Press of Virginia, 1999), p. 47.

3. See introduction in Takagi, Rearing Wolves, pp. 4–5.

4. Takagi, pp. 18–32.

5. An Act to Authorize the Manumission of Slaves, May 1782; Sidbury, Ploughshares into Swords: Race, Rebellion and Identity in Gabriel's Virginia, 1730–1810, pp. 34–35.

6. Lou Powers and Linda Rowe, Colonial Williamsburg, Rockefeller Library research files, 1993.

7. Ibid., p. 31.

8. George Cooke to John Eustace, May 24, 1836, Benjamin Brand Papers, Virginia Historical Society.

9. U.S. Bureau of Census, Population, 1820–1840.

10. Catherine McCall vs. George Ingles, March, 1815.

11. Takagi, *Rearing Wolves*, pp. 48–49.
12. Charles Weld, *A Vacation Tour of the United States and Canada* (London: Longman, Brown, Green and Longmans, 1855), p. 288.
13. 1860 and 1850 U.S. Manufacturing Census.
14. Frederick Douglass, *My Bondage and My Freedom*, edited by William Andrews (Urbana: University of Illinois Press, 1987), pp. 147–148.
15. Takagi, *Rearing Wolves*, p. 51.
16. Sidbury, *Ploughshares into Swords*, pp. 161–164.
17. Harry Ward and Harold Greer Jr., *Richmond during the Revolution: 1775–1783* (Charlottesville: University Press of Virginia, 1977), p. 121; Virginia General Assembly Laws, 1782, Richmond Common Council Laws, 1797–1798.
18. Takagi, pp. 62–63; James Sidbury, *Ploughshares into Swords*, pp. 6–7.
19. Douglas Egerton, *Gabriel's Rebellion: The Virginia Slave Conspiracies of 1800 and 1802* (Chapel Hill: University of North Carolina Press, 1993), pp. 106–108.
20. Egerton, *Gabriel's Rebellion*, pp. 136–137 (the *New York Spectator*, especially, carried numerous stories about the slave revolts); Charters and Ordinances of the City of Richmond, in Gregg Kimball, *American City, Southern Place: A Cultural History of Antebellum Richmond* (Athens: University of Georgia Press, 2000), pp. 193–200.
21. Takagi, *Rearing Wolves*, pp. 67–70; Various acts of the Virginia State Legislature and the Richmond City Council, 1801–1831.
22. Egerton, *Gabriel's Rebellion*, pp. 164–169.
23. Ibid., pp. 98–105; Kimball, *American City, Southern Place*, p. 129.
24. Takagi, *Rearing Wolves*, pp. 66–70.

Chapter 17. The Black and White Legal Codes

1. William Henning, *The Statutes at Large: Being a Collection of All the Laws of Virginia, from the First Session of the Legislature, in the Year 1619*, 13 vols. (New York: Samuel Pleasants Jr., 1810–1823), vol. 12, pp. 182–183; June Guild, *Black Laws of Virginia: A Summary of the Legislative Acts of Virginia Concerning Negroes from Earliest Time to the Present* (Richmond, Va.: Whittet and Shepperson, 1936), pp. 154–155.
2. Hugo Badeau, *The Death Penalty in America: An Anthology* (Chicago: Aldine, 1982), pp. 4, 24; *New York Daily Gazette*, December 31, 1791.
3. *Richmond Enquirer*, September 9, 1806.
4. William Hening, *Statutes of Virginia* (Richmond: Samuel Pleasants Jr., 1823), vol. 13, p. 22.
5. H. J. Eckenrode, ed., *Richmond, Capital of Virginia: Approaches to Its History* (Richmond, Va.: Whittet & Shepperson, 1938), pp. 258–259.

Chapter 18. Washington, October 1806

1. Thomas Jefferson to Alexander Donald, July 28, 1787, in Julian Boyd, *The Papers of Thomas Jefferson*, 33 vols. (Princeton, N.J.: Princeton University Press, 1950), vol. 11, p. 632.
2. Merrill Peterson, *Thomas Jefferson and the New Nation* (New York: Oxford University Press, 1970), p. 766.
3. Thomas Jefferson to his daughter Martha, October 20, 1806, in Edwin Betts and James Bear Jr, eds. *The Family Letters of Thomas Jefferson* (Charlottesville: University Press of Virginia, 1986), p. 289.

Epilogue

1. Edward Hemphill, *George Wythe: America's First Law Professor and the Teacher of Jefferson, Marshall and Clay*, dissertation, Emory University, 1933, p. 38; Littleton Tazewell, *Sketches of His Own Family, Written by Littleton Tazewell, for the Use of His Children* (Norfolk, Va., 1823), p. 121.
2. Julian Boyd, "The Murder of George Wythe," *William and Mary Quarterly* (October 1955): 26.

Bibliography

ARCHIVAL SOURCES

Brown-Coalter Papers. College of William and Mary Library.
Jefferson, Thomas. Papers. Princeton University Library.
Mordecai, Samuel. Papers. Duke University.
Prentis, Joseph. Papers. University of Virginia Library.
Shippen, William. Papers. Library of Congress.
Tazewell, Littleton. Papers. Virginia State Library.
Tucker-Coleman Papers. Rockefeller Library, Colonial Williamsburg.
Wirt, William. Papers. Maryland Historical Society.
York County (Virginia) Deed Book, 1787.

NEWSPAPER SOURCES

Aurora (N.Y.) *General Advertiser*. 1800.
Charleston (S.C.) *Times*. 1806.
Massachusetts Spy. 1778.
New York Gazette. 1799.
Norfolk Gazette and Public Ledger. 1806.
Paulson's American Daily Advertiser. 1806.
Pennsylvania Evening Post. 1777.
Petersburg Republican. 1806.
Philadelphia Public Ledger. 1840.
Pittsburgh Gazette. 1833.
Richmond Enquirer. 1806, 1859.
Virginia Argus. 1806.
Virginia Gazette. 1778.
Virginia Gazette and General Advertiser. 1806.

JOURNAL ARTICLES AND BOOK CHAPTERS

Listed by Titles

"Diary of a Little Colonial Girl." *Virginia Magazine of History and Biography* 11 (1903–1904).
"Glimpses of Old College Life." *William and Mary Quarterly* (January 1900).
"Horrid News from St. Martins, or, Unheard of Murder and Poyson." St. Martin's, England, 1677. Pamphlet.
"Journal of a French Traveler in the Colonies, 1765, I." *American Historical Review* 26 (1920–1921).
"Letters of George Wythe to Richard Taliaferro." *William and Mary Quarterly* (October 1903).
"London Coroner's Inquests for 1590." *Journal of the History of Medicine and Allied Sciences* 28 (1973).

"Some Remarks on the Use of Nitrate of Silver for the Detecting of a Minute Portion of Arsenic." *Transactions of the Medical-Chirurgical Society*. London (1812).

"Will of Richard Taliaferro." *William and Mary Quarterly* (October 1903).

Listed by Authors

Alber, Lin, and R. Henkelman. "Elemental Contents of Napoleon's Hair Cut before and after His Death: Did Napoleon Die of Arsenic Poisoning?" *Analytical and Bioanalytical Chemistry Journal* (May 2004).

Anderson, D. R. "Chancellor Wythe and Parson Weems." *William and Mary Quarterly* (July 1916).

Anderson, Dice. "The Teacher of Jefferson and Marshall." *South Atlantic Quarterly* 16 (1916).

Bartrip, P. "A Pennurth of Arsenic for Rat Poison: The Arsenic Act of 1851 and the Prevention of Secret Poisoning." *Medical History* (January 1992).

Bigsby, J. J. "On the Effects of Arsenic as They Appear in the Human Body after Death." *London Medical Repository*, 1816.

Boyd, Julian. "The Murder of George Wythe." *William and Mary Quarterly* (October 1955).

———. *The Papers of Thomas Jefferson*. 33 vols. Princeton, N.J.: Princeton University Press, 1950.

Breen, T. H. "Horses and Gentlemen: The Cultural Significance of Gambling among the Gentry in Virginia." *William and Mary Quarterly* (April 1977).

Bynum, W. F., and Roy Porter. *William Hunter and the Eighteenth Century Medical World*. Cambridge, Mass.: Cambridge University Press, 1985.

Campbell, Anthony. "Darwin's Illness Revealed." *Postgraduate Medical Journal* 81 (2005).

Crowfoot, W. J. "On the Effects of Poisoning with Arsenic." *Medical and Physicians Journal*, London (1815).

Cullen, Charles. "Completing the Revisal of the Laws in Post-Revolutionary Virginia." *Virginia Magazine* 82 (1974).

Davis, D. H. "Cases." *Medical and Physicians Journal*, London (1812).

Doelha, Johann. "The Doelha Journal," translated by Robert Tilden. *William and Mary Quarterly*. Series 2, vol. 22 (1942).

Eckenrode, H. J. *Richmond, the Capital of Virginia: Approaches to Its History*. Richmond: Whittet and Shepperson, 1938.

Ford, Washington, ed. "Thomas Jefferson and James Thomson Callender." In *New England Historical and Genealogical Register*, 1896.

Gill, Harold Jr. "Williamsburg and the Demimonde: Disorderly Houses, the Blue Bell and Certain Hints of Harlotry." *Journal of the Colonial Williamsburg Foundation* (Autumn 2001).

Gorby, Michael. "Clinical Conference: Arsenic Poisoning." *Western Journal of Medicine* (September 1988).

Gorman, B., and D. L. Kaplan. "The Affliction of Job: Poisoned!" *Journal of the American Academy of Dermatology* (January 1999).

Henley, Bernard. "Of Main Street, the Eagle Hotel and Gambling, c. 1830." *Richmond Quarterly* (Fall 1981).

Hoffman, R. J. "Classics in the Courts of the United States, 1790–1800." *American Journal of Legal History* 22 (1978).

Hughes, William. "The First American Law School." *William and Mary Quarterly* (January 1922).

Hume, J. "On Poisoning with Arsenic." *Medical and Physicians Journal*, London (1818).

Jarrett, Calvin. "Was George Wythe Murdered?" *Virginia Cavalcade* (Winter 1963–1964).

Kosnett, M. J. "Arsenic, the Old Poison Rediscovered." *Clinical Toxicology Journal* 42 (2004).

Lawrence, Christopher. "Ornate Physicians and Learned Artisans: Edinburgh Medical Men, 1826–1776." In W. F. Bynum and R. Porter, eds., *William Hunter and the Eighteenth Century Medical World*. Cambridge, Mass.: Cambridge University Press, 1985.

Macauley, Alexander. "Alexander Macauley's Journal." *William and Mary Quarterly*, Series 1, vol. 11 (1902–1903).

Mari, F., E. Bertol, V. Fineschi, and S. B. Karch. "Channelling the Emperor: What Really Killed Napoleon?" *Journal of the Royal Society of Medicine* 97 (August 2004).

Mattison, Lewis. "Life of the Town." In *Richmond, the Capital of Virginia: Approaches to Its History*. Richmond, Va.: Whittet and Shepperson, 1938.

McClurg, James. "On Reasoning in Medicine." In *Philadelphia Journal of Medical and Physical Sciences*. Philadelphia: M. Carey and Son, 1820.

Miller, Jonathan. "An Account of an Epidemic Fever which Has Prevailed in Certain Parts of Virginia for the Past Eight Years." In *Philadelphia Journal of Medicine and Physical Sciences*, vol. 5. Philadelphia: Carey and Lea, 1822.

Mott, V. "Observations on the Best Methods of Detecting Poisonous Substances Taken into the Stomach, Particularly Arsenic." In *Medical Repository of New York*, 1811.

Powell, Lewis. "George Wythe." In *Journal of Supreme Court History* (1990).

Quick, John. "Hell Open'd, Or the Infernal Sin of Murther Punished." Plymouth, England, 1676. Retrieved from OldBaileyOnline.org

Rayner, J. "Alleged Murder by Poisoning of the Body with Arsenic: Exhumation of the Body after Six Weeks." *Lancet*. London (1838).

Remer, W. "Uutersuchung einer sonderbaren Vergiftungsgeschichte nebst angehangtem Gutachten." *Geburtsh Surgigcal Journal*, Arjznk, Jena (1906).

Roget, P. M. "Case of Recovery from Arsenic, with Remarks on a New Mode of Detecting the Presence of This Metal." *Transactions of the Medical Chirurgical Society*. London (1817).

Saunders, Robert. "Crime and Punishment in Early National America: Richmond, Virginia, 1784–1820." *Virginia Magazine of History and Biography* 86 (1978).

Smith, James. "Sedition in the Old Dominion." In *Freedom's Fetters: The Alien and Sedition Cases and American Civil Liberties*. Ithaca, N.Y.: Cornell University Press, 1956.

Smith, J. A. "History of a Case in Which a Large Quantity of Arsenic Was Taken, with the Appearances on Dissection." *New York Medical and Philosophical Journal and Review* (1811).

Smith, William. "A Just Account of the Horrid Contrivance of John Cupper and Judith Brown, His Servant, in the Poysoning of His Wife." Shrewsbury, England, 1684. Retrieved from OldBaileyOnline.org.

Sturtz, Linda. "The Ladies and the Lottery: Elite Women's Gambling in Eighteenth Century Virginia." *Virginia Magazine of History and Biography* (Spring 1996).

Symonds, J. A. "An Account of the Examination and Appearances of a Corpse Fourteen Months after Death, and of the Detection of Poisoning by Arsenic." *Transactions of the Provincial Medical and Scientific Association*. London (1835).

Tachau, Mary. "George Washington and the Reputation of Edmund Randolph." *Journal of American History* (June 1986). Taylor, William. "William Wirt and the Legend of the Old South." In *Cavalier and Yankee: The Old South and American National Character*. New York: Braziller, 1961.

Thorwald, J. "The Winding Road of Forensic Toxicology." In *Century of the Detective*. New York: Harcourt, Brace & World, 1964.

Walker, Leola. "Officials in the City Government of Colonial Williamsburg." *Virginia Magazine* 75 (1967).

Washbourn, N. "A Case of Swelling, Accompanied with Sphacelation of the Scrotum, etc. from the Imprudent External Use of Arsenic, Successfully Treated." *London Medical Review and Magazine* (1799–1800).

Weider, Ben, and John Fornier. "Activation Analysis of Authenticated Hairs of Napoleon Bonaparte Confirm Arsenic Poisoning." *American Journal of Forensic Medicine and Pathology* 20 (December 1999).

Books

Adams, Charles. *The Works of John Adams, Second President of the United States, with a Life of the Author.* 10 vols. Boston: Little, Brown, 1856.

Adams, Eliphet. *A Sermon Preached on the Occasion of the Execution of Katherine Garret.* New London: T. Green, 1738.

Ammon, Harry. *James Monroe: The Quest for National Identity.* New York: McGraw-Hill, 1971.

Bailey, Robert. *The Life and Adventures of Robert Bailey, from His Infancy up to December, 1821.* Richmond, Va.: J. & G. Cochran, 1822.

Baillie, Matthew. *Morbid Anatomy of Some of the Most Important Parts of the Human Body.* London; Barber and Southwick, 1795.

Banner, Stuart. *The Death Penalty in American History.* Cambridge, Mass.: Harvard University Press, 2002.

Bartlett, Elisha. *An Introductory Lecture on the Objects and Nature of Medical Science.* Lexington, Ky.: N. L. and J. W. Fineall, 1841.

Bazin, Herve. *The Eradication of Smallpox.* New York: Academic Press, 1984.

Bear, James Jr., and Lucia Stanton. *Jefferson's Memorandum Books: Accounts, with Legal Records and Miscellany, 1767–1826.* 2 vols. Princeton, N.J.: Princeton University Press, 1997.

Beck, John. *Medicine in the American Colonies, and Historical Sketches of the State of Medicine in the American Colonies, from Their First Settlement to the Period of the Revolution.* Albany, N.Y.: C. Van Benthuysen, 1850.

Bell, Whitfield. *The Colonial Physician and Other Essays.* New York: Science History Publications, 1975.

Berman, Myron. *Richmond's Jewry, 1769–1976, Shabbat in Shockoe.* Charlottesville: University of Virginia Press, 1979.

Betts, Edwin and James Bear Jr., eds.,*The Family Letters of Thomas Jefferson.* Charlottesville: University Press of Virginia, 1986.

Beveridge, Albert. *The Life of John Marshall.* 8 vols. Boston: Houghton-Mifflin, 1916.

Bewell, Alan. *Romanticism and Colonial Disease.* Baltimore, Md.: Johns Hopkins University Press, 1999.

Billings, J. S., ed. *The Index of the Library of the Surgeon-General: Office, U.S. Army.* 16 vols. Washington, D.C.: U.S. Government Printing Office, 1880-1895.

Billings, Warren, John Selby, and Thad Tate. *Colonial Virginia: A History.* White Plains, N.Y.: KTO Press, 1986.

Binger, Carl. *Revolutionary Doctor: Benjamin Rush.* New York: W. W. Norton, 1966.

Blackburn, Joyce. *George Wythe in Williamsburg.* New York: Harper and Row, 1975.

Blanton, Wynham. *Medicine in Virginia in the Nineteenth Century.* Richmond, Va.: Garrett & Massie, 1933.

Bonet, Théophile. *Sepulchretum: sive anatomia practica ex cadaveribus morbo denalis.* Lyons: Sumptibus Cramer and Perachon, 1700.

Boudelais, Patrice. *Epidemics Laid Low: A History of What Happened in Rich Countries,* translated by Bart Hollad. Baltimore, Md.: Johns Hopkins University Press, 2003.

Boyd, Julian, and Edward Hemphill. *The Murder of George Wythe, Two Essays.* Williamsburg, Va.: Institute of Early American History and Culture, 1955.

Bradford, M. E. *Founding Fathers: Brief Lives of the Framers of the U.S. Constitution.* Topeka: University of Kansas Press, 1981.

Brodie, Fawn. *Thomas Jefferson: An Intimate History.* New York: W. W. Norton, 1974.

Brown, Imogene. *American Aristides: A Biography of George Wythe.* Teaneck, N.J.: Fairleigh Dickinson University Press, 1981.

Brown, Stuart, ed. *The Autobiography of James Monroe.* Syracuse, N.Y.: Syracuse University Press, 1959.

Burnaby, Andrew. *Travels Through the Middle Settlements in North America in the Years 1759 and 1760, With Observations on the State of the Colonies.* London: T. Payne, 1798.

Burstein, Andrew. *Jefferson's Secrets: Death and Desire at Monticello*. New York: Basic Books, 2005.

Butterfield, L. H. *The Adams Papers: The Diary and Autobiography of John Adams*. 3 vols. Cambridge, Mass.: Belknap Press, 1962.

Callender, James. *The Prospect before Us*. Richmond, Va.: M. Jones, S. Pleasants Jr. and J. Lyon, 1800.

Carson, Jane. *We Were There: Descriptions of Williamsburg, 1699–1859, Compiled from Contemporary Sources and Arranged Chronologically*. Williamsburg, Va.: Colonial Williamsburg Foundation, 1965.

Cartwright, Frederick, and Michael Biddiss. *Disease and History*. New York: Thomas Crowell, 1972.

Cassedy, John. *Medicine in America: A Short History*. Baltimore, Md.: Johns Hopkins University Press, 1991.

Chastellux, Marquis. *Travels in North America in the Years 1780, 1781 and 1782*, translated by Howard Rice. Chapel Hill: University of North Carolina Press, 1963.

Chitty, Dennis, ed. *Control of Rats and Mice*. 3 vols. Oxford: Clarendon Press, 1954.

Christian, W. Asbury. *Richmond: Her Past and Present*. Richmond, Va.: 1912.

Christison, Robert. *A Treatise on Poisons, in Relation to the Medical Jurisprudence, Physiology and the Practice of Physic*. 2nd ed. Edinburgh: Edinburgh University Press, 1832.

Conway, Moncure. *Omitted Chapters in History Disclosed in the Life and Papers of Edmund Randolph*. New York: G. P. Putnam's Sons, 1888.

Cooke, J. *A Treatise on Poisons, Vegetable, Animal and Mineral, with Their Cure*. London: Edward and Charles Dilly, 1770.

Copeland, David. *American Colonial Newspapers: Character and Content*. Newark: University of Delaware Press, 1997.

Corner, George, ed. *The Autobiography of Benjamin Rush*. Princeton, N.J.: Princeton University Press, 1948.

Crawford, William. *Report on the Penitentiaries of the United States*, Montclair, N.J.: Patterson Smith, 1969.

Dabney, Virginius. *Richmond: The Story of a City*. Charlottesville: University Press of Virginia, 1976.

Daniels, Jonathan. *The Randolphs of Virginia*. Garden City, N.Y.: Doubleday, 1972.

DeBow, J. D. B. *Statistical View of the United States . . . Being a Compendium of the Seventh Census*. Washington, D.C.: Beverly Tucker, 1864.

Dill, Alonzo. *George Wythe: Teacher of Liberty*. Williamsburg, Va.: Colonial Williamsburg Foundation, 1979.

Doig, J. P., S. Ferguson, I. A. Milne, and R. Passmore, eds. *William Cullen and the Eighteenth Century Medical World*. Edinburgh: Edinburgh University Press, 1993.

Douglass, Frederick. *My Bondage and My Freedom*. Edited by William Andrews. Urbana: University of Ilinois Press, 1987.

Dowdy, Clifford. *The Golden Age: A Climate for Greatness, 1732–1775*. Boston: Little, Brown, 1970.

Dreisbach, Robert. *Handbook of Poisoning and Diagnostic Treatment*. 2nd ed. Los Altos, Calif.: Lange Medical Publications, 1959.

Duffy, John. *Epidemics in Colonial America*. Baton Rouge: Louisiana State University Press, 1953.

Eaton, Clement. *Henry Clay and the Art of American Politics*. Boston: Little, Brown, 1957.

Egerton, Douglas. *Gabriel's Rebellion: The Virginia Slave Conspiracies of 1800 and 1802*. Chapel Hill: University of North Carolina Press, 1993.

Ellis, John. *Yellow Fever and Public Health in the New South*. Lexington: University of Kentucky Press, 1992.

Emsley, John. *Elements of Murder*. Oxford: Oxford University Press, 2005.

Evans, Richard. *Death in Hamburg: Society and Politics in the Cholera Years, 1830–1910*. Oxford: Clarendon Press, 1987.

Ewing, William. *The Sports of Williamsburg*. Richmond, Va.: Dietz Press, 1937.

Fabian, Ann. *Card Sharps, Dream Books and Bucket Shops: Gambling in Nineteenth Century America*. Ithaca, N.Y.: Cornell University Press, 1990.

Fithian, Phillip. *Journal and Letters of Phillip Fithian, 1773–1774: A Plantation Tutor of the Old Dominion*, edited by Hunter Farish. Williamsburg, Va.: Colonial Williamsburg Foundation, 1943.

Fitzpatrick, John. *Writings of George Washington*. 38 vols. Washington, D.C.: U.S. Government Printing Office, 1932.

Forrest, William. *The Great Pestilence in Virginia, Being an Account of the Origin, General Character and Ravages of the Yellow Fever on Norfolk and Portsmouth in 1855, Together with Sketches of Some of the Victims*. Philadelphia: J. B. Lippincott, 1856.

Gardner, Joseph, ed. *The Founding Fathers: Thomas Jefferson: A Biography in His Own Words*. New York: Newsweek Publishing, 1974.

Glassner, Gregory. *Adopted Son: The Life, Wit and Wisdom of William Wirt, 1772–1834*. Madison County, Va.: Kurt-Ketner, 1997.

Gordon, Maurice. *Aesculapius Comes to the Colonies: The Story of the Early Days of Medicine in the Thirteen Original Colonies*. Ventnor, N.J.: Ventnor Publishers, 1949.

Green, Elna. *This Business of Relief: Confronting Poverty in a Southern City, 1740–1940*. Athens: University of Georgia Press, 1993.

Grigsby, Hugh. *The History of the Federal Convention of 1788, with Some Account of the Eminent Virginians of That Era Who Were Members of the Body*. 2 vols. Richmond, Va.: Virginia Historical Society, 1855.

Grob, Gerald. *The Deadly Truth: A History of Disease in America*. Cambridge, Mass.: Harvard University Press, 2002.

Guild, June. *Black Laws of Virginia: A Summary of the Legislative Acts of Virginia Concerning Negroes from the Earliest Time to the Present*. Richmond, Va.: Whittet and Shepperson,1936.

Halliday, E. M. *Understanding Thomas Jefferson*. New York: HarperCollins, 2001.

Hayes, Wallace, ed. *The Principles of Toxicology*. New York: Raven Press, 1994.

Hays, J. N. *The Burdens of Disease: Epidemics and Human Response in Western History*. New Brunswick, N.J.: Rutgers University Press, 1998.

Hemphill, Edward. *George Wythe: America's First Law Professor and the Teacher of Jefferson, Marshall and Clay*, dissertation. Emory University, 1933.

Henning, William, and George Munford. *Reports of Cases Argued and Practice Decided by the Superior Court of Chancery for the Richmond District*, 2nd ed., 4 vols. Charlottesville: University of Virginia Press, 1903.

Henning, William. *The Statutes at Large: Being a Collection of All the Laws of Virginia, from the First Session of the Virginia Legislature, in the Year 1619*. 13 vols. New York: Samuel Pleasants Jr., 1810–1823.

Hewitt, Robert. "The Influence of Somatic and Psychiatric Medical Theory on the Design of Nineteenth Century American Cities," www.priory.com/homol/19c.htm, accessed July 2, 2008.

Hill, Rolla, and Robert Anderson. *The Autopsy: Medical Practice and Public Policy*. London: Butterworth, 1988.

Hopkins, Donald. *Princes and Peasants: Smallpox in History*. Chicago: University of Chicago Press, 1973.

Hughes, Thomas. *Medicine in Virginia, 1607–1699*. Williamsburg: Virginia's 350th Birthday Celebration Corporation, 1957.

Hume, David. *Treatise on Human Nature*. London: J. Noon, 1739.

Isaacs, Rhys. *The Transformation of Virginia, 1740–1790*. New York: W. W. Norton, 1982.

Jabour, Anya. *Marriage in the Early Republic: Elizabeth and William Wirt and the Companionate Ideal.* Baltimore, Md.: Johns Hopkins University Press, 1998.

Jackson, Donald. *The Diaries of George Washington.* 6 vols. Charlottesville: University of Virginia Press, 1976.

Jefferson, Thomas. *Notes on the State of Virginia.* London: John Stockdale, 1782.

Johnson, David. *Policing the Underworld: The Impact of Crime on the Development of the American Police, 1800–1887.* Philadelphia: Temple University Press, 1942.

Jones, Richard Glyn. *Poison! The World's Greatest True Murder Stories.* Secaucus, N.J.: Lyle Stuart, 1987.

Journals of the Continental Congress, 1774–1789. 34 vols. Washington, D.C.: U.S. Government Printing Office, 1904–1937.

Kahn, George, ed. *Encyclopedia of Plague and Pestilence.* New York: Facts on File, 1995.

Karlen, Arno. *Disease and Plagues in History and Modern Times.* New York: Touchstone Books, 1995.

Kaufman, Martin. *American Medical Education: The Formative Years, 1765–1910.* Westport, Conn.: Greenwood Press, 1976.

Kennedy, John P. *Memoirs of the Life of William Wirt, the Attorney General of the United States.* 2 vols. Philadelphia: Lea and Blanchard, 1849.

Kimball, Fiske. *The Capitol of Virginia: A Landmark in American Architecture,* edited by Jon Kukla. Richmond: Virginia State Library and Archives, 1989.

Kimball, Gregg. *American City, Southern Place: A Cultural History of Antebellum Richmond.* Athens: University of Georgia Press, 2000.

King, Lester. *The Medical World of the Eighteenth Century.* Chicago: University of Chicago Press, 1958.

———. *Transformations in American Medicine, from Benjamin Rush to William Osler.* Baltimore, Md.: Johns Hopkins University Press, 1991.

Kirtland, Robert. *George Wythe: Lawyer, Revolutionary, Judge.* New York: Garland, 1986.

Klaassen, Curtis, Mary Amdur, and John Doull. Casarett and Doull's *Toxicology: The Basic Science of Poison.* 3rd ed. New York: Macmillan, 1986.

Koch, Adrienne, and William Peden. *The Life and Selected Writings of Thomas Jefferson.* New York: Modern Library, 1949.

Krieg, Joann. *Epidemics of the Modern World.* New York: Twayne, 1992.

La Rochefoucauld-Liancourt, François. *Voyages dans les Etats-Unis d'Amérique, fait en 1795, 1796, et 1797.* 4 vols. Paris: DuPont de la Republique, 1799.

Lears, Jackson. *Something for Nothing: Luck in America.* New York: Penguin, 2003.

Lewis, William, ed. *The Great American Lawyers.* 8 vols. Philadelphia: John Winston Company, 1907–1909.

Lieutand, Joseph. *Historia Anatomico Medica.* 2 vols. Paris: I.S. Zolling, 1786.

Lilienfeld, Abraham, ed. *Times, Places and Persons: Aspects of the History of Epidemiology.* Baltimore, Md.: Johns Hopkins University Press, 1980.

Little, John. *History of Richmond.* Richmond, Va.: Dietz Press, 1933.

Lyons, Albert, and R. Joseph Petrucelli. *Medicine: An Illustrated History.* New York: Harry Abrams, 1978.

Mack, Arien, ed. *In Time of Plague: The History and Social Consequences of Lethal Epidemic Disease.* New York: New York University Press, 1991.

Macpherson, J. *The Annals of Cholera from the Earliest Periods to the Year 1817.* London: Ranken, 1872.

Mallory, Daniel, ed. *The Life and Speeches of Henry Clay.* 2 vols. New York: Van Amringe and Bixby, 1844.

Malone, Dumas. *Jefferson and His Time.* 5 vols. Boston: Little, Brown, 1974.

Marcus, Jacob. *Early American Jewry, the Jews of Pennsylvania and the South, 1655–1790.* Philadelphia: Jewish Publication Societies of America, 1953.

Marks, Geoffrey, and William Beatty. *Epidemics*. New York: Charles Scribner's Sons, 1976.

Mason, Francis, ed. *John Norton and Sons, Merchants of London and Virginia, Being the Papers from Their Counting House for the Years 1750–1795*. Richmond, Va.: Dietz Press, 1937.

Maxwell, Edward, ed. *The Virginia Register*. Richmond, Va.: McFarland, 1852.

McClurg, James. *Experiments upon the Human Bile and Reflections on the Biliary Secretions*. London: T. Cadell, 1772.

McGraw, Roderick. *Russia and the Cholera, 1823–1832*. Madison: University of Wisconsin Press, 1965.

McIlwaine, H. R., and John Pendleton Kennedy, eds. *Journals of the House of Burgesses of Virginia*. 13 vols. Richmond, Va.: Richmond Library Board, Virginia State Library, 1905–1915.

McLaughlin, Jack. *To His Excellency Thomas Jefferson, Letters to a President*. New York: W. W. Norton, 1991.

McNeill, William. *Plagues and People*. Garden City, N.Y.: Doubleday, 1976.

Mereness, Newton. "Journal of Lord Adam Gordon." *Travels in the American Colonies*. New York: Antiquarian Press, 1961.

Meyer, Clarence. *American Folk Medicine*. New York: Thomas Crowell, 1973. Mifflin Company, 1925.

Montesquieu, Charles. *Spirit of Law*. 2 vols. Translated by Thomas Nugent. London: J. Nourser and Peter Vaillant, 1750.

Morgagni, Giovanni. *De Sedibus et Causis Morborum*. 5 vols. London: A. Millar and T. Cadell, 1769.

Morgan, Edmund. *Virginians at Home*. Charlottesville, Va.: Dominion Books, 1968.

Munford, George. *Two Parsons, Cupid's Sports, the Dream and the Jewels of Virginia*. Richmond, Va.: J. D. K. Sleight, 1884.

Nevins, Allan. *The Diary of Phillip Hones, 1828–1851*. New York: Dodd, Mead, 1927.

Numbers, Ronald, ed. *Medicine in the New World: New France, New Spain, New England*. Knoxville: University of Tennessee Press, 1987.

Ogden, Horace. *CDC and the Smallpox Crusade*. Washington, D.C.: U.S. Department of Health, Centers for Disease Control, 1972.

Ottobone, Alice. *The Dose Makes the Poison*. Berkeley, Calif.: Vincente Brooks, 1984.

Palmer, William, ed. *Calendar of Virginia State Papers and Other Manuscripts, 1652–1869*. 11 vols. Richmond, Va.: State of Virginia, 1875–1893.

Paulding, James. *Letters from the South*. 2 vols. New York: James Eastburn, 1817.

Peterson, Merrill, ed. *James Madison: A Biography in His Own Words*. New York: Newsweek Publications, 1974.

———. *Thomas Jefferson and the New Nation*. New York: Oxford University Press, 1970.

Plenck, Joseph. *Elementa medicinae et chirurgiae forensis*. Vienna: Rudolphum Graeffer, 1781.

Population of the United States for 1860, Compiled from the Original Returns of the Eighth Census. Washington, D.C.: U.S. Government Printing Office, 1864.

Pringle, John. *Observations on the Diseases of the Army*. London, 1774. Retrieved from OldBaileyOnline.org. Last accessed July 15, 2007.

Proceedings of the Old Bailey. Available at OldBaileyOnline.org. Last accessed July 15, 2007.

Reardon, John. *Edmund Randolph: A Biography*. New York: Macmillan, 1974.

Reiss, Oscar. *Medicine and the American Revolution: How Diseases and Their Treatments Affected the Colonial Army*. Jefferson, N.C.: McFarland, 1998.

Report of the Minority of the Committee of Twenty Four on the Subject of Gambling in the City of Richmond. Richmond, Va.: T. W. White, 1833.

Roach, Mary. *Stiff: The Curious Lives of Human Cadavers*. New York: W. W. Norton, 2003.

Rosenberg, Charles. *The Cholera Years: The United States in 1832, 1849 and 1866*. Chicago: University of Chicago Press, 1962.

Rutland, Robert, ed. *James Madison and the American Nation, 1751–1836*. New York: Simon & Schuster, 1994.

Sanger, William. *The History of Prostitution: Its Extent, Causes and Effects throughout the World.* New York: Eugenics, 1939.

Schwarz, David. *Roll the Bones: The History of Gambling.* New York: Gotham Books, 2006.

Schwarz, Philip. *Twice Condemned: Slaves and the Criminal Cases of Virginia, 1705–1865.* Baton Rouge: Louisiana State University Press, 1988.

Shewmake, Oscar. *The Honorable George Wythe.* Williamsburg, Va.: Colonial Williamsburg Foundation, 1954.

Showman, Richard, and Dennis Conrad. *Papers of Nathanael Greene.* 12 vols. Chapel Hill: University of North Carolina Press, 1978–2002.

Sidbury, James. *Ploughshares Into Swords: Race, Rebellion and Identity in Gabriel's Virginia, 1730-1810,* New York: Cambridge University Press, 1997.

Smallpox in Colonial America. New York: New York Times-Arno Press, 1971.

Smith, Jean. *John Marshall: Definer of a Nation.* New York: Henry Holt, 1996.

Smith, Paul. *Letters of Delegates to Congress, 1774–1789.* 26 vols. Washington, D.C.: Library of Congress, 1976.

Southard, D. L. *Discourse on the Professional Character and Virtues of the Late William Wirt.* Washington, D.C.: Gales and Seaton, 1834.

Spear, Charles. *Essays on the Punishment of Death.* Boston: C. Gilpin, 1851.

Sprigg, June. *Domestick Beings.* New York: Alfred Knopf, 1984.

Stevens, Serita Deborah, and Anne Klarner. *Deadly Doses: A Writer's Guide to Poisons.* Cincinnati, Ohio: Writer's Digest Books, 1990.

Stewart, C. P., ed. *Toxicology: Mechanism and Analytical Methods.* 2 vols. New York: Academic Press, 1961.

Styron, Arthur. *The Last of the Cocked Hats: James Monroe and the Virginia Dynasty.* Norman: University of Oklahoma Press, 1945.

Takagi, Midori. *Rearing Wolves to Our Own Destruction: Slavery in Virginia, 1782–1865.* Charlottesville: University Press of Virginia, 1999.

Tansill, Charles, ed. *The Making of the American Republic: The Great Documents, 1774–1789.* New Rochelle, N.Y.: Arlington House Press, 1972.

Tazewell, Littleton. *Sketches of His Own Family, Written by Littleton Tazewell, for the Use of His Children.* Norfolk, 1823.

Teeter, Dwight, and Jean Folkerts. *Voices of a Nation: A History of Media in the United States.* 4th ed. Boston: Allyn & Bacon, 2002.

Thomas, F. W. *John Randolph of Roanoke and Other Sketches of Character, including William Wirt, Together with Tales of Real Life.* Philadelphia: A. Hart, 1853.

Thomas, Herbert. *The Doctors Jared of Connecticut.* Hamden, Conn.: Shoe String Press, 1958.

Thomas, Rolla. *Eclectic Practice of Medicine.* Colonial Williamsburg academic paper, 1993.

Thompson, C. J. S. *Poisons and Poisoners, with Historical Accounts of Some Famous Mysteries in Ancient and Modern Times.* New York: Barnes & Noble, 1993.

U.S. Bureau of Census Reports for Virginia and Richmond, 1790, 1800, 1810.

Van Heyningen, W. E., and John Seal. *Cholera: The American Scientific Experiment, 1947–1980.* Boulder, Colo.: Westview, 1983.

Wagner, E. J. *The Science of Sherlock Holmes: From Baskerville Hall to the Valley of Fear, the Real Forensics behind the Great Detective's Greatest Cases.* New York: John Wiley & Sons, 2006.

Ward, Harry, and Harold Greer Jr. *Richmond during the Revolution: 1775–1783.* Charlottesville: University Press of Virginia, 1977.

Washington, H. A., ed. *Writings of Thomas Jefferson.* 3 vols. Washington, D.C.: Baylor & Maury, 1858.

Weld, Charles. *A Vacation Tour of the United States and Canada.* London: Longman, Brown, Green and Longmans, 1855.

Wills, Christopher. *Yellow Fever, Black Goddess: The Co-Evolution of People and Plagues.* New York: Addison-Wesley, 1996.

Wirt, William. *Sketches of the Life and Character of Patrick Henry*. Philadelphia: Claxton, Remsen, Haffelfinger, 1878.

———. *The Letters of a British Spy*. 10th ed. New York: Harper and Bros., 1832.

Worrall, Jay. *Friendly Virginians: History of America's First Quakers*. Unpublished manuscript. Virginia Historical Society, 1992.

Wythe, George. *Decisions of Cases in Virginia by the High Court of Chancery with Remarks upon Decrees by the Court of Appeals Reversing Some of Those Decisions*, edited by Benjamin Minor. Richmond, Va.: J. W. Randolph, 1852.

Index

NOTE: Page numbers in *italics* refer to illustrations.

Abbott, Nelson, 127
Adams, John, 7, 8, 55–56, 57, 69, 72, 151–152
"Age of Arsenic," 191
Agrippina, 187
alcohol, 78, 83–85, 93, 97. *See also* taverns
Alexander, Prince (Russia), 188
Alexander, Robert, 158–159
Alexander V (Pope), 169
American Philosophical Society, 201
American Revolution, 54–58
antigaming laws, 95–98
Arnold, Benedict, 10
arsenic, 30, 126–127, 141
    historical accounts of poisonings, 171–172, 185–193, 202–203, 207–208, 211
    poisoning event in Wythe household and, 12–16, 209, 216–217
    ratsbane, 125, 127, 141, 197–198, 204, 215, 230
    survival from poisoning, 17, 104, 141, 212
    symptoms of poisoning, 167–168, 184–185, 205, 207–209
    tests for, 183–185, 203–205, 209–212, 213
    See also autopsies; medicine
assault-and-battery cases, 99
Ast, Frederick, 115
Atholl, Earl of, 202

autopsies
    of Brown, 183–184, 197, 206, 213–214
    conclusions of, 196–197, 206–214
    history of, 168–172, 198–203, *199*
    of Wythe, 183–184, 195–197, 205–207, 213–214
Ayres, Goody, 170–171

Bailey, Robert, 97
Bank of Alexandria, 233
Bank of Richmond, 123, 129, 233
Bank of Virginia, 232, 233
Bateman, Mary (Yorkshire Witch), 191
Bell, John, 193
Ben (slave), 49
Bible, accounts of poison in, 186
billiards, 91, 95
black and white legal codes, 225–227, 228–234
Blair, Reverend John, 25
Blandy, Mary, 189, *190*, 207
blood-letting, 27, 181
Board of Revisors (Virginia), 64–69, 106, 229, 231, 233–234
"body snatchers," 170
Bonet, Théophile, 200
Boughton, Sir Theodosius, 184
Bracken, John, 78
Breckinridge, John, 75
Brinvilliers, Marie d'Aubrey Marquise de, 188–189

Brittanicus, 187
Broadnax, Lydia, 9, 49, 64, 80, 114
　　move to Richmond by, 112
　　poisoning episode and, 12–16, 17,
　　　　104, 141, 212
　　Sweeney suspected by, 23–24,
　　　　36–37
　　testimony prohibition and,
　　　　216–217, 228–229, 234
Brooks, William, 171
Brown, John, 73, 75
Brown, Judith, 190
Brown, Michael, 114
　　autopsy of, 183–184, 193–194, 197,
　　　　206, 213–214
　　death of, 13–16, 36, 104–107,
　　　　124–125, 163
Brown, William, 23
Bruton Parish Church, 49
Buchanan, James, 171
Buchanan, Reverend John, 25
burglary, 99
Burnaby, 54
Burr, Aaron, 238

Cabell, William, 130, 214
Callender, James, 138
calomel, 182
"Cantarella, La," 187–188
capital punishment, 66–67, 101–102,
　　163–164, 187–192, 231
capitol building (Virginia), 220
Carr, Dabney, 135
Carr, Peter, 76
Carr, Robert, 189
Carter family, 148, 156
Cary, Wilson, 129
casinos, 89–90, 96–97
castor oil, 182
Cesare Borgia, 187
Chancery Court (Virginia), 6, 65
Chase, Samuel, 139
Chastellux, Marquis de, 44, 59
Chesterville Plantation, 45, 46,
　　49, 109

China, autopsies in, 169, 185, 199
Chinese Materia Medica (Shen
　　Nung), 186
cholera, 26–32
Christison, Robert, 204–205
Claiborne, William, 37, 212
Claudius (Emperor of Rome), 187
Clay, Henry, 22–23, 74, 74, 89,
　　112–113, 117, 237
Clements, Abel, 12, 128–129
Clements, Isaac, 128
Clement VII (Pope), 188
coffee, poisoning incident and, 13–16,
　　208, 209, 230
College of William and Mary, 40–45,
　　50, 58–62, 70
　　decline of Williamsburg and, 77–78
　　McClurg's career at, 177
　　Wythe and, 7, 48, 63–65, 69–77,
　　　　78, 81
Commonwealth v. Caton, 118–119
"conjurers," 192
Constitutional Convention
　　(national), 11, 78–79, 152, 157.
　　See also U.S. Constitution
Continental Congress, 6, 54–56, 92, 156
Cooke, J., 209
Court of Hustings (Virginia), 124–125
crime
　　punishment for, 66–67, 99–103,
　　　　101–102, 163–164, 187–192, 231
　　in Richmond, 11–12, 38–39,
　　　　98–103, 115
　　Virginia Board of Revisors on,
　　　　65–69, 229, 231, 233–234
Cupper, John, 190

dance halls, 86
Dandridge, William, 123
Darwin, Charles, 193
Dauphin François, 188
death sentence. See capital
　　punishment
Declaration of Independence, 5–6, 18,
　　56, 64, 110

Demeunier, Jean Nicholas, 67
Deshayes, Catherine (La Voisin), 189
Dinwiddle, Robert, 46
Diocletian (Emperor of Rome), 187
dissection. *See* autopsies
Donald, Alexander, 40
Donellan, John, 184
Douglass, Frederick, 222
Douglass, John, 175
Dunbar, Earl of (George Home),
 202–203
Dunmore, Lord (Governor of
 Virginia), 55, 88
DuVal, William, 3, 17, 130, *162*
 letters to Jefferson, 161–164, 184
 Sweeney suspected by, 23, 184

Eagle Hotel (Richmond), 89–90
Edwards, Ninian, 145–146
Elementa medicinae et chirurgiae forensis
 (Plenck), 205
Elizabeth I (Queen of England), 188
England
 American Revolution, 54–58
 capital crimes in, 66
*Engravings Explaining the Anatomy of
 Bones* (Bell), 193
Evans, Robert, 211
Evans, William, 211
Every Man His Own Doctor
 (Tennent), 201
*Exhortation and Caution to Friends
 Concerning Buying or Keeping of
 Negroes* (Keith), 45
exhumation, 213–214
*Experiments upon the Human Bile and
 Reflections on the Biliary Secretions*
 (McClurg), 178

family feuds, poison and, 190–191
Fanny (slave), 49
Farrar, Nancy, 91
Fauchet, Jean Antoine Joseph,
 149–154
Fauquier, Frances, 42

Federalists, 11
Fenning, Eliza, 207
fires, 115, 136
"fly powder," 204
forensics. *See* arsenic; autopsies
Foushee, William, 24–25, 34, 104,
 115, *173*, 180–181, 237
 autopsy conclusions of, 197,
 206–214
 cholera suspected by, 26–32
 at funeral, 20–21
 medical training of, 172
 reputation of, 176
 as Richmond mayor, 96
France
 American Revolution, 57
 Randolph and, 154
Franklin, Benjamin, 56, 57
freed blacks, 219
Freiburg University, 169

Gabriel's Revolt, 11, 163, 224–227, 228
Galen, 168
gambling, 12, 38, 87–89
 law enforcement and, 92, 95–98
 in Richmond, 83–95, 95–98
 by Sweeney, 87, 92, 93, 95, 96, 97,
 101, 103, 124
 in Williamsburg, 59–60
Garret, Katharine, 163
gender issues
 crime and, 100
 prostitution and, 85–87, 91
Giles, William, 76
Gilmer, George, 146–147
Goldsmith, James, 211
Gordon, Lord Adam, 59
Graeme, John, 90
Greece (ancient), 185
Greenhow, Sam, 105
Grigsby, Hugh, 112

Hamilton, Alexander, 151
Hay, George, 138
Henry, Patrick, 7, 20, 51, 149, 157

Hippocrates, 29
Historia anatomica medica
    (Lieutaud), 200
Hone, Philip, 116
horse racing, 83, 88, 93–94
horse theft, 99, 238–239
House of Burgesses (Virginia), 6, 46,
    47, 50–52, 64
Hudgins v. Wrights, 111
Hume, David, 69–70
Hunter, William, 201

India, cholera epidemic, 28–29
Indian tribes, smallpox and, 32
infanticide, 99
Instructions to the Coroner (thirteenth
    century), 169
insurance industry, in South, 115
Italy, poisoning history in, 187
Izard, George, 76

Jacob III, Count of Baden (Austria), 169
Jamestown, 176
Jefferson, Martha, 64
Jefferson, Peter, 40
Jefferson, Thomas, 3, 6, 7, 17, 18, *41*,
    235–236
  architecture of, 42, *220*
  education of, 44–45, 61
  gambling by, 89
  House of Burgesses, 50–52
  Monroe and, 75
  Mutual Assurance Society and, 115
  Nicholas and, 130
  Randolph and, 149, 151–152
  on slavery, 110–111, 225
  on Virginia Board of Revisors,
    64–69, 106, 229, 231, 233–234
  as Virginia governor, 10, 63, 75
  Wirt and, 146
  Wythe friendship, 36, 40–45, 48,
    50, 63–65, 69, 76, 105–107,
    156–157, 161–164, 184
  See also College of William
    and Mary

Jockey Club racetrack (Richmond), 94
Julius Caesar, 168

Keith, George, 45
Kelly, Elizabeth, 170–171
"King's Yellow," 204
Kulmus, Johann, *200*

larceny, 100
La Rouchefoucauld-Liancourt,
    François, 136
Lee, Richard Henry, 157
Letters of a British Spy (Wirt),
    140, 159
Lewis, Zachary, 46
Lieutaud, Joseph, 200
Livingston, Robert, 56
*London Medical Review and
    Magazine*, 211
Lorraine, Cardinal of, 188
lotteries, 87–89
love triangle poisonings, 189–190
Lucrezia, 187

Macon, Thomas, 95
Madison, James, 11, 68
  McClurg and, 177
  Randolph and, 148, 151–152
  Wirt and, 146, 238
magnesium, 209
"Manna of St. Nicholas," 188
Marbury v. Madison, 118
Marsh, John, 203
Marshall, John, 7, *70*, 72, 73, 75, 238
  Pleasants v. Pleasants, 111
  as student of Wythe, 118–119
  Wirt and, 146
mass poisonings, 192–193
McCaw, James, 34, *172*, 179–180, 237
  autopsy conclusions of, 196–197,
    206–214
  cholera suspected by, 26–32
  at funeral, 20–21
  medical training of, 172
  reputation of, 176

McClurg, James, 34, 170, *173*, 198, 237
  autopsy conclusions of, 195–196,
    206–214
  on bile, 178, 181, 194, 196, 206
  cholera suspected by, 26–32
  Constitutional Convention, 157
  at funeral, 20–21
  medical opinions of, 180–184
  medical training of, 172
  reputation of, 176–179
McClurg, Walter, 35
McCraw, Samuel, 105, 126–127, 184
Medici, Catherine de, 187–188
medicine
  colonial-era treatments, 27,
    175–176, 181, 209
  medical training, in early U.S.,
    172–176
  theories about bile, 178, 181, 194,
    196, 206
  See also arsenic; autopsies; Foushee,
    William; McCaw, James;
    McClurg, James
mills, 220
Monroe, James, 75, *75*, 182
  kidnap attempt, 224
  Randolph and, 157–158
  Wirt and, 146, 238
Montesquieu, Baron Charles Louis de, 69
Monticello, 42
Moore, Benjamin, 43
moot courts, 69, 72–73
moot legislature, 69, 72–73
Mordecai, Sam, 94
Morgagni, Giovanni Battista, 200–201
Morse, Reverend Jedidiah, 77
Morton (Scottish regent), 202
Munford, William, 7, 19–20, 23, 61,
  69, 74, 113–114
Mutual Assurance Society, 115
mystics, 192

Napoleon Bonaparte, 10, 193
Nero (Emperor of Rome), 187
Newgate Calendar, 211

New York City, 85
Nicely, George, 128–129
Nicholas, George, 76, 129
Nicholas, John, 128
Nicholas, Philip Norborne, 23, 125,
  129–131, 138, 157
Nicholas, William Cary, 156
Norfolk, Virginia, 85–86, 133–134

Observations on the Disease of the Army
  (Pringle), 201
Octagon (Randolph's home), 155
Olmstead, Frederick Law, 113
Orfila, Mathieu Bonaventure, 193
Overbury, Sir Thomas, 189

Page, John, 44, 130
Pendleton, Edmund, 6, 57, *58*, 64,
  229, 231
Percy, George, 176
Perrigo, Rebecca, 191
Perrigo, William, 191
Petersburg Republican, 130
Phi Beta Kappa Society, 70, 73
Philadelphia Gazette, 153
*Philadelphia Journal of Medical and Physical
  Sciences*, 178, 179, 181, 210
Phoebe (servant), 126, 184, 230
Pickering, Thomas, 150, 152–153
Pierce, William, 55
Pinard, John, 28
"Pink Alley," 86
Pleasants, John, 111
Pleasants v. Pleasants, 111
Plenck, Joseph, 205
poison. *See* arsenic
Powell, Lewis, 44–45
Price, William, 105
Pringle, John, 201
prisons, 102
property ownership laws, 70, 100
Prosser, Gabriel, 11, 163, 224–227, 228
Prosser, Thomas, 224
prostitution, 85–87, 91
Ptolemy I (Pharaoh of Egypt), 168

Quakers, 45

race issues. *See* slavery
racetracks, 83, 88, 93–94
Randolph, Edmund, 24, 36, 130–131,
    148–149, *150*, 238
    Sweeney defended by, 147, 158–160
    Treasury scandal and, 155–156
    as Virginia governor, 148–149,
        156, 157
    Whiskey Rebellion scandal and,
        149–154
    Wythe friendship, 106, 149,
        156–158, 159
Randolph, John, 149
Randolph, Peyton, 46, 149, 153
rape, 100
Reinsch, Edgar, 203
religion
    Religious Bill of Rights (Virginia), 18
    Virginia Board of Revisors on, 65,
        67, 68–69, 106
Richmond, Virginia, 3, 4, 4–5, 112–118
    clothing worn in, 112
    crime in, 11–12, 38–39, 98–103, 115
    "for hire" slaves in, 217–224, 226
    gambling in, 83–95, 95–98
    immigration to, 115–116
    map, 84
    population of, 10–11, 82–83, 115–117
    as Virginia capital, 75, 77–81
    Wythe in, 3, 78–81, 108–119
Richmond Daily Dispatch, 86
Richmond Enquirer, 4, 10, 18, 22,
    180, 232
Ritchie, Thomas, 22, 232
Rives, Nat, 90
Roane, Spencer, 75
Roman Empire, 168, 186, 187
Rose, William, 126–127
Ross, Ezra, 171
Ross, Valentin, 202
roulette, 91
Royal Society of London, 201
Rush, Benjamin, 27, 56, 175, 231

Sager, Joseph, 189–190
Sager, Phoebe, 189–190
Sancho (slave), 225
Scattergood, Tom, 103
Scheele, Carl Wilhelm, 202
Schoepf, Johann, 95–96
Secondat, Charles Louis de (Baron
    de Montesquieu), 69
second degree homicide, 68
*Sedibus et causis morborum,
    De* (Morgagni), 201
Sedition Act, 138–139
Sepulchretum (Bonet), 200
Serres, Antoine, 169
Shakespeare, William, 188
Shannon (client of Wirt), 142, 230
Shen Nung, 186
Sherman, Roger, 56
Shippen, Thomas, 73
Sixtus IV (Pope), 169
slavery, 10, 38, 137
    black and white legal codes,
        225–227, 228–234
    crime and race issues, 100–102, 116
    "for hire" slaves, 217–224, 226
    manumission, 111, 219
    poisonings and, 192
    revolts against, 11, 163, 224–227, 228
    Virginia Board of Revisors on,
        67–68, 229, 231, 233–234
    Wythe on, 41, 49, 61–62, 109–111
    See also individual names of slaves
smallpox, 32–34
Smith, John, 176
Socrates, 186
Spooner, Bathsheba, 171–172
Spotswood, Alexander, 83
Stamp Act, 51, 54
Street, Henry, 90
Stuart family, 192–193
suicide, by arsenic, 208
Sulla, 187
Sweeney, George Wythe (Wythe's
    grandnephew), 8–10, 49, 91,
    238–239

arrest of, 123–125
defense, 139–143, 147, 157,
  158–160, 198, 214, 230, 233–234
  (*See also* autopsies)
denounced by Munford, 20, 23
evidence against, 14, 36–39, 140,
  184, 204, 229–234
gambling habit of, 87, 92, 93, 95,
  96, 97, 101, 103, 124
lifestyle of, 11–12, 38, 114
poisoning episode and, 12–16,
  23–24, 30, 36–37, 209, 216–217
public opinion about, 163–164
thefts by, 92, 123–125, 141, 162,
  232–234, 238–239
verdict, 229–234

Taliaferro, Richard, 46
Taliaferro family, 109–110
"tasters," 188
taverns, 83–85, 92–93, 100, 222–223, 227
Tazewell, Littleton, 61, 76, 80,
  141, 237
temperance societies, 97
Tennent, John, 201
Tinsley, Peter, 117
tobacco industry, 218, 219
Toffana, 188
transportation law, 226
Treatise of Human Nature (Hume),
  69–70
Treatise of Poisons, A (Cooke), 209
Treatise on Poison (Orfila), 193
Treatise on Poisons, A (Christison),
  204–205
Tucker, Nathaniel Beverley, 52
Tyler, John, 70

University of Edinburgh
  *Edinburgh Medical and Surgical
    Journal*, 27, 210
  medical school of, 27, 170, 172,
    176, 198, 204
U.S. Constitution, 5–6, 11, 78–79,
  80–81, 152, 157. *See also*

Constitutional Convention
  (national)
U.S. Treasury, Randolph and, 155–156

Valeria, 187
Vindications (Randolph), 154
Virginia
  Board of Revisors, 64–69, 106, 229,
    231, 233–234
  capitol building, 220
  constitutional convention of, 10–11,
    56–57, 156
  Constitution of Virginia, 18
  courts of, 6, 65, 111, 124–125
  House of Burgesses, 6, 46, 47,
    50–52, 64
  yellow fever epidemic in, 33–35
  See also Norfolk, Virginia;
    Richmond, Virginia;
    Williamsburg, Virginia; *individual
    names of Virginia leaders*
Virginia Argus, 18
Virginia Gazette, 78, 80

wages
  of doctors, 176
  of "for hire" slaves, 217–224, 226
  of lawyers, 133–135
  of prostitutes, 86–87
Waller, Benjamin, 46
Washington, George, 6, 7, 53, 57, 78
  death of, 21, 27
  gambling by, 87–89
  McClurg and, 178
  Mutual Assurance Society and, 115
  Randolph and, 148, 149, 151–154
Weems, Reverend M. L., 130, 158
Whiskey Rebellion, 149–153
Wickham, John, 75, 159
Williams, Taylor, 127
Williamsburg, Virginia, 40–41, 44
  decline of, 77–78
  map of, 79
  Wythe in, 5, 46–50, 49, 58–60, 64,
    71, 109

Williamsburg (*continued*)
  See also College of William and
    Mary
Willis, Thomas, 169
Winthrop, John, Jr., 174
Wirt, Elizabeth, 135–137
Wirt, William, 130–131, 145–147
  career ambitions of, 132–139
  Letters of a British Spy, 140, 159
  stuttering overcome by, 143–145
  Sweeney defended by, 139–143,
    158–160, 198, 214, 230, 233–234
  as U.S. attorney general, 238
Witt, William, *134*
Wolcott, Oliver, Jr., 150, 152
Wrights (slaves), 111
Wyatt, Henry, 211
Wythe, Anne Lewis (first wife), 46
Wythe, Anne (sister), 9–10, 45–46
Wythe, Elizabeth Taliaferro (second
    wife), 46–49, 78–79
Wythe, George, 3–10, 45–54, 65,
    236, 239
  American Revolution role of,
    54–58
  autopsy of, 183–184, 195–197,
    205–207, 213–214
  on Board of Revisors, 64–69, 106,
    229, 231, 233–234

Chesterville Plantation and, 45, 46,
    49, 109
  funeral of, 17–23
  on his poisoning, 16, 25–26, 36–39
  Jefferson friendship, 36, 40–45,
    48, 50, 63–65, 69, 76, 105–107,
    156–157, 161–164, 184
  as judge, 113–114, 118–119
  as law professor/tutor, 7, 48, 63–65,
    69–77, 78, 81, 113, 117, 163
  love of books by, 42–43, 92,
    118–119, 124, 162
  marriages of, 46–49, 78–79
  McClurg and, 177, 179
  political career of, 11, 46, 54–56,
    64, 78–79, 156
  as practicing lawyer, 45–46, 52–53
  Randolph and, 106, 149,
    156–158, 159
  in Richmond, 3, 78–81, 108–119
  in Williamsburg, 5, 46–49, 49,
    58–60, 64, *71* (*See also* College of
    William and Mary)
  will of, 14–15, 38, 104–107, 124,
    162, 230
  Wirt and, 133, 159
Wythe, Thomas (father), 45

yellow fever, 33–35, 87, 136, 181